PATRICK BARKHAM was born in 1975 [...] for the *Guardian*. He is the author of [...] P[...]'s Mos[...] [...]tic *Animal*, whi[...] Prize and the W[...]wright Prize, *Coa[...]* Islander: A Journey Around Our Archip[...] Edward Stanford Travel Writing Award and a *BBC Countryfile Magazine* award. He lives in Norfolk.

'There's a simple driving narrative behind this book – how an amateur but extremely well-informed naturalist set out to see all of Britain's 60-odd native butterflies in a single year, and very nearly did so. It's humorous and packed with anecdote but also full of facts and ideas – and above all it shows us why we should give a damn. Excellent, in short. Just what's needed' Colin Tudge

'This is a delightful book – a bit butterfly-ish itself with magical moments of metamorphosis, exquisite precise detail, informative, lovely and unexpected. Barkham fulfils a childhood fantasy, as we all dream of doing, and fulfils it both dutifully and beautifully. It is indeed about butterflies, but also about obsession and learning and adventure and joy. Always grounded in the particular – of place, weather, history and other detail – it transcends these, so that even if you don't give a toss about butterflies you will care about his summer and its results. This is "the new nature writing" at its finest. *The* present you have been wanting to find for your friend, especially if your friend likes the countryside, but you will need to buy two because you will want to keep one for yourself' Sara Maitland

'The quintessential sense of natural history shines through this superb book' David Bellamy

'Charming, intimate and brimful of interesting facts and anecdotes' *Herald*

'By the end of Patrick Barkham's charming book you, too, will care about the differences between the Chalkhill Blue and the Silver-studded Blue, and the Skippers will be old friends ... *The Butterfly Isles* goes a long way to explain the delights of obsessive natural history ... after following Barkham's journeys nobody could fail to be enthralled by Ringlets and Painted Ladies' Richard Fortey, *Financial Times*

'[Barkham's] account is beautifully written and enormously entertaining, full of curious pieces of butterfly lore ... But it is more personal aspects of his quest which give depth to the book ... it is a splendid and accomplished account of all of Britain's butterflies, but it touches something deeper as a tribute from a son to his father, thanking him from the heart for a very special childhood' *Independent*

'A beguiling book ... [Barkham] criss-crosses Britain, recording his search in [a] vivid, adept, unapologetic voice, wonderfully catching the spirit of these ethereal creatures' *Guardian*

'[An] engaging account ... Barkham combines the patience and eye for detail of the naturalist with a vivid writing style that turns his 59 species into distinct characters' *Sunday Times*

'Suffused with engaging family anecdote and the genial humour of a patient man, this is amateur nature writing at its happiest' *The Times*

'A delightful account of a year chasing butterflies' *Metro*

'A delightful mixture of butterfly and personal biography' Richard Jones, *BBC Countryfile*

'Barkham writes with schoolboy excitement and his enthusiasm is infectious' Catherine de Lange, *New Scientist*

'As entertaining and effortlessly instructive as any nature book I've read' *Irish Times*

THE
BUTTERFLY ISLES

A Summer in Search of
our Emperors and Admirals

Patrick Barkham

Line drawings by Helen Macdonald

GRANTA

Granta Publications, 12 Addison Avenue, London W11 4QR

First published in Great Britain by Granta Books 2010
Paperback edition published by Granta Books 2011
This paperback edition published by Granta Books 2018
with preface and revised 'Watching butterflies' and 'Recommended reading' sections

A CIP catalogue record for this book
is available from the British Library.

1 3 5 7 9 10 8 6 4 2

ISBN 978 1 78378 458 5
eISBN 978 1 84708 239 8

Typeset by M Rules
Printed and bound by CPI Group (UK) Ltd, Croydon, CR0 4YY

www.granta.com

CONTENTS

SUMMER

AUTUMN

This book is for my dad, John Barkham

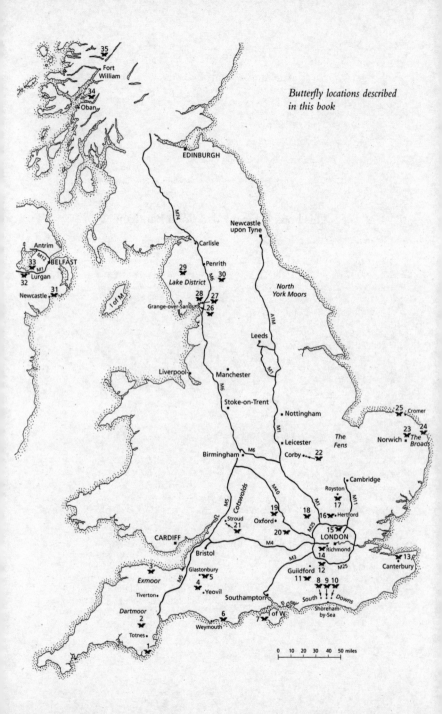

Butterfly locations described in this book

Sites and Named Butterflies

1 Start Point, Devon:
 Small Pearl-bordered Fritillary, Wall
 Brown, migratory butterflies including
 Painted Lady
2 Aish Tor, Devon:
 Pearl-bordered Fritillary, Small Pearl-
 bordered Fritillary, Dark Green Fritillary,
 Green Hairstreak, Silver-washed Fritillary,
 rare High Brown Fritillary
3 Bin Combe, Exmoor, Somerset:
 Heath Fritillary
4 Green Down & the Poldens, Somerset:
 Large Blue
5 Collard Hill, Somerset:
 Large Blue
6 Lulworth Cove, Dorset:
 Lulworth Skipper
7 Brook Bay/Compton Bay, Isle of Wight:
 Glanville Fritillary
8 Steyning, West Sussex:
 Brown Hairstreak
9 Mill Hill/Shoreham Bank, West Sussex:
 Adonis Blue, Chalkhill Blue, Clouded
 Yellow, Dingy Skipper, Grizzled Skipper
10 Newtimber Hill, West Sussex:
 Silver-spotted Skipper
11 Tugley Wood, Surrey:
 Purple Emperor, Wood White
12 Denbies Hillside, Surrey:
 Adonis Blue, Chalkhill Blue, Clouded
 Yellow, Grizzled Skipper, Dingy Skipper,
 Silver-spotted Skipper
13 Blean Woods, Kent:
 Heath Fritillary
14 Ham Lands, Twickenham:
 Orange Tip, Small White, Green-veined
 White, Speckled Wood, Comma, Holly Blue
 and other common spring butterflies
15 Durants Park, Ponders End, Enfield:
 White-letter Hairstreak
16 Waterford Heath, Hertfordshire:
 Grizzled Skipper
17 Therfield Heath/Royston Common,
 Hertfordshire:
 Chalkhill Blue
18 Aldbury Nowers, Hertfordshire:
 Grizzled Skipper, Dingy Skipper, Green
 Hairstreak, Marbled White
19 Whitecross Green Wood, Oxfordshire:
 Black Hairstreak, Brown Hairstreak
20 Bernwood Forest, Oxfordshire:
 Black Hairstreak, Brown Hairstreak, Purple
 Emperor, White Admiral
21 Rodborough Common, Gloucestershire:
 The Duke of Burgundy Fritillary, Small
 Blue, Adonis Blue, Marbled White, Green
 Hairstreak, Dingy Skipper
22 Fermyn Woods, Northamptonshire:
 Purple Emperor, White Admiral, Purple
 Hairstreak
23 Marsham Heath, Norfolk:
 Silver-studded Blue
24 Hickling Broad, Norfolk:
 Swallowtail
25 Kelling Heath, Norfolk:
 Silver-studded Blue, White Admiral
26 Arnside Knott, Cumbria:
 Scotch Argus, Northern Brown Argus,
 Grayling, High Brown Fritillary, Dark
 Green Fritillary
27 Meathop Moss, Cumbria:
 Large Heath
28 Latterbarrow & Yewbarrow, Cumbria:
 Northern Brown Argus, High Brown
 Fritillary, Dark Green Fritillary
29 Grey Knotts, Cumbria:
 Mountain Ringlet
30 Smardale Gill, Cumbria:
 Scotch Argus
31 Murlough, County Down:
 Marsh Fritillary, Réal's Wood White
32 Craigavon Lakes, Armagh:
 Réal's Wood White
33 Montiaghs Moss, Antrim:
 Réal's Wood White, Large Heath
34 Glasdrum Wood, Argyll:
 Chequered Skipper, Pearl-bordered
 Fritillary, Small Pearl-bordered Fritillary
35 Allt Mhuic, Loch Arkaig, Inverness-shire:
 Chequered Skipper, Pearl-bordered
 Fritillary, Scotch Argus

PREFACE TO THE NEW EDITION

It is nearly a decade since I set out to finish an uncompleted childhood quest, and see all 59 species of British butterfly in one summer.

'The past is a foreign country: they do things differently there,' wrote L. P. Hartley in *The Go-Between*. Already, the summer of 2009 looks like another country. Many butterfly species have been through eighteen generations or more since I searched for them. They are fast-moving insects, and a few have changed their haunts, or habits.

In subsequent summers, I've renewed my acquaintance with many of them. Hanging out together in warm corners of our countryside brings me as much joy as hearing the first swift in spring.

If you are meeting these old friends for the first time, here's how they are progressing. Britain's newest butterfly, Réal's Wood White, has since been identified as another almost-identical species and renamed the Cryptic Wood White. The Large Blue, which vanished in 1979 and was revived via a brilliant conservation effort, has continued its resurgence. There's a greater concentration of Large Blues in Somerset than anywhere else in the world. At the time of writing, another butterfly driven to extinction in England, the Chequered Skipper, is being restored to the romantic old forest of Rockingham, near the pub that bears its name. We can save species if we really try.

My near-fatal attraction for our most charismatic butterfly, the Purple Emperor, has endured. Happily, the Emperor is becoming less elusive and can now be spotted soaring through Essex, Suffolk, Norfolk and Lincolnshire. Other species moving northwards, assisted by climate change, include the Silver-washed Fritillary, the Marbled White and the Speckled Wood.

Butterflies are fine symbols of hope. But in the last decade our eyes have opened to a catastrophic loss of insect life. Michael McCarthy has written of the 'moth snowstorm' that once materialised before car headlights on summer nights. There are no such snowstorms today. A 2017 study of flying insects on German nature reserves identified a 76 per cent decline in abundance over twenty-seven years from 1989. Three-quarters of Britain's butterflies are declining, including once-common species such as the Small Tortoiseshell and Small Copper.

A decade ago, we suspected that pesticides were driving these losses. Recent scientific studies strongly suggest that one particular group of pesticides, neonicotinoids, are the prime cause of an insect Armageddon. But we can't simply blame farmers. A 2017 scientific study revealed that butterflies in urban Britain have declined more rapidly than in rural places. Climate change may help some butterflies but others are being killed by its milder winters or erratic weather.

It is easy to feel despair but we can take heart from butterflies, and take action. We can count them, join Butterfly Conservation, and embrace insect-friendly behaviours. I've banished garden chemicals, rewilded my small lawn and enjoyed their return.

I owe butterflies a great debt. Hunting for them in 2009 helped me reconnect with wild nature. I've since escaped London for the Norfolk countryside where I grew up. Curious readers of the following pages can be reassured that I still dream of finding a rare Camberwell Beauty in Britain, and I did repair my obsession-damaged relationship with Lisa. One of our daughters, Camilla, takes her name from the White Admiral, which scientists call *Limenitis camilla*. Another, Esme, is rearing Small Tortoiseshells and, more controversially for our neighbours, cabbage-munching Large Whites. Aged six, Esme puts me to shame with her moth-identification skills. Children are great connoisseurs of tiny creatures.

For the last three years, the first butterfly we've seen each spring has been a brilliant Brimstone – a symbol of hope for the coming season. I hope you enjoy the summer within this book and if butter-flies haven't yet brought you joy, or changed your life, I hope they may.

Patrick Barkham
Norfolk
February 2018

Introduction

How I learned to love little brown jobs

Behind the marram grass were twisted old pines and hollows that smelt of hot thyme. The warm ground was pebble-dashed with dry rabbit droppings. Holidaymakers splashed about on the beach; birders hunched in the hides. Only my dad and I crossed the empty no-man's-land of the rolling sand dunes, performing an odd, trotting dance, tracing random circles as we followed invisible darts of silver.

I was eight. For most of us, butterflies are bound up with childhood. Many of our earliest and most vivid memories of a garden, a park or flower will feature a butterfly and, perhaps, our pudgy hand trying to close around it. My love of butterflies began not with a blaze of colour but with a small brown job. That's what my mum called the common plodders of the butterfly world that would scarcely divert your gaze as they bimbled past. Meadow Browns or Hedge Browns or Wall Browns. Mostly brown and fairly dull.

This particular brown job was different: the Brown Argus. It was smaller, sharper and brighter than most butterflies with brown in their name. An arrow of silver grey in flight, its open wings were deep, dark chocolate with a border of dabs of orange. It was not exactly rare but was hard to find in East Anglia, where meadows had been ploughed into huge butterfly-unfriendly prairie fields during decades of intensive arable farming. It had not been recorded along this part of the coast in recent years. This may have been because no one had been looking, but it still gave us a mission: if we could find one, it would be a new sighting. Dad, I felt, could then Tell Someone. Who, it was not quite clear, but I had faith that he would.

We were on our summer holiday at Holme Dunes nature reserve. During the austere portion of the 1980s, the era of inner-city riots and the miners' strike, my mum, dad, sister and I would spend two weeks of the summer in a small damp flat at the end of a bumpy track on the corner of the coast where north Norfolk turns into The Wash.

Every morning, mum would march us through spikes of marram to the beach, where she would defiantly sunbathe behind a wind-break, whatever the weather, and my sister and I would dig in the sand for hours and hours. In the mornings and evenings, borrowing mum's heavy binoculars which banged against my chest, I would follow my dad down the paths to the wooden hides built overlooking shallow pools on the marshes and we would watch strutting green-shanks and avocets sweeping their bills methodically through the water. There is a photograph of Dad and me standing on the patio of the Firs, the rambling, isolated Edwardian house on Holme Dunes, which was divided into a flat for the nature reserve warden, a flat for holidaymakers and various dusty rooms filled with old signs and detritus from beach and reserve. Binoculars to his eyes, Dad stands there watching a heron on the channel close to the house. I'm at his side in little shorts and a mini-me pose, following my dad's line of vision, my mum's smaller binoculars pressed to my eyes.

The child of a broken home back when divorce was almost a social disgrace, my dad had found a solitary peace as a boy by running wild in the lanes and meadows of rural Somerset. He hunted out birds' nests in hedges and taught himself how to identify trees and grasses and flowers. As a young man, he lived in a caravan in the woods for weeks on end and studied wild daffodils. His career, inevitably, was rooted in the natural world – he taught environmental science to university students and, as a grown man, he spent his spare time seeking out wildlife and wild places. He often preferred to be alone.

In my eyes, Dad had the power to interpret every tremble of a leaf and every distant bird call in the countryside. His superpowers deserted him on butterflies, however. This particular year, on holiday, he created a little project for himself, which he seemed happy to share. He had a hunch that Holme was the perfect habitat for the Brown Argus. They were listed in old books as flying in this bit of north Norfolk but Dad was not sure when they were last seen here. It could have been decades ago. So we set out one hot afternoon on our first ever butterfly mission.

It was written in the stars that I would become a birdwatcher. Holme, where we holidayed every summer, was one of the best spots

3

in East Anglia for rare birds. Every year, exotic species would be blown far off course and end up lodged in a sea buckthorn bush on the dunes. Hundreds of birders from all around the country would descend on the reserve with their cameras and tripods. Here was a passion tailor-made for a small boy who loved nature like his father. Nature, but drama as well: scarcity, rarity, unpredictability and the boundless obsessive possibilities in creating lists and ticking things off, and trading gadgets, rare sightings and stories with the wider community of twitchers. My dad had a modest interest in football, took me to a couple of matches and I duly became obsessed with football. My dad had a grand passion for wildlife and took me bird-watching but, somehow, an obsession did not follow. I was always happy to go. I enjoyed peering at birds through binoculars. I liked the creosote pong of the hides, the lonely peen of waders and the empty sweep of marsh rising gently towards Holme church and village beyond. But nothing happened. In some receptacle of my brain, some small cell, the obsessive passionate cell, refused to twitch.

It took a small brown job to make that cell come alive. That first afternoon, hunting the Brown Argus, I could feel the heat radiating off the dunes onto my bare legs as I walked solemnly in my dad's footsteps, holding a blue biro and a piece of paper fixed to my pride and joy – a clipboard – to record everything we saw.

I kept a careful tally of each butterfly: I, II, III and we quickly clocked up some browns: the bland and slightly floppy Meadow Brown and the brighter, bustling Hedge Brown, also known as the Gatekeeper, a name which suits its friendly, busybody personality. There were dozens of Small Tortoiseshells – familiar to anyone like us who had a garden at home – and a few Small Heaths. I soon saw it was a bit unfair to call the Wall a 'brown job' because they were as elegant as Tortoiseshells, if less charismatic. There was a brilliant carroty flash as a Small Copper settled and opened its wings in the sunshine and the fine, bright midsummer hue of the Common Blue. Then we spied movement: a grey arrow flying low over clumps of marram. For a beginner, it is not easy to definitively identify a Brown Argus. The topside of its wings may be a striking dark brown but, in flight, thanks to its speed and the black and white dots on its beige underside, it looks grey, or silver, and uncannily like a female Common Blue.

Eyes down, as intent as an old couple at the bingo, we followed the promising silver grey dart for several minutes. This was harder than it sounds. Blink, and we would lose its flight path. We continued our circling, trotting, staring dance. Eventually, it settled on the ground just as a cloud swept across the sun and there it stayed, with its wings huffily closed. There are subtle differences in the pattern of orange studs and small eyes of black ringed by white that appear on the underwings of both Brown Argus and female Common Blue but I was not nearly expert enough to distinguish them.

Even when the sun reappeared and the little silver dart opened its wings wide, I was not certain of its identity. Unlike the showy male, the female Common Blue's wings are brown rather than bright blue. Some females are bluer than others but some are so brown they could almost be a Brown Argus, apart from a dusting of blue in the very centre of their wings. This silver dart had that dusting of blue.

The female Common Blue is far more shy and retiring than its man, flying fast and low over the ground, as elusive as enemy aircraft.

Four or five times during the next hour, my dad and I repeated our chase after different butterflies that flew like this. Several times, the insects lost us; on other occasions we caught up with them only to take one step too close when they finally settled, causing them to take fright and zip off again. When we got close enough, as a police officer might put it, to make a positive identification, it was always to put another line of biro in the column marked 'female Common Blue'.

Finally, we followed a silver shape that appeared determined to lose us by flying over a thorny patch of brambles. Then it eased off and glided for a split second, before dropping smartly onto a tiny flower of thyme in front of the brambles. There, in the sunshine, it opened its wings. A deep chocolate colour spread from the orange studs bordering the wings right into the soft brown hairs of its delicate body. Brilliant brown, with one little black dot in the middle of each upper wing, and no trace of powdery blue.

Here, unmistakably, was a Brown Argus. It was thrilling. I believed we were recording something brand new, which was enough to make a small boy feel quite self-important. I was a naturalist pioneer noting his discovery as earnestly and excitedly as Joseph Banks sketching new species during his Pacific voyages with Captain James Cook on the *Endeavour*. Later, Dad told the warden on the nature reserve about the Brown Argus. I was not sure if he told other environmentalists as well; the grown-up world of conservation was still a vague thing of meetings and telephone calls and interminable adult conversations that were beyond my perception. For me, then, it was not just a sense of discovery: seeing the Brown Argus was also intrinsically satisfying. It was beautiful to look at. And its beauty presented an unexpected puzzle: how could something so small and grey in motion become so rich and brightly coloured brown and orange when it settled down and opened its wings?

I went on to record five or six Brown Arguses that day on my scrap of paper, and a pattern was set. Dad and I returned to the dunes every day during our holiday, just after lunch, and walked and ran and stopped and started on our own secret mission all over the dunes, chasing, identifying and recording every butterfly we saw. My butterfly brain cell fluttered into life.

Every summer, when we returned to Holme, Dad and I would count butterflies. Gradually, we began taking little trips around Norfolk to look for other unusual species. After a couple of years, Dad set up a more ambitious trip, which involved evening telephone calls to friends in Oxford, Brighton and Surrey. Before we left, he presented me with the very latest piece of butterflying technology: Jeremy Thomas's *Butterflies of the British Isles*. With a photograph of a Peacock on the front and graphs and distribution maps inside showing the flight seasons of butterflies and where they are found, this increasingly battered paperback guidebook is still in my pocket today when I hunt for butterflies. Inside the cover, in faded pen, it says in my dad's spidery writing: 'Pad, for the 1 July 1988 Expedition to the south east'.

That trip was the first of our annual butterfly expeditions. Over the next six summers or so, Dad and I would go away to different corners of the countryside searching for butterflies we had not seen before. We set ourselves the task of seeing all fifty-eight species of British butterfly. If we were in any earlier decade, we would probably have run around with nets, catching, killing and setting our prizes on boards of cork carefully placed in mahogany drawers. But in the 1980s, we did not dream of collecting live butterflies. My dad may have grown up hoarding birds eggs but by then, like other environmentalists of his generation, he was acutely aware of the disappearance of our native wildlife in the face of industrial agriculture and forestry, and urbanisation. As butterflies became more scarce, so too did the old robust engagement with nature. In the two decades between the 1950s and 1980s, butterfly collecting all but vanished as mysteriously as the disappearance of rare butterflies. Collecting went from being an expression of a love of nature to being judged not merely environmentally damaging but socially deviant. Nature lovers' rejection of collecting was hastened by technology, too: like other butterfly lovers, my dad and I collected our rare butterflies in the form of photographs.

As a child, I saved up £40 and bought a clunky second-hand Praktica camera, and we travelled to woods, meadows and bogs in the Lake District, Oxfordshire and Surrey. We went on long walks, talking about this and that, waiting, trotting after and taking photographs of the butterflies we saw. We tracked down the very rarest species, and one, the Large Blue, which was supposed to be extinct. But we never saw all fifty-eight. We ran out of summers, or steam, and my personal tally of British species got stuck at fifty-four.

For more than a decade, I left butterflies behind. I went to university, moved to London to work and lived abroad for a while. A sniff of sweet cut grass in June or sour damp leaves in November could cause a jolt of recognition and regret for the rural existence I had left behind. I felt guilty at living so far removed from my roots, so far from leaves and earth and the small, free wonders of the natural world. Wherever I went, I snatched moments in green spaces and under trees, but I was caught up in cities and careers and had little time to luxuriate in the countryside. I would go on holidays with friends and point out butterflies when we were in the countryside. If asked about it, I would dismiss my observations as drawing on the remnants of knowledge acquired when I was young. Sometimes I would admit in a desultory sentence or wave of the hand that my dad and I used to go looking for different species of butterfly.

Like lost loves, butterflies still flew through my dreams. These were not merely the handful that had got away – during my child-hood I had never seen the Duke of Burgundy, the Chequered Skipper, the Glanville Fritillary, the Mountain Ringlet or Réal's Wood White – but some I had caught a glimpse of and desperately needed to see again. Above all else, the insect I most wanted to come to an accommodation with was the Purple Emperor. It eluded and taunted my dad and I for years before I eventually caught sight of it for precisely two of the 315 million or so seconds of my twenties. This butterfly cast a mysterious curse over me, and it haunted my dreams. I was not sure what it represented but I had suppressed the power of the countryside and I had been in denial about my child-hood passion for too long.

Finally, I decided I must complete this unfinished business, in the course of one summer. Butterflies, I hoped, could be a way to unlock the ordinary, everyday beauty of the natural world that I hoped could still be experienced on our small island, if only I took time to seek it out. This is the story of my search for every British butterfly (fifty-nine now, since the discovery of Britain's newest butterfly, Réal's Wood White, in Northern Ireland in 2001), from the spectacular rarities to the common-or-garden butterflies; from emerald green to canary yellow, from beaches to forests; from central London to the Highlands of Scotland.

Fifty-nine seems an attractively accessible figure. Britain is not particularly blessed with butterflies. There are about 18,000 species of butterfly in the world, including 7000 in South America and more than 500 in Europe. Because Britain is a northerly country, and because it was cut off from the Continent by rising seas 8000 years ago, most of these sun-loving insects never made it to our shores. The ones that did tended to be small and hardy, better able to cope with our mendacious summers than the huge, flapping tropical butterflies we can see in the humid greenhouses of butterfly farms.

A search for all fifty-nine species is, however, deceptively difficult. It is not the sort of mission you can accomplish in an afternoon sitting in a sunny garden in the south of England. There is no single day on which you can see every species; like spring and summer flowers, different butterflies emerge at different times of year. The Orange Tip, for instance, appears in April and is never seen again after May, while the Brown Hairstreak does not usually emerge as an adult butterfly until August. Most butterflies are on the wing for a week or two, but some barely manage three days. Others may live longer or appear and reappear in several broods across the summer but few are permanent presences in our hedgerows and woodlands in June, July and August. Like exotic rock stars visiting music festivals, several bold migrants fly across oceans to make surprise guest appearances in the middle of our summers. Meanwhile, many stay-at-home natives have led obscure lives for centuries, basking at the tops of trees like the Purple Hairstreak or lurking in the bottom of bogs like the Large Heath. Some furtive insects, such as the Black Hairstreak, rarely dance more than a few metres from where they hatch during their short lives; in bad summers they hardly seem to appear at all.

I also wanted to see all fifty-nine before it was too late. As the countryside has shrunk, so species have become confined to isolated fragments of land. Driven to extinction in England in the 1970s, the Chequered Skipper is now only found in the Highlands of Scotland around Fort William. Over the last century, the Swallowtail, our largest and most spectacular butterfly, has been forced into glorious isolation on the Norfolk Broads. Other butterflies never leave their headquarters in Cumbria or the West Country, or a sliver of Surrey and Sussex. A few of our native species, particularly the Duke of Burgundy and the Wood White, are teetering on the brink of extinction, leading incredibly precarious lives and depending for their survival on one tiny plant or one species of ant or an apparently arbitrary constellation of weather, rabbits and largely forgotten ways in which we once worked the land. One species, the Large Blue, became officially extinct when I was a boy, but was deliberately reintroduced in a secret location known only as Site X. Another, the High Brown Fritillary, is both endangered and devilishly hard to distinguish from other species. Everything, ultimately, depends on the weather. Remove sunshine and install the typical weather of a British summer, and you won't see many butterflies on the wing at all. The previous two summers had been sunless and joyless and disastrous for our native butterflies. Few butterflies will fly in the rain; some, such as the Silver-spotted Skipper, usually need temperatures in excess of 19°C to give them the energy they need just to get off the ground.

My mission was a bit like an ultra-marathon. Seeing every species in the course of one summer was perfectly possible. Compared with moths or dragonflies, say, Britain's butterflies are wonderfully accessible: fairly straightforward to identify and easy to learn about. Anyone could train themselves to find them all in a summer but, like running a hundred miles, most people would think you were a little bit deranged to try. There are far fewer butterfly enthusiasts than, say, the twitchers who follow birds. Every summer, one or two obsessives with a lot of time on their hands may try and find all fifty-nine; many more, like me, have long wanted to see every species but have never accomplished it in their lifetimes, let alone in one season. Butterfly seekers expend more energy than you could imagine on long, fruitless journeys to inaccessible places that stubbornly fail to give up their jewels because the forecasters got it wrong and the clouds and rain sweep in.

Juggling my mission with a full-time job, much of my butterfly-ing would be undertaken at weekends, so I would need fine weather, good luck and a lot of patience. This did not come naturally to me. Nor did another state of being that butterflies demanded: spontane-ity. I like order and plans. Butterflies hatch out at their own pace, determined by the weather. Each is as unpredictable as the other.

Species may emerge two weeks earlier than expected, and disappear again long before they should. I could not plan this mission; I needed to be spontaneous. If a day dawned sunny, I must take advantage of it. If I did not, I might miss my only chance to see a certain species. Short on time and long on obscure locations far from train stations or reliable buses, I guiltily realised I would be more reliant on my car than was healthy for myself, or for our resident butterfly populations. I also needed help. I had not gone searching for butterflies in earnest for more than a decade. My identification skills were decidedly rusty and I could not rely on books, even my faithful Jeremy Thomas guidebook. With the changing climate, many butterflies are changing their habits. Guidebooks quickly fall out of date. Besides, they seldom give precise locations where rare species are found. I would need the advice of more people than just my dad if I was to track down the rarest species.

Unlike a marathon, there was no absolutely clear finishing line. The figure of fifty-nine butterflies native to Britain includes two regular migrants, the Painted Lady and the Clouded Yellow, but if I saw other, much rarer migrants I could clock up more than fifty-nine. Scarce migrants are little twists of fate: you cannot just visit a particular woodland or meadow to see them. You cannot choose to find them; they find you, once in a lifetime. Perhaps this year would be my time and I would chance across a giant Monarch racing over the ocean from North America or stumble on a Large Tortoiseshell, a tragic butterfly which became extinct in the UK shortly after the Second World War for reasons no one understands but which occasionally, at random, reappears in the south of England. I might become one of barely 500 people in 300 years who has seen a Queen of Spain Fritillary in Britain, one of the most gracious members of the golden-coloured fritillary family which continues to baffle lepidopterists by thriving just across the water in Holland and France but rarely deigning to visit this island. The most magical sixtieth species would be the Camberwell Beauty. Like many butterfly lovers, since I was a boy I had longed to see one of these large, romantic butterflies with brown wings so rich they were almost purple, bordered by lemon yellow. My heart still lurches every time I spot a dark silhouette against the sky that is big enough to be a Beauty; so far, it has always turned out to be a common Red Admiral or Peacock.

A rare migrant I could not plan for. Finding the fifty-nine regular residents would be challenging, and rewarding, enough. I would have to spend as much time as possible in some of our most acclaimed and beautiful nature reserves but also lurk around motley scraps of land in cities and overlooked patches of our precious, ordinary and unprotected countryside. I hoped a journey around our overcrowded and overheating isles would help me better understand our relationship with these beautiful insects; how they depend on us and how we may be more dependent on them than we realise. The brief lives of our butterflies are amazing miracles and minor tragedies; romantic, sad and strange. Wondrous in themselves, for their own will to survive, butterflies are also colourful canvasses for all our projections. A journey in search of every species of butterfly is about our need to celebrate and capture fleeting moments of wonder as we fly through our lives.

WINTER

1

In the beginning was an egg

Over banquets of roast swan and sweet port, the butterfly obsessives of the eighteenth century would slide open their mahogany collecting drawers and show off their bright, dead specimens to fellow members of their newly formed entomological societies. This was one way Aurelians, a rather foppish term passionate collectors once used for themselves (taken from the Latin *aureus* or *aureolus*, meaning golden and referring to the golden hue of some butterfly chrysalises), navigated the dark, depressing winter months. Trays of dried butterflies carried colour, beauty and vivid memories of warm days into drawing rooms not yet caressed by television, electricity or central heating.

Few butterflies are on the wing, flying as adults, from October through to March. In the chill of winter, their existence, like summer days, seems a complete chimera. It is too cold and wet and there are

17

few flowers and almost no nectar for them to feed upon. Lacking sunshine, and the objects of their adoration and desire, many butterfly enthusiasts sink into a mild despondency in the winter months. As a boy, I was a seasonal enthusiast. Like cricket, butterflies sprang into my life during the summer. While the Aurelians of today no longer catch and kill butterflies, many of the most committed do not push their passion from their minds in winter. Because collecting is beyond the pale to modern sensibilities, they have had to find other ways of communing with butterflies in the off-season. Counting eggs is one. Which is why I began my year in search of butterflies by looking for minuscule eggs in the freezing cold and snow, in the shadow of a prison.

The Brown Hairstreak is one of a small number of British butterflies that survives the winter as a mass of nutritious fluid inside a tiny egg with an unusually robust shell. It was these cream pin-pricks, lodged in the crook of twigs, that I was hoping to find when I drove across the Chilterns towards Oxfordshire on an uncompromising, old-fashioned winter's day in early February. Snow lay in the shade of every hedge and in grimy piles outside Bullingdon Prison, where pale relatives visiting those locked inside clambered out of small hatchbacks. Desiccated and crunchy, the snow stained yellow when you thumped a boot on it. Bullingdon welcomed its first guests in 1992 and looked older than it should, scarred by hard life and surrounded by a hotchpotch of overgrown military land belonging to Bicester Garrison.

The desire to search for these microscopic eggs on an icy day would be unfathomable to most ordinary minds. A group of seven people poking about in the bushes by the prison walls would certainly arouse the suspicion of the regular security patrol seeking to ensure that no friends of the inmates were throwing mobile phones or drugs over the walls.

'Ah, officer. I am just looking for the eggs of the Brown Hairstreak butterfly,' is an explanation so strange it might just buy you enough bewilderment to scarper. Butterflies? Eggs? In February? Eh? On this day, the prison knew all about the egg-hunting mission I had joined. Slightly surprisingly, a burly senior prison staffer was a big butterfly enthusiast. He was keen to manage the prison hedges to help Brown Hairstreaks thrive there and had invited local members of Butterfly Conservation, a friendly and very active small charity that has a membership of 14,000 across the country, to count eggs, an activity only likely to enhance butterfly lovers' reputation for eccentricity.

Every butterfly lives its life in the same miraculous cycle described by Eric Carle in his classic children's book, *The Very Hungry Caterpillar*. A caterpillar hatches from an egg, eats a lot, locks itself into a chrysalis, or pupa, and emerges some time later in a dramatic summer outfit: a fully grown, four-winged insect. The adult stage, the part we particularly admire, comes when the weather is warm. That is the easy bit. Winter is more challenging. The cycle of egg–caterpillar–chrysalis–adult is always the same but different species of British butterfly tackle the cold in different ways.

Butterflies fly, mate, lay eggs and grow as caterpillars at different times and at different rates. In favourable conditions in the UK, a Painted Lady can race through its life cycle in a flash: from egg to rapidly growing caterpillar, to chrysalis and then adult in barely eight weeks. Other butterflies, such as the Chequered Skipper, may spend a hundred days feeding up as a caterpillar and take a year to go through one turn of its life cycle.

Most British butterfly species spend the winter in the form of a caterpillar, which is surprising because they seem at their most vulnerable when a soft, juicy worm. We think of butterflies in their most visible adult, winged form, but the caterpillar is the longest stage of many butterflies' life cycle: this is when they eat, feed and grow. In the year a Purple Emperor is alive, it may be on the wing as an adult for barely two weeks. The rest of the time it is egg, caterpillar and chrysalis. The Purple Emperor is one of the most handsome and slow-growing of caterpillars, hatching from the egg in August, changing its colour to remain camouflaged as the leaves it feeds on change from green to brown, hunkering down for winter and resuming its feeding and growing in the spring. Caterpillars, which move through instars, or stages of growth, shedding their exoskeleton as they go, tend to be solitary, although some species cope with winter by huddling together in specially constructed tents or discrete webs which they spin; others snuggle up with species of ant, such as the Large Blue, which spends the winter as a parasite, reclining underground in the safety of an ants' nest, where it feasts on ant grubs.

One adaptable butterfly, the Speckled Wood, can choose to tackle winter either as a caterpillar or a chrysalis, while a few, such as the Swallowtail and the Grizzled Skipper, only take on winter in their pupal stage, secure within their chrysalises, which are attached to twigs or half-buried in the ground. Butterflies begin to develop adult characteristics, such as putative wings, inside their bodies while they are caterpillars. But the chrysalis is that magical moment in metamorphosis in which the green or brown grub transforms itself into a winged chariot of many colours. Chrysalises may look stiff and dead but they are very much alive, concealing the great changes that unfold behind their discrete ribbed shells of black, brown, green or grey. These pupae are tougher and more adaptable than they appear: a Swallowtail chrysalis can survive submerged in water, while the pupa of various Blues and Hairstreaks produce audible squeaks to attract ants. Butterflies need warmth and sunshine to hatch from the chrysalis; when they do, they cannot fly immediately but must pump haemolymph (a butterfly's equivalent of blood) into their crinkled wings to inflate them, spreading them out until they are dry, firm and ready to take to the wing.

A small, robust elite of British butterflies – the Small Tortoiseshell, Comma, Peacock, Red Admiral and Brimstone – spend the winter hibernating as adults. These butterflies have jagged edges to their wings or cunning brown patterns on their underwings so that when they are hibernating with their wings shut tight they look just like dead leaves. We may chance upon them, motionless, tucked neatly in our woodpile, attic or shed.

We have long seen ourselves in the miracle of metamorphosis, whether we are Chinese or ancient Greek, Christian or Hindu. Psyche is the Greek word for butterfly. It is also Greek for soul. The demi-goddess Psyche appeared as a butterfly and both ancient and modern societies have seen butterflies as our souls, elevated from the earthy constraints of living in a body and liberated from suffering. In seventeenth-century Ireland, an edict forbade the killing of white butterflies because they were seen as the souls of children. During the Second World War, Jewish children in Nazi concentration camps wrote poems about butterflies and carved them on walls. In late-twentieth-century China, single white butterflies were found in the cells of executed convicts who had recently converted to Buddhism.

If an adult butterfly is, symbolically, an elevated soul, the caterpillar is more down to earth. In the eighteenth and nineteenth centuries, when butterfly collecting became a sociable, fashionable pastime in Britain, good Christian collectors – and many early Aurelians were clergymen – saw their prey as a small but brilliant part of God's work. They spotted something that repulsed and bewitched them in the life cycle of a butterfly: themselves.

Caterpillars were loathsome and greedy worms, doomed to perpetual toil on the Earth – mankind, in other words. Yet the miracle of the butterfly gave hope and purpose to our meaningless crawling. From wriggling maggot, man too could hope to ascend to a higher life in the skies, via a chrysalis-like coffin, as long as he sought out a purposeful life on Earth devoted to the enlightened study of the wonders of God's creation.

I've always quite liked plump, green caterpillars busying around on leaves with their appealing wiggly walk. But an anonymous motto at the beginning of Victorian collector Edward Newman's *An Illustrated Natural History of British Butterflies* describes an encounter with caterpillars in a verdant meadow:

Great was their toiling, earnest their contention,
Piercing their hunger, savage their dissension,
Selfish their striving, hideous their bearing,
Ugly their figure.

Later, our anonymous author and caterpillar-hater returned to the meadow to find creatures:

Hued like a rainbow, sparkling as a dewdrop,
Glittering as gold, and lively as a swallow,
Each left his grave-shroud, and in rapture winged him
Up to the heavens.

And so man was not doomed to remain on Earth:

No! like these creatures, trouble, toil, and prison
Chequer the pathway to a bright hereafter
When he shall mount him to the happy regions
Made to receive him.

Back on Earth, Bullingdon's designers tried to put its inmates out of sight, and mind, by planting shrubs around the high curve of the prison wall to screen it from passing traffic. Beside scrawny teenage poplars and beeches was the diffident presence of straggly blackthorn trees. In February, before much hint of their brief blossoming, these looked as tired and careworn as the prison they feebly screened. Over the years, however, the blackthorn had spread, its suckers fighting through brambles and hawthorn and, at some point, an inquisitive female Brown Hairstreak flew past the prison, spotted the blackthorn, the food plant of its caterpillar, and pushed through its dark green leaves to lay eggs on its branches. In summers since, the stubby bushes that circle the prison came to support a thriving colony.

There are five butterfly species called hairstreaks in Britain. All are small, elusive butterflies of middle England: private, understated and overlooked, they tend to keep their wings closed when at rest but can surprise you with their flamboyance and vivacity. Unlike most British butterflies, all five hairstreaks have dinky little tails, trailing from the bottom of their hindwings. The Black Hairstreak is small, dark and rare. The Purple Hairstreak has wings of brilliant iridescent purple, like its bigger friend-in-purple, the male Purple Emperor. The Green Hairstreak is emerald green and has a violent temper; the White-letter is named after the delicate white 'w' on its underside.

Despite its dull name, the Brown Hairstreak is the biggest and most beautiful of all the hairstreaks. The undersides of its wings are decorated with bright slivers of silver and ginger while its uppersides are a deep, rich brown. The female's upper wings are enlivened by large and brilliant panels of orange. Like a few other strikingly handsome or charismatic British butterflies, it attracts a cult following among Aurelians. Its eggs, however, are rather less compelling: microscopic dots stuck to the underside of a twig all winter (like the tiny bud of a flower) that will eventually explode into a colourful butterfly.

A handful of people in bulky winter coats, hats and gloves had joined David Redhead, a Butterfly Conservation volunteer, for the search by Bullingdon Prison. Redhead used to work for Thames Water and only discovered a latent passion for butterflies, and the Brown Hairstreak in particular, in retirement. He thought it came from childhood memories of a buddleia festooned with summer butterflies and was also inherited from his grandfather, who was a great butterfly enthusiast. 'A seed was sown then. I don't think I realised it at the time,' he said.

In my thirties, I was the youngest in the group by some margin, but there were as many women as men. As Michael Salmon reveals in *The Aurelian Legacy*, a brilliant history of British butterfly collecting, in 1750 a quarter of the subscribers to Benjamin Wilkes's *English Moths and Butterflies* were women. Around the same time, however, all members of the first Aurelian society were men. For the two centuries that it was the height of fashion, butterfly collecting was a male, if not especially masculine, preserve. The virtual extinction of collecting seems to have been followed by a steady growth in the number of women nursing a passion for butterflies.

There are about two thousand particularly dedicated enthusiasts like Redhead in Britain who do things such as count eggs and, once a week during the summer, undertake butterfly transects. These are a specific, walked route at a particular location – a local wood, for instance – along which they record every butterfly they see. Their data is supplied to scientists who monitor butterfly populations and distribution for Butterfly Conservation. Every winter, the charity gathers its volunteers together and reports back on the numbers and health of the British butterflies. The datasets which these volunteers help produce have provided a unique and detailed record of butterfly numbers in Britain since the system was devised by scientists in the mid-1970s. This has been a huge help in all kinds of conservation projects; the only disheartening thing is that the figures they produce only too accurately chart the alarming decline of most our butterfly species.

There were certainly no butterflies on the wing on this February day in Oxfordshire. There was, however, something of the fervour of the Aurelians of old. Redhead quickly focused on his group's mission. 'If we start getting really excited you know we will have found a Black Hairstreak egg,' he explained to me. 'The holy grail,' murmured another member of the group. Every egg hunter nodded, bouncing the small magnifying lenses strung around their necks. Luckily, Redhead had a spare hand lens he could lend me. If we saw a tiny egg with our naked eye, we would need to look closely to identify it: rather than a Brown Hairstreak egg, it could be the more oblong-shaped egg of a Blue-bordered Carpet moth or, possibly, the duller white eggs of the Black Hairstreak, which was much rarer than its brown relative but was known to frequent this part of Oxfordshire.

After mating carried out in the canopy of a taller tree, usually a nearby ash, female Brown Hairstreaks descend to young branches of blackthorn. They deposit eggs one at a time against the crook formed by a twig and a thorn between knee and head height. These are glued so hard to the branch they withstand leaf fall, gales and snow until May, when the caterpillar eats its way out of the tiny pinprick of an egg through an even tinier pinprick in its roof. After fattening up, the caterpillar wanders to the ground under the cover of darkness and retreats into its pupal stage. Little is known about the Brown

Hairstreak's chrysalises; they are considerably harder to find than its eggs. Only in late July or August does the butterfly emerge and take to the wing.

Like many butterflies, a female Brown Hairstreak can lay more than 100 eggs. It is believed that up to 99 per cent of these eggs are destroyed before they have a chance to hatch. Predators include other insects, such as the alien Harlequin ladybird, but many get bashed or drop off. Brown Hairstreak eggs are particularly vulnerable to hedge cutting. Redhead talks to local landowners to persuade them to rotate their trimming and cut blackthorn once every three or four years rather than slashing it back every year.

We started on a small section of blackthorn round the corner from the prison entrance. Despite the chill, honey-coloured catkins and an expectant stillness in the air, along with an indefinable quality of light, suggested spring was almost in sight. The group fanned out, concentrating and silently competing to be the first to find an egg. I struggled to distinguish bare hawthorn and blackthorn twigs; the female Brown Hairstreak can tell where it should lay its eggs by drumming its feet on the top of a leaf to 'taste' it. After five minutes, the egg hunters began calling out that they had spotted eggs. Redhead kept a tally in a small notebook. On the branch below each egg, they hung a small white plastic tag so they could return later in the spring to see how many had successfully hatched.

Here, egg spotting, I tried to do what I thought my dad would do: I lightly held a slender branch of blackthorn, turned it gently to the light and systematically ran my eye along it, checking at every joint of a twig. After about ten minutes, I found my first-ever butterfly egg: in the cradle formed by two twigs on a branch of blackthorn already sprouting tiny lime-green leaves and a creamy flower that would shrivel and burn under the next frost. The egg was a minute waxy white dot. Through the hand lens, you could just about see a raised pitted pattern of pentagonal cells. In the roof was a tiny indentation, the micropyle, from where the caterpillar would emerge. The egg was strangely unmistakable. Once you had seen it, if you backed away you could still pick it out from two metres. 'Once you get your eye in, they look like footballs,' said one of the group.

We continued shuffling our way along the hedge in the shadow of the prison wall. The snow was dotted with the prints of deer and, incongruously, discarded sachets of margarine. Prisoners would leave them on the windowsills of their cells and magpies and other birds would snatch them, carry them into the trees outside the prison and peck out their oily insides.

On this rubbishy patch of prison land, we were steadily clocking up dozens of Brown Hairstreak eggs. One of the group, Tony Croft, discovered one on a high branch, so Redhead measured its height from the slushy ground: 2.2m, 'a new world record' for the height of a Brown Hairstreak egg, he said, joking in a serious kind of way. 'Well, an Upper Thames record.' While the women in the group talked of how they enjoyed this kind of spotting trip because it placed you in the wild for a couple of hours, a spirit of competition sparked up among the men. The fourth egg I found was an impressive 2.3m high, on a branch decorated with discrete blooms of grey and yellow lichens, another new record. Croft came back with the last word: an egg laid at 2.7m. When we reached exactly a hundred eggs, Redhead called it a day. I had contributed just seven. These Brown Hairstreak eggs did not count in my hunt for all fifty-nine species. The fifty-nine had to be seen in their adult form, not as eggs. If all went to plan, and these eggs became voracious caterpillars and then adults later in the summer, the Brown Hairstreak butterfly, traditionally the final species of the summer to emerge, might become my final, fifty-ninth sighting of the year.

At this moment, after three hours of methodical searching, I could only think of my numb hands and desperation for the toilet. These egg hunters were tougher than I had imagined. They must have bladders of steel. Something odd had happened to my eyesight too. It was, I imagined, like the submariners who are unable to focus on distant horizons when they resurface after weeks underwater with only the walls of their machine to stare at. After all this squinting at spindly branches, it might not have been so safe to jump in the car and drive back over the Chilterns. With glazed eyes and hands of ice, I headed home anyway.

It was not merely metamorphosis that was an everyday miracle. The ground was so hard and cold and the hedges so barren, I wondered how there could be millions of butterflies out there, from caterpillars crouched motionless on twigs or tucked up in tents sawn from blades of grass to chrysalises bobbing from the underside of a branch looking exactly like the twist and curl of a dead leaf. I wondered how they and the microscopic egg and the hibernating butterfly with its tatty wings clenched tight above its slender thorax survived, alive, patiently waiting for the sunshine and the green leaves that would signal it was time to fly into our lives again.

SPRING

2

The first butterfly of the year

The year I set out to see every species of British butterfly began with the coldest winter since my boyhood butterfly expeditions. February offered little prospect of seeing anything at all. Even though the dun brown countryside looked utterly inhospitable to sun-loving insects, the light finally began to lift. As the nights shortened, and my thoughts turned to this butterfly year, my dreams were, for the first time since childhood, populated by butterflies. Swarms of them, night after night, as if the environmental catastrophe of the twentieth century had never happened and a gently tilled countryside was again enlivened by millions of insects. In one dream, a Holly Blue was disappearing high over the overhanging ivy of a London backyard. On the same ivy bush appeared a rare Duke of Burgundy, its wings expansively spread in the sun, and then another. The ivy was festooned with butterflies. The collective noun we have invented for this kind of group is perfect: a kaleidoscope of butterflies.

Unfortunately, some kind of consciousness shook up this colourful assembly and, even as I dreamed, I understood that the presence of so many Duke of Burgundies on ivy, in London, in winter, could not be real and even before I woke up I was wrestling with the disappointment of the dream not being true.

Butterfly obsessives seem peculiarly susceptible to vivid dreams. Are these triggered by the depths of their obsession or the gaiety of the subject? The naturalist and illustrator Frederick William Frohawk described a friend who went butterfly collecting in Bude in 1891 and stumbled upon a new colony of Large Blues. 'After a good nights rest, when he had a pleasant dream of catching three examples of the Large Blue in his wanderings, he thought no more about it,' wrote Frohawk. That morning was overcast but, to the astonishment of his friend, he saw and caught three Large Blues. 'Again turning dull with rain about to fall, he returned to his room at the cottage to meditate over the queer coincidence.'

The anticipation of seeing my first butterfly of the year grew. I hoped it would be a memorable first sighting. In an imaginary kingdom populated by funny white creatures that resemble hippopotami, the small beasts of the woodland declare you can tell the fortune of your year by the colour of the first butterfly you see in spring. Tove Jansson's world of Moomintroll, Snufkin and the Snork Maiden may be slightly trippy but the Swedish-Finnish author beautifully documents our passage through the seasons and shows how north Europeans are lifted by the dazzling spring change after a long dark winter.

Even if it was a common species, the first butterfly of the year was always laden with significance. Shortly after waking from their long winter hibernation, Moomintroll and the Snork Maiden sat in the spring sunshine and discussed this special event. A brown butterfly does not augur particularly well for the year ahead. They are not spoken of. A white butterfly is better. This means you will have a peaceful, if unspectacular, summer. A yellow butterfly heralds a happy year but best of all is a bright, golden butterfly. Moomintroll and his friends see a golden butterfly and their summer, as Jansson relates, certainly turns out to be a memorable one.

One year, when I was a child, my first butterfly was a Holly Blue, as pale as the spring sky. I'm not sure how Moomintroll would analyse that; it may imply a rather cool summer. As a boy, most of my first sightings occurred when I visited my granny in North Curry, a pretty village sensibly plumped on a hump of land above the watery flats of the Somerset Levels. The first shoots of cow parsley and goose grass would stretch out in the lanes and I would see an Orange Tip zig-zagging along a grass verge or a Red Admiral warming itself on the stone wall in granny's garden.

Only one first sighting of the year sticks in my mind. When I was fifteen, I accompanied Dad on a trip to Monks Wood, in Cambridgeshire. We stayed overnight with one of my dad's friends who was a fellow of Gonville and Caius College and had rooms in an old quadrangle in the centre of Cambridge. On his wall was a large map of eighteenth-century London: it showed all the old villages, from Putney to Highgate, and the meadows and heaths, such as Hampstead and Enfield Chase, which were rich hunting grounds for the first butterfly collectors. The next morning was one of those days in mid-February that held the promise of spring, but only from behind a car windscreen. Outside, everything was chilled by the winter air. Bare branches were cold and damp to touch. The elaborate greenery of summer seemed a delusion. The countryside shrinks in winter; there really is less of it.

If you drive north on the A1 and glance right soon after the junction with the A14, you can see the massed ranks of Monks Wood, still impressive in size but long cut off from the royal hunting forest to which it once belonged. The wood is famous for its butterflies – and its extinctions. Since it became a national nature reserve in 1953, it has lost ten of the forty-one species recorded there, a scandal given its proximity to the ground-breaking butterfly science which has been undertaken for decades in the biological research station right next to the wood. In this year, 1990, Dad was checking on the progress of one of his research students, who was working in the wood, and so I tagged along. When we walked down a broad ride in the shelter of the trees we felt that first heat of the year from the sun. In the dusty grey coppice, the only colour was the pale yellow of catkins, dangling from twigs of hazel like earrings. Then, through the catkins charged an immaculate golden brown Comma. Pristine, it rested on the bare branch of a tree in the sunshine, its jagged wings looking like a shape cut out from a piece of folded paper by a small child.

I did not expect Moomintroll's gold, I did not demand a portent of happiness, but I would happily settle for an ordinary yellow butterfly. White would be a bit boring and I would rather not think on the implications of seeing a dark brown butterfly. That would not prefigure much of a summer. Miriam Rothschild, the zoologist and polymath for whom butterflies were probably her second grand passion after fleas, wrote about the special character of yellow butterflies. For some reason, three of the five yellow butterflies we might see in Britain are intrepid adventurers that fly to us across the ocean. 'They are great migrants and follow primaeval uncharted routes, which they have taken for thousands of years, ignoring the march of time, the destruction of forests, and the dangers of dual carriageways and motorised transport,' wrote Rothschild. She was referring to the Clouded Yellow, one of two regular migrants in our list of fifty-nine butterflies, and two other much rarer migrants, the Pale Clouded Yellow and Berger's Clouded Yellow. Vladimir Nabokov, too, was captivated as a boy when he spotted a rare Swallowtail, 'a splendid, pale yellow creature with black blotches, blue crenels, and a cinnabar eyespot above each chrome-rimmed black tail. As it probed the inclined flower from which it hung, its powdery body slightly bent, it kept restlessly jerking its great wings, and my desire for it was one of the most intense I have ever experienced.'

A Swallowtail does not emerge until the end of May at the very earliest, and the chance of seeing a Clouded Yellow in the spring, before anything else, was almost nil. I was not greedy, though; a Brimstone, lemon yellow and one of our most common butterflies, would suit me fine as the first butterfly of the year.

By the first weekend of March, the air held real promise of spring. Daffodils bowed their heads on suburban roadsides. When I ran along the old railway line that curves up from Finsbury Park to Highgate, in north London, one small hawthorn bush had burst into a brilliant, but lonely, green. Dark was not falling until after 6 p.m. This London landscape was bereft of butterflies. So too, more surprisingly, were the North Downs, just west of the famous Box Hill, to where Georgian day-trippers such as Jane Austen would rattle with their picnic hamper-laden carriages. In early March, I went for a walk with my girlfriend, Lisa, through the woods around Ranmore Common. In summer, this famous mix of woodland and downland would be laced with an intricate dance of butterflies. Now there were mountain bikers, motorcyclists, dog walkers, hikers, tractors and horse riders in the dappled sunshine. The air in the woods, however, remained silent and empty. Bereft of insect life, the woods seemed to lack a dimension. Without wings, it was like watching the scene on a black-and-white television.

I was missing butterflies but I did not think they were alive, or awake, to be missed, not yet. Then I checked Butterfly Conservation's website, where enthusiasts log their first, and latest, sightings of each species. Here, butterfly obsessives compete for the honour of being the first person to spot a particular butterfly every year. The very first butterfly of 2009? A Red Admiral: several were found flying on 13 January in Dorset, Hampshire and Oxford. Towards the end of February, butterfly spotters had already clocked up sightings of Small Tortoiseshells, Commas, Peacocks, Large Whites, Small Whites and Brimstones. These first sightings were always freakishly early, the work of people who dedicated every

waking hour to searching for butterflies. Uncharitably, I also wondered how reliable these records were. I had not yet set out
deliberately looking for butterflies but then these common, early
spring species were not the sort of insects you visited a specific nature
reserve to find. They should be flying everywhere.

I was beginning to wonder if there were any butterflies left in
Britain. I nursed lepidopteral dreams again that week and, on a
work trip to Margate, saw hares chasing each other across the ruts of
a recently sown field. The following weekend, I visited my mum in
Sheringham, a small seaside town on the north Norfolk coast. A tiny
fishing hamlet until the railway arrived, it swelled to a genteel resort
of 9000 people, living above sandy cliffs and below a belt of steep –
by East Anglian standards – wooded hills. Apart from its trains,
Sheringham was best known in recent years for its high street's stoic
defence of traditional family-run grocers, butchers and bakers against
plans for a Tesco supermarket.

Sitting in my mum's conservatory, in a Sunday morning stupor, I
was oblivious to the perfect butterfly weather – a calm, bright spring
day – unfolding around me. The sun was moving higher in the sky
each day; it had a polite, very English kind of punch behind it now.
Mum's small garden was dotted with the first daffodils and, in the
shade, purple crocuses. Against the wooden fence, delicate yellow-
green hellebores were in bloom. Perfume poured from the tiny cream
flowers of winter honeysuckle.

I was only drawn into the garden by a low-pitched warbling
which sounded like a dozen collared doves with a serious throat
infection. This weird, amorous cooing came from the centre of the
garden, where a small boggy pond was bordered by moss and irises.

The dark water was alive with frogs. There were more than fifty. Like teenagers in a crowded swimming pool, they eyed each other up, flirting and splashing and chasing. Some jumped on each other's backs; others casually dangled long limbs in the water; most hurtled around cooing and groaning and fervently trying to find someone to love. Fat handfuls of jewelled spawn were already piling up in the shallows. There was something obscene about such fecundity; their vibrating throats bashing out croaky love songs; their grabbing and fondling and threesomes, with one poor frog submerged below the bodies of two others crouched in triumph above it.

As I crept closer, fifty frolicking frogs froze. Slowly, lugubriously, a hundred froggy eyes turned on me. Chastised, I backed away and, whoosh, they flipped and turned and dived into the tangle of grey-green weed and dead leaves at the bottom of the pond. Every single frog vanished. All was still. Then I saw the Small Tortoiseshell.

It was sunning itself on a smooth stone by the water's edge, its wings laid so flat they were almost bent back on themselves. It took me a few seconds to recognise that this was a moment I had eagerly anticipated. The first butterfly of the year. Brilliant. Being so pleased by something so simple felt like becoming a child again. Its tortoiseshell patterning of orange, red, brown, black and white looked faded and crisped, as if it had been left in the sun too long. Apart from that, it was in good shape, its wings not at all tatty, despite spending the winter hibernating, clenched against the cold in a crevice of bark or a garden shed. On the flower bed was a movement: a second Tortoiseshell was sniffing a daffodil as if it were a tasty bone.

All this sunshiny pleasure was followed by a pang of disappointment. I am not sure where the Small Tortoiseshell stands on the Moomintroll scale of first butterflies but it must signal an unsurprising, everyday sort of year. The Small Tort, as my dad and I used to call it, is colourful and courageous and common, the Labrador of the butterfly world. A friendly butterfly that seems to love human company; a democratic butterfly that pops up in gardens all the way through spring and summer and autumn, feasting on our buddleias and basking on our fences and hibernating in our sheds. It is resilient and cheerful, and the male is quite feisty. You can tell the sex of a Small Tortoiseshell by gently throwing a stick over where it is resting. Males will fly up and attack the missile (the butterfly-as-Labrador again); females won't. The male needs to have his wits about him because the female leads him on a merry dance before agreeing to mate: he patiently waits behind the object of his desire all afternoon, fending off other males, and striking her hindwings with his antennae. Sometimes the female will shrug off her man by dropping into the nearest patch of nettles – where she lays her eggs – and running along the ground, with the male in pursuit. If the male successfully stays with the female, and fends off the advances of other rivals during the course of the afternoon, he is finally rewarded with a mating session that can last all night.

The Small Tortoiseshell will be the first butterfly many of us see in our lives, and will be the first that most of us see every year. If we can't name many butterflies, we can probably identify a Small Tortoiseshell in the garden. Like most common things, we take their beauty for granted. We probably shouldn't because, like the sparrow in the bird world, there has been an alarming decline in Small

Tortoiseshell numbers in recent summers. Clearly, the Small Tort is well adapted to our crowded, suburban island, so butterfly scientists believe this fall in numbers could be linked to an alien invader, 'a grisly parasite reminiscent of the *Alien* films,' as the *Daily Mail*, never slow to panic about the perils of immigration, put it.

In 1998, a fly called *Sturmia bella* was recorded in Britain for the first time. Since then, it has spread across England and Wales with an awful modus operandi. The fly lays its microscopic eggs on nettles close to where Small Tortoiseshell caterpillars are feeding. The caterpillars unwittingly eat the eggs, which hatch into grubs and grow inside them. These parasites wait until the Small Tortoiseshell caterpillar has fed itself up before bursting out of the host chrysalis as a fly, killing the Tortoiseshell just before it can become a butterfly. Other parasites are thought to have caused sudden reductions of butterflies in the past and could again in the future, particularly with climate change. The arrival of this fly and its successful colonisation of Britain may be due to our milder winters. In this way, the Small Tortoiseshell could be one of the first victims of climate change. By 2008, *Sturmia bella* had flown as far north as Merseyside, and that year was the worst year ever recorded for the Small Tortoiseshell, its population falling by 45 per cent compared with the previous summer. In the scientific sampling of areas where *Sturmia bella* was found, the fly killed 61 per cent of Small Tortoiseshell caterpillars, according to research by Dr Owen Lewis, an ecologist at Oxford University.

But scientists are not convinced that the parasitic fly is the only reason for the butterfly's population slump. The Small Tortoiseshell is also declining in Scotland and the Netherlands where there is no record of *Sturmia bella* yet. In most instances where new predators arrive, the attacked species eventually adapt to elude them. Other research suggests that, before the last two wet summers, the dry summers of a warming world also hit the Small Tortoiseshell because low moisture reduced the nutritional quality of nettles, meaning fewer caterpillars reached the weight required to transform themselves into adult butterflies. If the riddle of this disappearing butterfly shows how little we know of our commonest insects, we know even less about newcomers like *Sturmia bella*. Scientists do not yet have any idea how it even survives the winter, when there are no Small Tortoiseshell caterpillars to feast on. What does it eat then? Could it live off another butterfly host? We have marvelled at butterflies for centuries and yet there is still so much about them we do not understand.

So I should have been grateful to see two lovely Small Tortoiseshells that had not fallen victim to *Sturmia bella*. In truth, however, I felt slightly disappointed because I had self-indulgently set my heart on seeing a yellow butterfly. I had convinced myself that Moomintroll's scale of first butterfly sightings mattered and that a yellow butterfly would bring me luck. It was an achievable goal: a Brimstone is as common a sight in February or March as a Small Tortoiseshell. I also wanted to see a Brimstone first because it was, in a sense, the First Butterfly.

As well as being one of the first on the wing each year, the Brimstone may have been the insect that gave English-speaking nations the name 'butterfly'. It was, after all, a 'butter-coloured fly'.

While there is a link between the word 'butterfly' and the medieval superstition that they were fairies, or witches in winged form, who stole butter and cream – the German for butterfly, *schmetterling*, is derived from a Slavic word for cream – the *Oxford English Dictionary* suggests its origins refer 'to the yellow or creamy-white colour of familiar species such as the Brimstone.'

There are as many theories about the origins of the word 'butterfly' as there are British species. One that holds no appeal among those who champion butterflies' more elevated qualities is that the word comes from the old Dutch word *boterschijte* – butter shitter – because the excrement from certain caterpillars looks like butter. From the Norwegian *sommerfugl* to the Russian *babochka* (suggestive of witches again, with *baba* meaning old woman) there are a wealth of beautiful words for butterfly around the world. Investigating this, one etymologist noticed that many, from *pili-pala* in Welsh, to *bimbi* in Papua New Guinea pidgin and *pinpilinpauxa* in some areas of the Basque country, incorporate a basic repetition of sounds, which symbolically represent a butterfly opening and closing its wings.

The Brimstone's scientific name, *Gonepteryx rhamni*, means 'the angle-winged butterfly of the buckthorn'. The Brimstone does have a distinctive flourish to its wing, as if it were carved by a flamboyant carpenter. But because it shows up everywhere and almost any time, it does not belong to anywhere or any season. It is probably overlooked because it lacks a romantic association with a particular region, a lovely wood or a moment in May or June. When I was a boy, I saw enough Brimstones knocking around in the garden to never bother to sit down and read about it then. And as soon as I did, as an adult, I was fascinated by its strength, beauty and zest for long life. If I were an insect, I would want to be a Brimstone. It is our most resilient butterfly. As an adult, it lives longer than any other butterfly in Britain. Like other species that hibernate as adult butterflies, the Brimstone has one incentive to get through the winter: to breed and lay eggs in the spring. Unlike others, though, it is believed that a Brimstone can experience a full year. It does not merely hatch out in September and die in the spring. It can emerge from its chrysalis in early July and after surviving the winter may live until the following July. It is nomadic, will fly great distances and prefers its own company unless there is a spectacular source of nectar to feed on. A solitary butterfly has a forceful kind of integrity: it eschews crowds, and squabbles with other insects, and bounces on, high along hedges, content in its own company.

Years ago, I remember playing football in the garden on a bright January day and hearing wings crashing against the inside of the garden shed window. The sun had warmed the shed and woken a Small Tortoiseshell from hibernation. I opened the door, felt the heat and let it out before it became hopelessly tangled in dusty old cobwebs. You could almost see the poor Tortoiseshell flinch as it hit the wintery air outside. The Brimstone, however, is particularly tough. It will breeze out of wherever it is hiding on mild sunny days during winter, take a gulp of the crisp winter air, and then happily bed down again, wherever it chose to hide, until spring really starts. In this butterfly year, a Brimstone was sighted on 26 January in Oxfordshire, shortly before the infrastructure of southern Britain was amusingly paralysed by the heaviest snowfall for eighteen years. I would wager more Brimstones survived that cold snap than flashier Red Admirals and Tortoiseshells.

If the Brimstone is more resilient than the rest, it also has a criminal record. It was an accessory to the first ever entomological hoax. In 1702, James Petiver, an apothecary who gave many of our species their first English names, wrote of a mysterious butterfly which exactly resembled the Brimstone apart from black spots and blue moons on its lower wings. Petiver lived in some squalor and had a shaky grasp of Latin but doggedly identified and listed the English names of fifty British butterflies. He called modern-day Skippers hogs, pronounced 'ogs', but many of his names, from Admirals to Arguses, have endured. Carl Linnaeus, the Swede who is the father of modern taxonomy, honoured Petiver's mysterious blue-moon-and-Brimstone butterfly with its own scientific name, *Papilio ecclipsis*, in 1763. It took another thirty years before another entomologist, Johan Christian Fabricius, denounced the original specimen as a fake. Further inspection revealed that this rare butterfly was a Brimstone with spots and patterns painted on its wings. A cunning fraudster may have made good money by selling these exotic, highly desirable specimens to gentlemen collectors.

Another surprising quality in the Brimstone, I later learned, was that the female was desired by the male for her smell. This turns the male Brimstone into a crazed sniffer: he may be drawn to a spot by her scent, unaware that she is hidden on the underside of a leaf directly below his perch. It is possible for us to smell the aroma emitted by certain butterflies. When I read Nabokov's short story 'The Aurelian', I imagined that his hero's dreams of a 'Chinese "skipper" said to smell of crushed roses when alive' were an hallucinogenic fantasy. I only realised Nabokov was not inventing this when I read E. B. Ford, an eminent geneticist at Oxford University, whose scientific study of butterflies was the first volume of the famous 'New Naturalist' series of natural history books. Despite its high seriousness, Ford's book was a great success, selling more than 30,000 copies when it was published in 1945. In it, this startling passage jumped out: 'My friend the late Dr F. A. Dixey made a survey of butterfly scents in collaboration with Dr G. B. Longstaff. He found that the decisions which they reached independently, as to the nature of the various odours, nearly always corresponded, as far as the difficulties of describing them allowed.'

The image of Doctors Dixey and Longstaff, moustaches aquiver, leaning over the prone downy body of a butterfly and inhaling deeply is irresistible. The scents they detected are wonderfully of their time: the Marbled White is 'distinctly musky', the Meadow Brown is 'old cigar-box' while the Wall Brown is 'heavy and sweet, like chocolate cream'.

We can, apparently, pick up the attractive smell of the male butterfly – the male Green-veined White emits a strong scent of lemon verbena – but not the females, according to E. B. Ford. The reason for the perfume is simply to attract the opposite sex. Scents are not produced by every male butterfly. It depends on his age and the state of his secretory cells. It is almost as if the male goes through a kind of menopause and ceases to be sexually, and sensually, active.

After watching the Small Tortoiseshells, I returned to the conservatory and resumed reading. An hour later, my mum tapped on the window and motioned me to come outside. She had seen her first butterfly of the year: a Brimstone, and there it was, a perfect blend of daffodil and early spring leaves. It was smaller and greener than most Brimstones I had seen in the past and when it landed on yellowing leaves of ivy, it disappeared as surely as the frogs in the pond. Perfectly camouflaged. Whenever it settled in the sun it, characteristically, refused to open its wings. Brimstones are one of several butterflies which never bask in the sunshine by spreading their wings wide open. I watched until it meandered on its way again, flying along the fence all floppy and careless, as if loosening its limbs for a long summer ahead. Hopefully, it would herald a good summer for mum.

On the final weekend of March, I was back on the north Norfolk coast. In late afternoon, in the sheltered garden of the cottage in Wells-next-the-Sea which had recently become my home when I was not working in London, I watched two slightly faded Small Tortoiseshells embroiled in the theatre of mating. One, the male I presumed, chased another, twisting upwards together in a spiralling flight. For a hibernating butterfly, winter must be like a war. This was like a scene after a long conflict and an interminable separation: a man and a woman, exhausted and past their best, getting together for the first time. The female's show of reluctance appeared only that; in reality, they were locked together in dance, wanting to make the most of spring, of the remains of their day.

1. Small Tortoiseshell, Sheringham, Norfolk, 15 March
2. Brimstone, Sheringham, Norfolk, 15 March

3

Spring butterflies

By the end of March, a fake summer had taken hold across much of England and Wales. At the start of a magical week of unseasonally warm weather I was in Stoke Newington, where I lodged for work. While packing my bags to visit my dad, who lives in Devon, I glanced idly out of the window. Wobbling down the city street like a small boy on a bicycle was a white butterfly. It was so far away, I couldn't hope to identify which species of white it was. By the time I humped my bags down three flights of stairs and burst out into the sunshine of Stoke Newington, it was long gone. It would have been a Large, Small or Green-veined White. Most people call all three Cabbage Whites. They are common butterflies which you don't need to go looking for, but every one is special at the start of the year. I had missed it.

A walk on Dartmoor was too chilly for any butterflies but on the second day at my dad's house in Ashburton, Lisa and I drove through a warren of country lanes to Prawle Point in South Devon, an inaccessible slab of coastline between the estuaries of the Dart and Kingsbridge. Even in the era of satnav, few tourists take these roads. They mess with your mind. You are always three miles from where you want to go. Slapton, the sign said, was three miles away. Ten more minutes of switchback corners and hidden valleys and Slapton, the next sign said, was three miles away, still. Sometimes the hedges almost met over our heads; at other times, a strip of overgrown grass marched down the middle of the tarmac.

As the land approached great cliffs and the ocean beyond, fields rolled into submission like friendly puppies, sloping steeply into rough meadows bruised purple with bluebells. It was a warm spring day, brazen with primary colours. The blackthorn, braced against the prevailing westerly wind, flowered white and gorse showed brilliant yellow. In the shelter of a rocky cove, the warmth of the sun was enough to lure us into a short, sharp swim. The icy water pinched my chest and grasped at my throat.

Decades ago, collectors traipsed these cliffs looking for rare Large Blues. Today, the conditions were perfect for butterflies and yet there was none. There were insects – dozens of large black beetles had crash-landed on the coast path – but it was, still, a fraudulent summer, catching you out with its chilly air. All the plants and insects were far too underdeveloped to be offering up the gift of an early Holly Blue or Orange Tip, let alone an exotic migrant from over the waters.

The following day, we read the papers in my dad's small garden. A church meeting of rooks chuntered in the big firs by the cemetery.

The sickly smell of *daphne odora*, a squat flowering shrub, hung in the air. A beat of wings caught my eye and a Comma dipped down onto one of its flowers. For the next two hours, this golden garden butterfly probed its long tongue into the flowers of the *daphne odora* before looping over the wall into a neighbouring garden. With its perfect little white 'c,' or comma, scribbled on its underside and its ability to perfectly impersonate a dead leaf, the Comma will always be a special creature. No other butterfly has such finely crafted raggedy wings. What is a hop cat? A jazz fiend? A three-legged moggy? Or someone turned crazy by beer? This lovely expression is Victorian slang for the caterpillars of the Comma, which once stretched out lazily in the sun on hop fields across the nation. Hop was listed as the major food plant for the Comma in the butterfly books of the day. With the decline of commercial hop fields outside Kent and the West Midlands in the nineteenth century, it is thought that the Comma suffered.

When I looked in old guides, there was an odd reversal to today's narrative of species declining towards extinction. Rather than lyrical tales of the sun being blotted out by thousands of Commas, grave accounts spoke of the rarity of what is an increasingly common butterfly today. Writing in 1871, Edward Newman noted its absence from species lists in Norfolk, Suffolk, Sussex, the Isle of Wight, Dorset, Devon, Cornwall and, mysteriously, Kent, where there were a great number of hop fields. If it did occur in these locations, it was of 'great rarity', he concluded. The Comma became even scarcer in the early twentieth century. It is thought that climatic changes and harsh winters caused its temporary decline, despite the fact that the Comma is found inside the Arctic Circle.

Inexplicably, around 1914, its population started to increase. Since then, its population has swollen and moved northwards as well, probably assisted by a warming climate: its numbers increased by 350 per cent between 1976 and 2004. Since the turn of the century, the Comma has been recorded again in Scotland for the first time since the 1870s. Its reappearance has been as baffling as other butterflies' disappearance, although there is a theory that it switched to alternative food plants, such as nettles and elms, just one of many examples of butterflies confounding us with their resilience and adaptability.

After a morning with the Comma in Dad's garden, it seemed too fine not to drive to the beach again. Nabokov declared that hiking was his favoured form of locomotion for hunting butterflies 'except, naturally, a flying seat gliding leisurely over the plant mats and rocks of an unexplored mountain, or hovering just above the flowery roof of a rain forest'. Many Victorian entomologists refused to travel to butterfly hunting grounds by train because there was no chance of halting an engine to pursue a butterfly sighted from the window. Instead, they would trundle to their destinations by horse and cart, poised to rein in the horses if there was a chance of slipping their net over a prize specimen.

Few collectors would approve of a car as an entomologically useful engine. Only butterfly geniuses see anything from a speeding car: Matthew Oates, who is the National Trust's Nature Conservation Adviser and an Aurelian with the romantic fervour of old, once spotted a warring pair of White-letter Hairstreaks darting high around a scrubby elm at Gordano services on the M5. He was driving at 70mph. (It sounds an improbable boast but the White-letter Hairstreak males stage a distinctive spiralling battle around treetops. In contrast, another treetop butterfly, the Purple Hairstreak, has a tumbling flight. I'm not sure I could distinguish spiralling and tumbling from the fast lane.)

We were doing barely 20mph past the delicate church of St Nicholas and St Cyriacus in the pretty village of South Pool and up the single-track lane twisting its way out of the valley. The car grumbled and Lisa spotted a movement between the hedges. I braked and a butterfly dropped low enough for us to see the unmistakable yellow and blue eyes on each deep red wing: a Peacock, motoring along almost as briskly as us.

Like the Comma we had just seen, the Peacock was one of those colourful garden butterflies many of us messed with as children. After our fish died, for several summers my sister and I collected Peacock caterpillars from the nettles in the meadow at the bottom of our garden, placed them in the empty fish tank, fed them fresh nettles and watched them eat and then disappear into a chrysalis. These Peacocks were much more robust than our short-lived exotic fish. Without fail, apart from one year when we let the soil in the tank get too dry, they hatched into a butterfly every bit as beautiful as the creature exploding from the final pages of *The Very Hungry Caterpillar*. As adults, we lose our sense of wonder about these spectacular, and common, garden Nymphalidae. Peacocks are probably only properly appreciated by those true connoisseurs of butterflies: children.

After that first sighting, Peacocks seemed plentiful, this spring at least. This butterfly had a way of making its presence felt. Several times in fields and woodland edges, a Peacock flew directly at my head, as if to attack me. On another occasion, I watched one zigzagging dementedly after a bumblebee, as if it had been stung. Often Peacocks will rise from their resting place to chase off a rival insect, returning to exactly the same leaf. Flicking through *The Aurelian's Fireside Companion*, by Michael Salmon and Peter Edwards, I read that Peacocks will hiss at you like a snake or, as one entomologist put it, like 'the sound sometimes made by a goose on the approach of a dog'. This revelation in *The Entomologist* magazine of 1939 encouraged other lepidopterists to publish their tales of Peacocks hissing when disturbed during hibernation. E. J. Salisbury wrote: 'In December last, when my gardener and I were moving some logs from a woodstack, one near the base was seen to bear a hibernating Peacock butterfly. So we placed this log carefully to one side where it was in bright sunshine. Almost immediately our attention was recalled to it owing to the production of a hissing sound which can best be described as something between that produced by an angry cat and the hissing of a disturbed snake.' According to Frohawk, the noise was produced by the rubbing of the inner margin of the forewing against the costal margin of the hindwing.

With these defences, the Peacock would seem a match for any predator. Even *Sturmia bella*, the parasitic fly, does not so far seem to have affected its numbers even though, like the Small Tortoiseshell, the Peacock caterpillars' fondness for nettles means that they too are infected by the parasite. Instead, like the Comma, the Peacock has steadily moved northwards over the past century and is now a common sight in parts of Scotland where it was once as rare as a Camberwell Beauty.

In London, spring, as usual in the urban heat island, danced ahead of the west, east and north of the country. By the first weekend of April, the pear tree behind the flat in Stoke Newington was heavy with white flowers, chestnuts unfurled the first leaves of spring and the daffodils meekly lost their heads in the gathering shade. A great spotted woodpecker hammered on the bare ash tree by the reservoir and grey squirrels and magpies twitched, thuggishly, in the trees. Looking out, I spotted a white butterfly moving through the gardens below, seized my new binoculars and chalked up the first Large White of the year – and my fifth species out of fifty-nine. I was so rusty I had to double-check in my old Jeremy Thomas guidebook but it was a functional name for a functional butterfly: large and plain white, with black tips on its forewings. which also bore a black dot. Males had no black dot so this was a female.

These binoculars had not yet seen serious action. I had not wielded them in public. They were a spare pair with special butterfly powers: they could focus on a small insect from a short distance away and had a small, embarrassing sticker of a butterfly on them to prove it. They belonged to my dad and he gave them to me to help with my butterfly spotting. I took them with thanks and secret reluctance.

Ever since that picture was taken of me as a child on holiday, mimicking my dad's every move, I have resisted binoculars. As a teenager, on our butterfly expeditions, I took the Jeremy Thomas field guide and my pride and joy, my Praktica camera. But binoculars belonged to birdwatchers. They were the ultimate symbol of geekiness. No matter how chic your clothes or how hip your haircut, the moment you slung a pair of binoculars over your neck you showed the world you were a prize nerd. My dad carried binoculars most of the time when out walking. He also wore a white floppy-brimmed cricket hat and a terrible pair of sunglasses from America which were huge square blocks of dark plastic that fitted over his ordinary glasses. I was desperately – and futilely – fearful of looking like my dad. I hoped that by avoiding binoculars I could escape that fate. As an adult, I stuck by this principle.

So far I had seen five species of spring butterfly without trying. There were not many about, though. I walked with Lisa all day along Esk Dale in the North York Moors and did not see a single butterfly. On another couple of bright days, I ran along the old railway to Highgate in north London and, again, did not find anything. By mid-April, I was concerned I was yet to see an Orange Tip. These, and Holly Blues, are the sort of butterflies we should stumble across in spring. I was worried, too, because by May they might be gone from our skies for the rest of the summer. I could miss them. These common species do not live in special nature reserves. Wardens do not tend to their every need. Professors do not study their conservation. They are simply here and there, materialising in our gardens and hedgerows to tell us as clearly as blossom that spring has arrived and the earth is changing faster than we can imagine.

I had seen so few butterflies I was beginning to worry that chancing across one was no longer an easy, everyday experience: that all butterflies had to be sought out, special sanctuaries had to be visited, and we were toppling into an era in which climate change would finish off the last butterflies as yet unbowed by our industrial farming and incorrigible urban lifestyles.

I picked up the binoculars Dad had given me and braced myself. I really should undertake my first butterfly expedition of the year. It was only the second time in fifteen years I had set out with the sole purpose of seeing butterflies and I felt about fifteen years old again. I picked up my runner's rucksack, which was fluorescent and reasonably cool as rucksacks go, and filled it with the very uncool kit of a butterfly watcher: a packed lunch, a pen and notepad, Jeremy Thomas, my camera with a new zoom lens and those binoculars.

It was a sunny Saturday in mid-April. I decided to visit the newly established sensory gardens of Imperial Wharf, a flash development on the banks of the Thames, before heading to Ham Lands, a series of damp meadows across the Thames from Twickenham. Reading the local Butterfly Conservation website, there had been reports of Orange Tips at both locations.

Two minutes out of the Tube at Fulham Broadway, on the busy Harwood Road, a businesslike breeze from the east tossed blossom in the air. Sent in unpredictable directions by the turbulence of the city, each speck resembled a butterfly. It took a second glance before I realised one tumbling speck of blue was insect, not petal: a perfect, fresh new Holly Blue.

Keats must have watched the Holly Blue when he wrote of 'little bright-eyed things That float about the air on azure wings'. This courageous little wanderer was the first butterfly I had ever noticed in Zone One of London. There were probably plenty in parks and on canal-sides and railway embankments but I had never expected to see them and had never opened my eyes to them. Not here. It seemed cruel. How could it survive the tarmac and the scooters and the shouting? It was probably as happy as an urban fox. Better nourished, perhaps, because behind a modern office block I spotted the back of a Georgian terrace and a high garden wall completely covered in ivy. Last summer's Holly Blues would have laid their eggs here. Its name is inaccurate. It is actually the holly-and-ivy blue, and its love of these rugged plants which have colonised our cities sustains it in the most inhospitable environments known to butterflies. This small, triangular butterfly was once called the Azure Blue, which better suited its lovely shade of dusty pale blue. It was the colour of the sky and seemed always to frequent it, flying high and seldom bothering to settle so that clumsy mortals could take a closer look.

I walked on to Imperial Wharf, where the wind scythed through the 'Mediterranean style' boulevard between flats with windows tinted like those in a footballer's car. The modern restaurants were closed and did not look like they ever wanted to reopen. Scratch-scratch-scratch went the claws of a pug dog dragged unwillingly along the pavement. On the riverfront, the developers had mercifully allowed space for a fancy little 'sensory' garden. Red campion and ragged robin was already flowering in tiny, rough flower meadows skirted by miniature pines and silver birch. A goose was plumped contentedly in the middle of springy new turf like an ornament and I stopped, sat, stared, became self-conscious and left. There were no butterflies to be found.

I took the train to Twickenham. When I reached the riverbank, I was thrown into a shiny, hyper-real spring paradise. It was a forgiving time of year: fresh greenery smothered rubbish and garnished the bleakest of housing estates. But this part of London needed no help. The river scene looked like paintings from Victorian or Georgian times: high on the cliff at Richmond, the dark windows of huge houses looked sedated as they gazed blankly over the water. Framed by chestnuts and limes, Marble Hill House looked splendid, Ham House serene. The only difference from an old painting was that roughly every ninety seconds a plane heaved itself up from Heathrow and turned its belly overhead, spewing jet engine noise across the whole scene.

I had been told that the little boat taking passengers from the north to the south bank of the Thames just east of Twickenham – from Middlesex to Surrey – was more expensive per metre than the Orient Express. I paid my £1 and the boatwoman sighed as her son sorted through another passenger's fare which had been paid in 5p coins. Once, she recalled, a tourist spent the whole crossing – it is not very long – counting out his fare in coppers. 'Thank you very much,' she said when he handed her the fare and then, to his astonishment, she flung all the pennies and two pennies over her shoulder into the water.

On the south bank, the Thames path was busy with cyclists juggling plastic bottles of water. Affluent couples wrapped their faces in dark shades, their glossy children scampering behind the cavalcade of three-wheeled buggies. 'Money', 'price', 'product' and 'supply' featured in every conversation I overheard. An elderly jogger picked his way along the path, head bowed as if ducking gunfire.

I felt a teenage self-consciousness as I took off my rucksack and got out my notepad, Jeremy Thomas and my camera. The binoculars stayed in the bag. I was a geek but worse, I was a lone man, not walking with any purpose but rather loitering close to happy families and then scampering through thickets of unseen nettles in pursuit of something not visible to a casual onlooker's eye. I tried not to catch the eye of any casual onlookers.

At least I did not have a butterfly net. In the old days, Aurelians invited mockery with their foppish garb and outlandish equipment. Simple pursuits may be comically over-accessorised today thanks to modern capitalism's brilliance at manufacturing desires (when a humble walker requires GPS and breathable Gortex), but it was no less so in the nineteenth century. So laden with butterfly gear was the nineteenth-century collector that, in an 1822 guide, William Swainson recommended a collector should employ a 'little boy' to carry his gear, as a caddie might bear golf clubs. An advert for the naturalist retailers Watkins & Doncaster on the Strand (where hung a painted sign of a Swallowtail) advertised essential equipment in 1892. These included a wire or cane ring net and stick, an umbrella net (self-acting), a pocket folding net (cane), corked pocket boxes, zinc collecting boxes, chip boxes, entomological pins, pocket lanterns, sugaring tins (with brushes) – to capture moths – killing bottles (1 shilling and 6 pence), steel forceps, scalpels, scissors and larva boxes.

'A butterfly net was to some almost a badge of frivolity and oddness, especially when it was accompanied by a stove-pipe hat (lined with cork), collecting tins, a few yards of sheeting and a pincushion bristling with pins, worn like a medallion,' writes Salmon in his history of butterfly collectors. Guides of the day warned aspiring entomologists to expect catcalls and stares from the ignorant. So as well as all this kit, the Aurelian needed something else: a thick skin.

Edward Newman, my favourite Victorian butterfly writer and a prodigiously energetic man who rose at 4 a.m. on summer mornings so he could marshal his butterfly collection in peace, recommended a green butterfly net for its inconspicuousness: 'White never fails to attract a crowd, which causes some slight inconvenience to the entomologist, as well as loss of time, for he is invariably under the necessity of explaining to the bystanders exactly what he is doing.' For once, Newman's good humour is shot through with an irascibility you can sense in some butterfly obsessives today when their labours are interrupted by passers-by who are oblivious to the ecstasy that is chasing a small dun brown butterfly.

The first butterfly I saw by the Thames was a Comma sunning itself on a tree stump and, half to avoid other walkers, I then swung away from the path and onto a wet patch of meadow. Ham Lands nature reserve was once a series of gravel pits, feeding the city's great hunger for expansion. Extraction ceased in 1952 and the pits were filled with chalky rubble, which accidentally created rather good alkaline conditions for chalk-loving, butterfly-friendly plants.

At first glance, I saw nothing. If I had strolled straight through the meadow, I would have only picked up the two hefty Peacock butterflies pursuing each other around a patch of brambles. The lovely thing about looking for butterflies, however, is that it gives you an excuse to dither and then just be. I stood there, in the sunshine, in a meadow of pink and white flowering nettles and creamy cow-parsley flowers with their delicate, slightly bitter, scent, with young hops and sticky goose grass straining to climb over it all.

From one side, I could hear the distant roar of the crowd in Twickenham stadium, watching a rugby union cup final. From the other, an amateur football match on the pitches beyond the reserve. This was being taken so seriously that everything was shouted three times. 'Yes-yes-yes', 'feet-feet-feet' and 'time, time, time', followed by a single, strangled 'Oi!'

It was when I saw two small, white butterflies that I realised just how rusty my butterfly identification skills were these days. I pursued this pair up and down the sunny side of the meadow for twenty minutes. They kept speeding off. I could not tell whether they were Small Whites, Green-veined Whites or female Orange Tips, which do not have the male's unmistakable orange triangles on their wings. Finally they landed. Both looked like Small Whites. I flicked through Jeremy Thomas. Yes. But then so did a third butterfly. At this point, I started to doubt myself. This was the perfect spot and ideal time for an Orange Tip, so they couldn't all be Small Whites, could they? Was I getting it all wrong?

The whites were patronising a thick overgrown patch of nettles at the very boggiest point of the meadow. Squelching through the longest, wettest grass, I tripped on several hidden trunks of dead elms. Right in front of me, a fox jumped out of the undergrowth. It had the nonchalance of an urban fox and the healthy bushy coat of a country fox; it was a suburban fox, the sort of fox that lived in Surrey. Confused for a moment by a raucous screech from the trees that heralded the unexpected sight of a bright green ring-necked parakeet – an alien species that has made itself very much at home in south-west London – I paused, and an unmistakable male Orange Tip puffed self-importantly past with its fluorescent high-vis safety markings flashing in the sunshine. 'You beauty,' I said out loud. (The eccentricity of butterfly hunting is contagious. It spreads to all aspects of your being.)

The Orange Tip always reminded me of Easter walks at my granny's house in Somerset, but it seemed less benign the more I read about it. Its caterpillars are cannibals, born in solitary confinement: the mother will only lay one egg on each plant to try and stop them eating each other. This does not always work. To prey such as birds, the Orange Tip is also one of the least palatable of all British butterflies, and its brightly-coloured wings warn potential predators of its toxicity. The first Orange Tip I had seen for at least a decade was certainly more lurid than I remembered. It was also a relief. Everything was all right with the world, for another year at least, if the Orange Tips were dancing through a meadow by the Thames in April. The Apocalypse was not nigh, not quite yet.

I set myself the time-consuming task of running down every white butterfly I saw until I could confidently distinguish Green-veined Whites from Small Whites, and both these from female Orange Tips. The trick with butterfly hunting is not to follow too closely. Keep your distance, let them settle and then move in more slowly, treading more softly than you imagine you need to. It is surprising how well butterflies can see us, and appear to fear us. Some take alarm at blundering human beings from ten metres away, or more. All these whites reared skywards in alarm like a bolting horse when they got close to me. Gradually, I remembered to stop still, and move much more smoothly and cautiously. Finally, I found another white at rest and even though it would not close its wings I could see mottled grey on its hindwing and hints of green underneath. It was a female Orange Tip, and quite different from the Small Whites I had seen earlier.

The butterflies kept coming. A friend from work who recently learned of my mission sent me a text of two words: 'Speckled Wood'. I did not know he knew that much about butterflies but he had seen one of these, probably our most common woodland butterfly. An hour later, so had I: in the shade of the ramshackle old willows by the Thames, two Speckled Woods sat companionably together, their mottled beige and brown wings wide open in the sunshine, showing their cheerful black and white eye spots in the corner of each wing. The Speckled Wood stands out from other species for its willingness to fly around in the kind of shady woodland no other butterfly would tolerate. It has been one of the few butterflies to prosper as many woodlands have become more overgrown and tangled in recent decades.

I was relieved that Londoners are so famously incurious. No one glanced at me, let alone asked me what I was doing, even though I was behaving weirdly. I moved slowly through a more shrubby part of Ham Lands, my feet wet and my shins stinging from the virile young nettles on the damp meadow. I noticed several other men, on their own, with rucksacks and the slow-but-intent look of a butterfly hunter about them. Were they birdwatchers or perhaps even lepidopterists recording insects for Butterfly Conservation? One caught my eye and nodded, knowingly, perhaps companionably.

I leaned over another small white butterfly laid out on a grass stem. This one had wings decorated and divided by dark veins. Here, very satisfyingly, was a Green-veined White. It was so distinct, at rest at least, that I now knew that all my previous Small Whites had, indeed, been Small Whites. My identification skills were not as blunt as I feared.

A mid-afternoon warmth spread. One nature lover I had seen earlier was now sunbathing in a glade between hawthorn bushes. He lay on his back with his knees spread apart in the air. I bent over my Green-veined White. When I glanced behind me, the sunbather was looking at me through his legs. I ambled onwards. A Peacock butterfly, its wings expansively spread in the sunshine, encouraged me to pause again and take its photo. I looked around and now the sunbather had risen to his feet and was following me slowly and very intently up the deserted path through the bushes.

Solitary men. Wandering through the shrubbery. No binoculars. Too smartly dressed for walkers. Too aimless for birders. It belatedly dawned on me: these were men looking for love, with other men, in the bushes. I, too, was frolicking around the meadows, cruising these bushes, doing a lot of pausing and coquettish glancing. Imagine my protests: 'No, no, officer, I was not looking to commit acts of public indecency with strangers in the bushes. I was looking for the Orange Tip butterfly.' I had inadvertently attracted the advances of men on innocent walks across Hampstead Heath in London in my younger days. I took no offence. This time, no one even chatted me up. My butterfly-hunting manoeuvres must have been far too camp for most gay men's taste. On the other hand, I was slightly concerned about the signals I had been inadvertently sending, lurking in the bushes on my own and shiftily glancing around all the time.

My teenage self-consciousness returned like a blush, so I set off briskly for the Thames path and did not look behind me until I reached Richmond. Step by step, the rough edges of the river turned into a riverside park of pristine lawns and flowering trees. Normally these well-manicured gardens full of spring flowers would seem bountiful but, in my eyes, they now seemed barren and devoid of wild plants and insects. The rough meadows of Ham Lands might look nondescript at first, but after spending a couple of hours there I could see they were so much richer and more full of life than the most prolifically floral piece of park.

3. Comma, Ashburton, Devon, 22 March
4. Peacock, South Pool, Devon, 22 March
5. Large White, Stoke Newington, London, 5 April
6. Holly Blue, Fulham, London, 18 April
7. Small White, Ham Lands, London, 18 April
8. Orange Tip, Ham Lands, London, 18 April
9. Speckled Wood, Ham Lands, London, 18 April
10. Green-veined White, Ham Lands, London, 18 April

4

Baffled by Britain's dowdiest 'butterfly'

When I was a boy, the first ever trip Dad and I undertook to see a butterfly we could not just bump into on holiday was in search of two spring skippers. We drove twenty miles to an old railway line at Narborough in west Norfolk to look for the Grizzled Skipper and the dowdiest butterfly in Britain, the aptly named Dingy Skipper. An ugly butterfly is a fascinating oxymoron.

Both these little skippers are less common now than when I first saw them nearly a quarter of a century ago. They are not the sort of butterfly you chance across in a manicured garden or park. They prefer rough grassland and the flower-rich poor soil of brownfield sites, railway lines or disused quarries. I had not seen either butterfly since that trip. When I got a Monday off work late in April, I searched for a good skipper site close to the capital. Scouring the 'first sightings' pages of local branches of Butterfly Conservation on the web, I found an account of numerous Dingy Skippers seen flying at Waterford Heath, a mile outside Hertford. They had been spotted that very weekend.

It was late April and in the fields by the A1, oilseed rape was beginning to turn yellow in the warmth of the hottest spring for ten years. This boded well for chasing butterflies. Hidden from view, caterpillars would be hard at work eating their own bodyweight and more in green shoots and leaves, fattening quickly in the sunshine. Pupae would be warm and dry and butterflies would soon be hatching out everywhere.

At the entrance to the heath stood an old corrugated-iron shed, a scruffy reminder of industrial days. On the edge of the Beane valley, Waterford Heath was an amphitheatre of former sand and gravel pits, worked from the 1930s and abandoned in the 1990s. Now a community nature reserve, it had been colonised by plants and animals that appreciated poor, sandy soils. On a Monday morning, nothing stirred except for two magpies shifting uneasily in a hawthorn bush. The see-sawing call of a great tit rang out loudly and repetitively and the echo of geese drifted up from the river. The grass glistened with dewy spiders' webs and on the steep banks flowered wild strawberries, one of the food plants enjoyed by the Grizzled Skipper caterpillar. Dusty heads of musk thistle stood to attention, dry and dead reminders of last summer.

It was twenty-five minutes before I saw any insects. A grey-brown, moth-like butterfly flew over my shoulder and weakly but indefatigably paraded around the amphitheatre: a skipper, but which kind? It was hard to follow against the sun, and it just kept going and going. It landed on a dead thistle and whizzed off again as I closed in seeking its photograph. Four or five of these little grey insects sent me spinning around the heath in circles for an hour. All of them materialised from the steep sheltered side of the old pit. Some I would follow as they raced out purposefully over the short grass. They would keep going in a graceful arc until they returned to exactly where they had started out. No matter how slowly and carefully I moved, or how much respectful distance I kept, they would not settle, but would dance into the hawthorn more quickly than I could run.

Finally, I got a couple of photographs. Skippers are characterised by their brisk, buzzing flight. Small Blues and Brown Arguses are also really difficult to follow with the naked eye at times. I did not, however, remember Dingys being quite this difficult. Looking at them more closely, however, I was puzzled. I checked the images on the back of my camera as well. If this was a Dingy Skipper it had very bright chequered markings, almost as bright, in fact, as a Grizzled Skipper. You can look at guidebooks as much as you like but there is no substitute for seeing something in the wild and being able to compare it with something else in the wild. So far, I had found the differences between white butterflies surprisingly obvious when you saw two different species in the same hour. Here again, I consulted Jeremy Thomas. The Grizzled Skipper usually emerges two weeks before the Dingy Skipper. Even if butterflies are coming out earlier because of climate change, this would be a very early Dingy. The information boards at the entrance to the heath said there were Grizzled Skippers here but made no mention of Dingys. So these, I thought, must be Grizzled Skippers.

The absorption of an Aurelian in the midst of their mania is comic. Henry Attfield Leeds hunted Chalkhill Blue aberrations at Royston Heath. On one occasion, he was so preoccupied by a pair of feeding moths that he was butted from behind by a deer. I too was lost in this more modest challenge. These little grey flashes were taunting me, flying, flying, flying and never settling. When they did, they disappeared, and I only saw them again when they flew off after I disturbed them. Eventually, I saw a smaller, darker and some-how more substantial, well-defined grey-brown shape. I followed it. This time, it landed within seconds, and obligingly posed for a photo. With its pristine dark-grey-and-white chequered pattern, this was a beautiful little Grizzled Skipper. And it definitely was not what I had just been pursuing for the last hour.

'If you go BA, I can get you some air miles,' puffed a lunchtime businessman jogger to his lunchtime pal as they heaved past. I sat down, frustrated. If you cannot find your butterfly, or get him to settle for a photograph, sometimes it is best to find the sunniest and most sheltered spot and sit and wait for them to come to you. This delivered my first Red Admiral of the year. I heard the flick of its wings before I saw it and when it hove into view it was like meeting an old friend after a number of years. I had forgotten how charming and attractive he was.

Named by Petiver in 1699, the Red Admiral was once called the Scarlet Admiral, a nicely scandalous name for its black-brown wings garnished with slashes of bright red. Despite being one of our more common garden butterflies, entomologists believed that until recently few survived our winters and most specimens flew in from the Continent. Milder winters have encouraged more to successfully hibernate. This one probably had, because most immigrant Admirals arrive in May and June and their offspring are what we see on fallen fruit in orchards or basking on ivy blossom in autumn.

After the welcome distraction of the Red Admiral, disappointment in myself for failing to identify the other grey butterfly returned. What was it? The mystery skipper was bigger and paler than the Grizzled, which would suggest a Dingy. Was it simply the male or the female? I flicked through Jeremy Thomas again but there did not seem much difference between the sexes. Was it a weird Hertfordshire variation? I managed to snatch another photo, and looked at it again on the back of my camera. The mystery skipper had a distinct chequered pattern, quite unlike a Dingy Skipper. The background colour of its wings was predominantly cream, rather than the dark grey of a Grizzled Skipper. Against the sunlight, its wings were almost translucent. I did not know what it was. So I gave up.

At home, that night, I mulled it over. Suddenly, I was struck by an obvious thought. The mystery skipper must be a moth.

Lepidoptera is the name given to the order of animals that includes butterflies and moths. Lepidopteron is formed from two Greek words: *lepis* meaning a scale and *pteron* denoting a wing. Butterflies and moths are distinguished from other insects by having wings made of tiny scales: if you ever trap one in your hands, the dust spilled in its distress are its scales. These give colour to a butterfly or a moth. Butterflies and moths also have a proboscis, a long tube coiled beneath the head which can be unfurled to take in liquids or nectar, rather like a straw.

We tend to imagine butterflies are brilliantly coloured, love the sunshine and fly during the day unlike moths, which are dull and grey and skulk around at night. From this basic distinction flower all kinds of assumptions and symbols and thinking which we attach to the two types of insect. Moths do tend to be drab and nocturnal, with plump bodies compared with the slender thoraxes of butterflies and moth wings flop down flat whereas butterflies tend to hold their wings rigid, above their backs. Around the world, however, there are insects that test the boundaries of this scientific classification: butterflies that look and behave just like moths, and even fly at night, and vice versa. In Britain, the moth most easily confused with a butterfly is probably the Six-Spot Burnet, which is brightly coloured and flies during the day; while the butterflies that most resemble moths belong in the skipper family, and the Grizzled and Dingy Skippers in particular. Curiously, the other butterfly I had seen that day, the Red Admiral, is one of the few butterflies to have been occasionally spotted flying at night. With a bit of practice, it becomes easy to distinguish our fifty-nine butterflies from the 2400 species of moths recorded in Britain. Most of the time, moths fly in a far more wayward, fluttering style than butterflies. But the most reliable way to separate the two is to check the antennae: butterfly antennae end in a distinct club, whereas almost all moths have fine, feathery antennae, with no clubs at the end.

With this basic rule belatedly returning to my brain, I went to my camera again and checked: the dingy 'butterfly' I had chased around Waterford Heath did not have clubbed ends to its antennae but feelers: here, obviously, was a day-flying moth. Why had it not occurred to me before? Clearly, I had been a bit crap. In my defence, I had not seen a Dingy Skipper for twenty-four years. I had also assumed that the enthusiastic posting by a Butterfly Conservation member was correct. In this case, whoever had recorded Dingy Skippers at Waterford Heath that weekend was almost certainly wrong: once one had been misidentified, it would be easy to assume every similar little grey butterfly would be the same.

Regressing to helpless little boy, I decided to email the photographic evidence to my dad. He would know for sure. Back came the reply. Yes, the elusive insect was a Lattice Heath moth. 'It would take a pretty unobservant amateur to mistake that for a Dingy Skipper,' wrote my dad, mildly. I felt chastened. My dad had a much deeper but also much more rounded knowledge and appreciation of natural history than I; as a new project, he had recently begun trapping moths to identify them (releasing them unharmed afterwards). Unlike him, I had never taken an interest in moths. They just did not move me. At least I could console myself with two more new species, taking me to twelve, but this could be a long, taxing summer. I had forgotten there was so much uncertainty in a world of just fifty-nine butterflies.

If that escapade made me feel foolish, there was another uncertainty I felt more excited about. That afternoon, I had driven on Arbury Nowers, a majestic hill in the Chilterns overlooking Tring Park, where Charles and Walter Rothschild had amassed an extraordinary collection of two and quarter million butterflies and moths, which now forms part of the vast collection belonging to the Natural History Museum in London.

I was hoping for a Dingy Skipper or a Green Hairstreak but found none. Nevertheless, it was so lovely that I felt optimistic about the year ahead and there were plenty of other butterflies. Brimstones are usually solitary butterflies and yet here on the Chilterns I saw twelve. There were battalions of Peacocks roaring about, too. After the dire summers of 2007 and 2008, perhaps this year would herald a miraculous recovery for our butterfly species.

I was on the western side of the steep down, at the end of the day, when, with a bang-bang-bang of wingbeats, a large ginger butterfly flew past in tearing haste. I gave chase up the chalky downland in my walking boots. The butterfly disappeared over the horizon in seconds. It was every bit as unequal a contest as that described by W. S. Coleman in 1860 who chased a Clouded Yellow when it crossed his path on the North Downs. He confessed the contest between 'a heavy biped, struggling and perspiring about a slippery hill-side' and 'a winged spirit of air, to whom up-hill and down-hill seem all one' was completely one-sided.

Five minutes later, another, similar butterfly zipped past. Again, I gave chase, with exactly the same outcome. Overhead, periodically, an easyJet plane rising from Luton cast a fast-moving shadow over the grass. Standing on the Chilterns, I was under an entomological flight path. These two impatient butterflies were too pale to be Peacocks and too large to be Small Tortoiseshells. It was far too early for a fritillary. They were flying with such purpose, they had to be great migrants. I could not be sure, I had not got a proper look, but they must be Painted Ladies, all the way from France, Spain or even Africa.

Just as a few exceptional years are graced by hundreds of

Camberwell Beauties or Clouded Yellows, so some of our summers are blessed by extraordinary invasions of migratory Painted Ladies. A day or so later, when I phoned Matthew Oates, the National Trust's butterfly expert, to arrange a day out searching for the rare Duke of Burgundy, he sounded more excited about something else. He had been walking on the Quantock hills in Somerset that weekend when he encountered a Painted Lady moving at speed. It was very early in the year and already there was a stream of sightings across southern England. 'Something is going on,' he whispered. Would this summer see another great migration event?

11. Grizzled Skipper, Waterford Heath, Hertfordshire, 20 April
12. Red Admiral, Waterford Heath, Hertfordshire, 20 April

5

The Duke and the Duchess

When I climbed into the passenger seat of his car, I knew it would be a special day. Pinned carefully to the upholstered interior roof of Matthew Oates' red Honda Civic were two dozen paper butterflies, an empire of Purple Emperors. Further back was a Painted Lady, carefully cut from a butterfly poster or old guidebook. The sky of his vehicle was filled with butterflies.

We were hoping to see 'His Grace', the Duke of Burgundy, which Oates believed was now Britain's most vulnerable butterfly. This was one of the five butterflies I had never seen before. My dad and I had never even attempted to see it together because it tended only to fly in May, when I was busy with exams at school and Dad was busy with exams at university. Oates, it turned out, was another of probably many Aurelians still tormented by the painful memory of all the butterflies he had never seen as a child because of the miserable strictures of the exam hall.

There are probably fewer Duke of Burgundies than any other species in the country, Oates reckoned, because our other rarities tend to occur in larger colonies. In 2000, it was calculated that this butterfly's total flight area in Britain was 2.66 square kilometres, which equates to 0.001 per cent of Britain's land surface. That year, there were thought to be about 200 colonies; by 2009 there were only 80 colonies left. All bar five of these isolated populations were tiny, and therefore extremely fragile, liable to be erased by one or two bad summers. This noble little butterfly was on the very edge of existence.

A twinkly man, perpetually amused by the rich ironies of life, Oates met me at Kemble station in the Cotswolds. I had taken a 7 a.m. train from Paddington because he advised me that His Grace was an early riser and liked to be tucked up in bed by 3.30 p.m. Before this day, I had only met Oates once, briefly, in Birmingham at a pleasingly ramshackle gathering of amateur and professional butterfly recorders who provide annual records of numbers and distribution for ecologists and Butterfly Conservation. My dad knew Oates through conservation work and had said I must seek him out because he was an amazing man. So I was a little deflated when we first met and he seemed rather diffident as I enthusiastically outlined my mission to see all species of British butterfly in one summer. Oates, whose professional title is the National Trust's Nature Conservation Adviser but who had carved a unique niche for himself as the Trust's roving butterfly man, was probably deluged with approaches from ill-informed authors and idiotic journalists like me who always wanted something for nothing. I imagined he was fatigued by it all. After another couple of emails, however, he seemed to warm to the idea of a butterfly trip and mentioned he would show me the Duke of Burgundy and, later in the summer, his true love, the mysterious and magnificent ruler of our butterfly kingdom, the Purple Emperor, 'His Imperial Majesty', as Oates called it.

Murky grey morning cloud was shielding the sun but the forecast for 23 April, St George's Day, was optimistic. At least our hunt gave Oates the excuse to escape his office for a day – the flashy, eco-friendly National Trust headquarters in Swindon – and wander through his real domain, the downs and the woods. He was in a far jollier mood than when I had first met him balancing a small pyramid of sand-wiches on a paper plate in a stuffy room at the butterfly recorders' symposium. Searching for butterflies should be as spontaneous and instinctive as these insects in flight. Nabokov loved to 'drop in, as it were, on a familiar butterfly in his particular habitat, in order to see if he has emerged, and if so, how he is doing'. We were going to drop in on Oates' favourite spot for the Duke and his Duchess.

At this time of year, the Cotswolds looked young and vigorous and exceedingly well groomed, rather like the disconcertingly self-assured teenagers who studied at the Royal Agricultural College we drove past. 'A den of iniquity,' said Oates dryly. 'All equine studies and pratology.' It looked like an Oxbridge college in its dress of smug, mellow stone. Dinky wooden signs on the verge advertised cream teas and jazz and, in a lay-by a man was carving a wooden barn owl by an old blue van. Scattered in front of him were poiso-nous-looking wooden toadstools he had created: twee new age tat for the gardens of retirees with vast disposable incomes.

We pulled into the local Waitrose supermarket for a cup of tea while waiting for the cloud to clear. Oates quickly turned the conversation to our quarry for the day and His Grace's attitude to sex. 'I won't call it the courtship habits of the Duke of Burgundy fritillary. He does not ask her for her name,' he said. 'Being a male Burgundy is all about sex. It's mating.' Oates then explained a fact which was obvious but of which I had hitherto been oblivious: for all its beauty, every second of almost every butterfly's winged life is about mating. A caterpillar is dedicated to eating and growing; on the wing, a butterfly is fully grown so its sole purpose now is to find a mate and, if female, lay eggs. (There are a few exceptions among the late-summer generations of hibernating butterflies such as the Small Tortoiseshell, which take nectar before finding a good place to hibernate, only mating when they emerge again in the spring.)

The Duke only gets one shot: during its short life in the spring, when the weather is often erratic. Perhaps this makes the males more priapic and pugnacious than others, although the Duke has not been as successful in his mating affairs as many human aristocrats. This butterfly is on the decline across most of Europe. In the beginning, in Britain, it was known as Mr Vernon's Small Fritillary. It was called a fritillary because of its superficial resemblance to other fritillaries, but this was a misnomer for it was decided that, unlike Britain's eight resident fritillaries, the Duke actually belonged to the Riodinidae family of butterflies (more recently, taxonomists ruled that it is actually a member of the Lycaenidae family alongside the hairstreaks and blues but it is still not a fritillary). Butterfly books now excise the fritillary part of its name but romantics such as Oates continue to use it: rightly or wrongly, he argued, it is part of His Grace's history. The most intriguing bit – why it took its name from an unidentified aristocrat – is unfortunately completely unfathomable.

Oates first got to know the Duke during the 1970s. He worked at Noar Hill, a nature reserve in Hampshire which remains a rare stronghold for the butterfly. This, for Oates, was one of his early scientific assignments after a misspent youth studying poetry. As a child, his very first memory was of an insect: being viciously bitten in his playpen by an army of red ants. Another early memory was catching in his hands a Small White that, in his memory at least, was sitting on a red rose. Later, he chased an Orange Tip around the cricket pitch at school and swiped it to the ground with his cricket jumper, giving his prize catch to another boy who collected butterflies. His love for natural history really began, however, when he became a precocious birder. Aged four, he joined a bird-nesting group run by the biology teacher at the school where his father was headmaster. 'It completely changed my life,' he said, and with 'a small gang of delinquent boys' he ran wild in Crewkerne, Somerset, looking in nests for eggs and the ultimate prize, a cuckoo's egg in a robin's nest.

Dispatched to boarding school in West Sussex aged eight, he eventually defected from the school's bird group to its butterfly- and moth-collecting group, run by his formidable old maths master. After the freedom of Crewkerne, Oates found his school 'a prison surrounded by the most incredible landscape imaginable'. In the woods close by, 'we had Pearl-bordered Fritillaries, Small Pearl-bordered Fritillaries, White Admirals and best of all, the monarch of the woods, the Purple Emperor.' He sighed with pleasure. 'Forty years ago this year, I saw my first Purple Emperor. There was no going back after that.'

The dry science of biology, as it was then taught, 'bored the pants' off him and Oates ended up studying the Romantic poets and Samuel Taylor Coleridge in particular. Although he skived off work to go butterflying throughout the hot summer of 1976, he only became a professional conservationist after years of volunteering on nature reserves. Eventually it turned into a high-profile position at the National Trust. During the 1980s, like many entomologists, he undertook studies of heroic-sounding complexity to better understand the needs of the Duke. He performed a mark-and-recapture study (capturing, marking and recapturing 600 individual butterflies) and studied the immature stages of the butterfly's life, which was complicated by the fact that the caterpillars only come out at night.

These labours were against a backdrop of growing concern for the Duke. Over recent decades, the Duke performed a startling adaptation to its changing environment. During the twentieth century, it moved from being a butterfly predominantly of the woodlands to being a butterfly found on dry downland and rough pasture. This was very unusual. Butterflies do not usually transform their behaviour and habitat so quickly. The decline of coppicing probably drove it out of the woods and Oates believed we had now almost lost it as a woodland butterfly. Its bold switch to pasture, however, had not halted its decline. 'The Oates motto is "never underestimate a butterfly",' said Oates. One source of hope for some species is climate change. Better summers will make some butterflies more capable of travelling across our decimated landscape to look for new sites. 'But I am seriously worried for Burgundies. The figures are very alarming. What's messed it up in the last twenty years is conservation management.' In creating nature reserves and carefully managing land to better conserve rare plants and animals in recent decades, we have actually damaged populations of Dukes, Oates argued. 'The track record of conservation management on this butterfly is bloody awful. I really think we could lose it.'

If I were a conservationist, I would be exasperated by His Grace the Duke of Burgundy for being as fussy as the most indulged aristocrat. As Oates has documented, males live for just five days on average. Females appear rarely and will spend three-quarters of their day hidden in vegetation, wings snapped shut. Oates once watched a female for three and a half hours. It did nothing. Eggs are laid on cowslips but they must be a very particular size: females select cowslips with at least four medium-sized leaves. The cowslips must then have grass growing over them in summer to prevent the leaves turning yellow before the caterpillars are fully fed. Droughts, and the resurgence of rabbits, have drastically reduced Burgundy populations.

Before climate change, another man-made event, the introduction of the rabbit-killing disease myxomatosis in the 1950s, caused the decline of many grassland butterflies which relied on large rabbit populations to keep the grass short and full of flowers. Conservation strategies saw a widespread reintroduction of grazing to help rare plant species and butterflies such as the Adonis Blue. But the Duke of Burgundy required longer, rougher grassland; overgrazing has caused its population to plummet. The ongoing problem is conflicting conservation aims. Many grasslands managed for the conservation of other flowers and butterflies have been too overgrazed for the Duke's exacting tastes. Even with Oates at the helm, Burgundies have disappeared from National Trust land. 'Burgundies,' he observed, 'have been slipping through the conservation net spectacularly.'

We juddered over a cattle grid and parked at the start of what Oates called 'a completely nebulous' lane that wound around the bottom of Rodborough Common. The folds of the Cotswolds were deep and intimate. Every Friday, in the little gap where we pulled over, an executive and his personal assistant would park up to conduct a ritual every bit as clandestine as the coupling of the Duke and Duchess. The first leaves of the beech trees were unfolding, as luminous and delicate as the wings of a butterfly freshly emerged from its chrysalis. Oates was almost singing with delight as the cloud lifted. 'They are out there, I can feel it.'

Rodborough Common had been donated to the National Trust by a butterfly lover who feared that quarrying could destroy it. It was one of the best sites left for the Duke. But you could easily walk around the common on a sunny day in April or May and never see this perky little aristocrat, so discreet are its colonies. Oates pointed to a slope which held a small population. The Duke had not been so plentiful here since a winter's day ten years ago when the common's warden had the flu, he explained. This meant he left the cows on the slope over a weekend, three days longer than planned. A few too many cowslips were trampled and the plants have not returned to their former abundance. Nor has the Duke.

Unlike the collectors of old, Oates carried nothing but a camera, although his straw sunhat with a vivid blue ribbon around the rim gave him the look of an Aurelian of old. The blue ribbon was from hunting second-generation Adonis Blues late last summer. He should have changed it to burgundy for the day; he would never dare search for the Purple Emperor without a band of purple around his hat.

Five minutes up the path, where ash, turkey oak and dogwood gave way to grassland, Oates immediately picked out two Green Hairstreaks in a dogfight, smudges of grey in the sky. 'That is a vicious little thing and their sexual morals are terrible. They are a disgrace,' said Oates, beaming. The caterpillars are cannibalistic and the pupae squeak if disturbed. These small, emerald butterflies are not to be trifled with.

I had not seen a Green Hairstreak for a decade and while I remembered they always landed with their wings closed, exposing their brilliant, iridescent green underwings, I had forgotten they always tilt themselves rather melodramatically to best soak up the sun. A female rubbed its wings together in a self-satisfied circular motion as it drank from a tiny flower of milkwort.

We walked slowly up the slope to Manor House Combe, a cleft in the steep grassy common midway between top and bottom, where the north-facing slope turned west. Oates breathed deeply. 'This is the still point of the turning world, not just for me but for Burgundies.' It was a particularly peaceful corner of Rodborough Common, well chosen by the Dukes. The males have territories to

THE DUKE AND THE DUCHESS

which successive generations return each year. They wait in this sheltered, warm spot for the Duchesses, who tumbled down the slope on their maiden flight. The males have to seize their chance because if they don't someone else will.

So far, the only thing that had tumbled down the slope was a fawning black Labrador. Above us, the steady stream of weekday dog walkers were completely out of sight, sticking to the flat top of the common. Dogs can do it but modern man, remarked Oates, cannot cope with a slope.

We saw the first Small Heath of the year, a butterfly with a happy expression thanks to the black eye spot on its forewing, which is the colour of a polished oak chest. Like the Green Hairstreak, the Small Heath always settles with its wings closed although it is rather more modestly clothed in brown and beige. We waited. The sun shone and the sense of peace was gently broken by the very English sound of Woodchester church bell striking eleven. It only bore a hazy relation to the actual time. The previous week it had chimed twenty-three times.

'Hello precious,' whispered Oates. He had found one. 'They are little jewels.' Two male Duke of Burgundies rose up, spiralling into the sky like helium balloons, until they were the height of the downs. As if they were teenagers pushing and shoving and finally separated in the playground by the wrench of a teacher's arm, they were repelled by an invisible force, and looped away from each other in the sky. Then each butterfly folded its wings together and plummeted like a meteor back to the warm grass.

A rush of emotions funnelled into the combe: a buzz of pleasure I had not felt since a child, sparked by searching for and then finding a rare butterfly; surprise, at the diminutive stature of the Duke, which had loomed in my mind far larger because of the grandness of its name and its scarcity, rather like celebrities who are surprisingly small if you see them in the flesh; and a sensation of completeness, that this jabbing little prize-fighter was the crowning piece of a cowslip-filled Cotswolds combe on a perfect April morning.

The sparring between the Dukes over this fine territory was nothing, reckoned Oates, to the disputes between the Dukes and Dingy Skippers. Some butterflies just do not get on and, where they flew together, the similar-sized Dukes and Dingys enjoyed a fierce rivalry. 'That's real hate,' sighed Oates, with the satisfaction of a circus ringmaster watching his charges. 'In football terms, you're talking Manchester United versus Liverpool or Portsmouth versus Southampton.'

There, in the combe, we followed six Dukes until each came to rest. Oates could instantly tell they were male, and how many days each butterfly had been out. One pristine male crouched on a bent piece of grass, swaying slowly in the stillness, as if it was tucked in a baby bouncer. A tiny male landed on a curled-up beech leaf from last autumn. It was so unusually small that in the old days it would have been classified as an aberration and therefore eminently collectable. 'I can see the fascination with collecting aberrations,' said Oates. In a different era, conservationists like him would almost certainly have been butterfly collectors.

When he was a boy, he spent winters finding out what the classical names of butterfly taxonomy actually referred to. Some were derived from the physical character of the butterfly. The Green Hairstreak's scientific name is *Callophrys rubi*. *Callophrys* means 'beautiful eyebrow' in Greek, a tribute to the butterfly's delicately adorned forehead; *rubi* means 'of the bramble' in Latin, which is not actually the Green Hairstreak's main food plant but was the first known to Aurelians. The Duke's name, *Hamearis lucina*, appears rather meaningless although it is a spring butterfly and Lucina is the Roman Goddess of the spring and of childbirth. 'I'd call it a Visigoth because that's what it is,' said Oates with relish. 'It's a bastard.' Every butterfly seemed to be pushing and shoving in the sunshine that morning. The males were all fighting to hold the best piece of territory. As we watched the Dukes, an aggressive intruder approached. Here, at last, was a Dingy Skipper. Small, dowdy and up for a scrap, it was definitely not a Lattice Heath moth. No moth would be that combative.

We moved to another part of the common, Swellshill Bank, where early purple orchids rose from the grass and the white rump of a roe deer disappeared into the scrub below. 'Now, who are you?' enquired Oates, stooping to find a female and a smaller male sitting companionably together. I lay on the turf to peer at the six legs of the female. Unusually, the male Duke of Burgundy can be distinguished from the female by the fact it only has four visible legs. (Butterflies, as insects, have six legs but in many species only four are easily visible, with two tucked up against the thorax and used for tasks other than walking, such as tasting, rather like our hands and arms.) The ground was springy and smelt damp and delicious. This pair had just mated. When a Duke chased off another Dingy Skipper, Oates turned ringmaster again. 'That's better. That's much better. He sorted out the Dingy Skipper! He beat him up!'

Watching Oates in the field, interpreting the insect life around him, was immensely satisfying. Knowledge and enthusiasm are attractive qualities in any setting but the way he also moved smoothly and lightly among these insects was more unusual. Oates was not there on the outside, pointing at the Dukes with an academic distance; he was among them, almost one of them. His absorption in our task and the pleasure he took in it reminded me of how much I enjoyed communing with nature through looking for butterflies. I felt a pang of regret that I had exiled myself from this pleasure by spending my twenties being busy doing other things. I had hardly been butterfly watching in earnest for more than fifteen years. This summer, at least, I hoped to make up for lost time.

The Duke of Burgundy was the first of the five British butterflies I had never seen before in my life. This was a prized sighting, and the unexpected views of Green Hairstreaks, Dingy Skippers and Small Heaths took my tally for the year up to teenage respectability: sixteen in total, before May had even begun. We celebrated with nothing stronger than an orange juice and lemonade over lunch at a pub with a stuffed pike on its dark wall. A century ago, it would have been packed with butterfly collectors; we sat in the garden, alone. We have to reforge our relationship with natural beauty, argued Oates. 'To us, nature is something we do through the BBC Natural History unit and a television screen. It scares me rigid what's going on. Our whole relationship is remote and not experiential. We underestimate the importance of beauty and wonder in our lives at our peril.' Oates' theory was that we are so alienated from nature that we need a reason to engage with it, and something to concentrate our minds, like prayer beads for a believer. 'We need our hand holding and butterflies can be that guide.'

Oates may conduct butterfly science and write papers for ecological journals, but he described his relationship with butterflies as a spiritual, religious and philosophical one. As one might expect from someone who studied the Romantic poets, for him, butterflies were about aesthetics and passion. 'I am addicted to them and I admit it and confess it. They are the focus of my relationship with nature and natural beauty. They are a conduit into natural beauty. Whether I could have a relationship with nature without them hasn't been tested. It is a passion but never underestimate the importance of passion in our lives. I wonder if football is a substitute for true passion. I'm not denigrating it but I wonder whether we can do better than that and nature does offer considerably better than that. As much as I love football it's no substitute for the real thing.'

Butterflies were part of the spirit of a place. 'Imagine a National Trust garden deprived of song birds or imagine a garden without butterflies. There would be a dimension missing.' Oates told me about the Welsh concept of *cynefin*. There is no direct English translation but the word refers to a place of personal belonging – heartland, perhaps. Butterflies can be part of this, particularly when they are such vivid presences in early childhood memories. If individuals are separated from their place of belonging, and are deprived of *cynefin*, they can long for home so intensely that they suffer spiritual breakdown, or *hiraeth*. This is what happened to John Clare, the poet son of a farm labourer from rural Northamptonshire, when he found success and moved to London at a time when the Acts of

Enclosure were destroying his beloved homeland. 'It's a poetic concept and it's bloody lost on scientists,' said Oates with sudden fierceness. 'I'm convinced there is something more important than DNA.'

Perhaps we could learn from beekeepers, mused Oates. They often enjoy a deeply empathic relationship with their charges. Like Prince Charles to his plants, some keepers will talk to their bees. The words may not matter but the tone does. Oates said he believed that butterfly species have a communal soul. Perhaps our souls could commune with theirs. 'What fascinates me in life is the relationship we have with species. Man and dog. Woman and horse. Man and butterfly. One to one. There is something there. It's ineffable but we know it's there.'

13. Green Hairstreak, Rodborough Common, Gloucestershire, 23 April
14. Small Heath, Rodborough Common, Gloucestershire, 23 April
15. The Duke of Burgundy, Rodborough Common, Gloucestershire, 23 April
16. The Dingy Skipper, Rodborough Common, Gloucestershire, 23 April

6

A kaleidoscope of Painted Ladies

The invasion began on a Thursday in the middle of May at Portland Bill. A south-westerly was blowing and on it sailed the first of an army of Painted Ladies. Purposefully, steadily, one by one, they appeared over the heads of walkers on the Dorset coast. And then they disappeared as quickly as they came, zigging left and zagging right but broadly sticking to a predetermined course – north, north-west – as if guided by an invisible hand.

'Angels' visits are few and far between,' wrote the Victorian lepidopterist Edward Newman of rare migrants. Over the years, however, Britain has been blessed with many strange and surprising visits from foreign butterflies. Most summers, a few dozen exotic migrants – a Monarch, a Queen of Spain Fritillary or a Camberwell Beauty – defy the logic of latitude or longitude, altitude or atmosphere, and pitch up on our shores. These are magic events.

Occasionally, there is an invasion of stunning magnitude, an incomprehensible number of tiny insects travelling an unfathomable distance, traversing seas and deserts and swamps and rivers and roads and cities and railways and giant prairie fields to settle, for some unknown reason, on a field in the centre of England. In 1508, Richard Turpyn recorded at Calais 'an innumerable swarme of whit buttarflyes cominge out of the north este and flyinge south-estewards, so thicke as flakes of snowe'. In 1846, the *Canterbury Journal* reported a similar invasion of Small Whites: 'One of the largest flights of butterflies ever seen in this country, crossed the Channel from France to England on Sunday last. Such was the density and extent of the cloud formed by the living mass, that it completely obscured the sun from the people on board our Continental steamers, on their passage, for many hundreds of yards, while the insects strewed the decks in all directions. The flight reached England about twelve o'clock at noon, and dispersed themselves inland and along the shore, darkening the air as they went.'

Every few decades, Britain succumbs to a huge invasion of Painted Ladies or Clouded Yellows when there are perfect breeding conditions on the Continent and favourable winds and weather to ensure the success of mass migrations. The great Clouded Yellow migrations are known as *Edusa* Years, after the butterfly's old scientific name. During the Second World War, military observers spotted a great golden ball drifting over the waves. They feared it was a cloud of poison gas; it turned out to be a huge phalanx of migrating Clouded Yellows. The lepidopterist L. Hugh Newman recollected how his father encountered a similar flock of Clouded Yellows. 'Imagine his surprise when, one sunny June morning, he saw what looked like a yellow cloud drifting over a field of lucerne which he passed every day. He realised in a moment that there was a vast swarm of Clouded Yellow butterflies, something which is the dream of every entomologist.'

Matthew Oates had already alerted me to the possibility of Painted Ladies being on the move. 'My Painted Lady count opened with a threesome and that's not normal at all,' he said. More significantly, he heard word of them moving in great number overseas. This year, rumours of an impending invasion began circulating in late winter. The Painted Lady is one of the most widely distributed butterflies in the world. The only places it does not favour are tropical rainforests and parts of South America. In February, a leading Spanish lepidopterist, Constanti Stefanescu, recorded hundreds of thousands of adult Painted Ladies emerging in the Atlas Mountains of Morocco. Unusually heavy winter rains in North Africa had triggered a germination of food plants devoured by its caterpillars. New generations hatched in great numbers. These butterflies flew to southern Europe. Some missed Portugal and, with unimaginable reserves of stamina, carried on flying across the Bay of Biscay all the way to Britain. 'Even for an albatross that's quite an achievement, never mind something the size of a Painted Lady,' said Richard Fox, a lepidopterist who works for Butterfly Conservation and studied the invasion. More sensibly, most of the African Painted Ladies settled in Spain and Portugal and bred again. If conditions are favourable, Painted Ladies can race through their life cycle, moving from egg to caterpillar to pupae to adult in just six weeks – far more quickly than most butterflies. (In laboratory conditions, eight generations of Painted Ladies have been produced in a year, although this rate cannot be sustained in the real world.) In southern Europe, their caterpillars quickly gained weight and, by April, large numbers of a new generation of adults hatched out and, like relay runners, moved northwards through France.

On May 3, Kevin Goodwin, a butterfly lover who had relocated from Britain to the south of France, sent an email to one of his old pals in the Wiltshire branch of Butterfly Conservation. In the last few days, he wrote, he had seen thousands of Painted Ladies flying past his house, each bent on a northerly course. 'It would be interesting to see if this year turns out to be a good one for Painted Ladies in Britain. If it is remember where you heard it first! From the Wiltshire branch "agent" in south-west France.'

More than a dozen British butterflies are migrants. Our resident populations of Large and Small Whites and Small Tortoiseshells are regularly topped up with visitors from the Continent, who arrive in summer and breed on our shores. These species and, to a lesser extent, the Red Admiral, are all able to survive the British winter, unlike the Painted Lady which can reproduce during our summer but cannot live through our cold winters. In this sense it, like the Clouded Yellow, is a pure migrant and not able to live all year round in this country, even though both are classed as members of our fifty-nine native butterflies.

I had already been tormented by the two mysterious butterflies ripping over the Chilterns at Aldbury Nowers. During the second week in May, I visited my dad in Devon to hunt for more emerging species. Saturday dawned darkly and Dad decided we should drive to

Start Point for a speculative walk along the South Devon coast and see if things brightened up. We parked high up by Start Point, a slab of rock into which was poked a lighthouse like a candle in a cake. Every set of boulders and each rocky inlet had a name: Sea Rock, Chap & Crater, Foxhole Cove, Gull Island, Great Sleaden Rock, Barler Rock, Frenchman's Rock. Scrubby patches of blackthorn and cherry were sculpted by the winds. Gorse flung coconut scent into the sky. The sun came out. We walked westwards along the coast and then looped back inland, where Large Whites, Green-veined Whites and Orange Tips graced the sheltered lane. We rejoined the coast at Hallsands, the remnants of a fishing village that had fallen into the sea. The most westerly house in the village had recently been drastically renovated and transformed into expensive holiday apartments. 'Important, iconic and historic,' boasted an advertising hoarding as we walked past a small, shouty sales office.

We were almost back at the car when we met four blokes on mountain bikes, sprawled on the path in exhaustion after a day-long ride, for charity, they said, up and down the coast path. Then, across them in a blink, flew a very pale orangey-brown butterfly. Just like the two mysterious butterflies that had hurtled past me on the Chilterns, this butterfly did not dally on a flower or settle in the sun. This time, however, in trainers rather than walking boots, I gave chase and could get close enough to catch a glimpse of its open wings as it powered inland at shoulder height. This was definitely an incoming Painted Lady.

It was only one. And that was all I saw for a couple of weeks, because I was stuck on a treadmill of work, in the city, with no time for the countryside. On the Whitsun bank holiday at the end of May, I took Lisa away for a non-butterfly break. My life this year had quickly become extremely butterfly orientated. I spent all evening reading about butterflies and all night dreaming about them and every week-end pursuing them. Lisa found the geekiness of all this quite cute. 'Butterfly boy' was her new nickname for me. But she preferred to relax by flitting around parties in fancy dress with all her mates and I no longer had time to do any of this. So I treated her to a break from all this nerdiness: I took her for a weekend on a steam train. It was, in my defence, in North Wales, which to use the Welsh concept first mentioned to me by Matthew Oates, was her place of *cynefin*, a land to which she felt an intense spiritual connection. Even she enjoyed being a geek for a day as she drove a steam train and then, on 25 May, a gloriously clear bank holiday Monday, we joined the crowds walking up Snowdon. At the beginning of our ascent, on the rough pasture to our right, I saw another, rather faded Painted Lady. This was odd, I thought. I had never seen one on a mountainside before.

It turned out that this particular Painted Lady was an advance party. Several days ahead of its peers, it presaged the influx to come. Unknown to me, further south, the invasion had already begun. On the Sunday while I was away in Wales, Matthew Oates emailed me. 'Massive PL invasion, seemingly bigger than that of 1996!' he wrote. 'Feel I'm knockin on heaven's door . . .' He had seen 241 in an afternoon working in the middle of a wood close to Cirencester, Gloucestershire. Few were settling or taking any nectar; all were heading north, and their numbers built by the hour. By 4 p.m., he was seeing five every minute. Many were faded, their bright orange turned pale and ghostly from their great travels; Oates called them grey pilgrims.

Painted Ladies spilled across southern England that weekend, seemingly coming in from all directions, but only heading one way: north. I rather wished I had been at home in Norfolk. Up to 18,000 were spotted sailing on the breeze across Scolt Head Island on the north Norfolk coast. Nature reserve staff clocked fifty arriving every minute. In East Sussex, a steady 133 were counted in one hour dancing over a gate in a wood. At Melbury Down, in Dorset, 128 were counted over ninety minutes by a butterfly enthusiast who recorded: 'When they arrived at the dry west-to-east valley bottom, there was a moment of indecision for each individual – some turned right and some left – before each one plucked up courage and climbed vertically northwards up the other side and over a dense and tall beech wood.' Valleys, mountains, motorways, forests and urban jungles were no obstacles to these indefatigable creatures.

In the last week of May, Painted Ladies turned up everywhere, not just in Britain but across Europe. I had to fly to Frankfurt for work. In woods just south of the city, I saw three of the migrants, which had moved north into Germany rather than across the Channel to Britain. Returning to London the following day, I found twelve flopping all over the white blooms of the cotoneaster hedge at the end of my street in Stoke Newington. I had never seen any butter-flies at this spot before. Another two raced each other up the road, heading, once again, due north. Every day, even in central London, you could see a Painted Lady: St James's Park, King's Cross, I bumped into them everywhere. This was definitely not normal.

The following weekend, Butterfly Conservation coordinated a special two-hour count. One volunteer in East Sussex clocked up 1500 in that time. From this count, scientists extrapolated that twenty million Painted Ladies had flown into Britain. This was exceptional compared with recent summers: in the previous year all the butterfly recorders in the Wiltshire branch of Butterfly Conservation counted a grand total of fifty-six Painted Ladies in their county during the whole year. One week into this invasion, the biggest numbers were recorded in West Wales, a sign there had been a second wave of butterflies beating their way through Cornwall and across the Bristol Channel on a more westerly line. The butterflies appeared to take a week to plough through England to Scotland. My sighting at the foot of Snowdon was nothing; a week later, a walker spotted a Painted Lady on the summit of Fionn Bheinn in Scotland, at 933m. Painted Ladies were seen on the Orkneys and right at the tip of the Shetlands. They were seen on the Isle of Man, still flying in the last of the sunshine at 9.30 p.m. By early June, they had arrived in Ireland. On the coast of Donegal, in the far north west, forty were counted every minute flying overhead. Where were they going? North-west from Ireland, after hundreds of miles of Atlantic Ocean, the first land they would find is Iceland. They found it. On 4 June, a Painted Lady was recorded in Iceland. Others followed in the subsequent weeks, part of an elite band of butterflies that had travelled from desert to glacier.

In the weeks to come, the Painted Ladies would be a constant companion, an emblem of the summer. One excited tabloid reported the invasion of a 'giant butterfly'. The Painted Lady is one of our bigger butterflies and certainly one of the strongest fliers but it is not a giant. While 1996 was another big year for migrating Painted Ladies, this summer's event was probably the biggest migration of any butterfly into Britain in living memory. 'I've never seen a migration like it,' said Martin Warren, the chief executive of Butterfly Conservation, who watched 200 pass him in an hour on a patch of downland, all heading due north. 'Normally when you see Painted Ladies you see one or two come in and then they head off but they don't necessarily head off in the same direction.' What, I wondered, made them stop and settle in a certain spot? In mid-June, at home on the north Norfolk coast, everywhere I went I saw Painted Ladies. Driving through the countryside, one would hurtle across the road every few hundred metres. Some were creepily immaculate, like Dorian Gray, mysteriously untarnished by the torrid journey they must have endured. Lepidopterists have noted that butterflies can look remarkably fresh after long migrations. They may be buffeted by the wind but they do not scratch themselves against plants or injure themselves during the rough and tumble of mating. Perhaps Painted Ladies have particularly smart survival strategies. One day in June, there was a torrential thunderstorm. When the rain ceased I heard the crashing of a Painted Lady against the inside of my living-room window. It had flown in the small, opened window and into my cottage to shelter from the storm.

Other Painted Ladies, however, were very much the grey pilgrims. Some did look like the picture of Dorian Gray in the attic. When I walked along the Norfolk coast one day, I found a Painted Lady with no orange, white or black markings left. As grey and ragged as a Victorian vagabond, its wings had almost wasted away. I could just make out the tracings of its old markings on what was left of its wings. It looked utterly wretched as it clung, like other Ladies, to the head of a thistle, but then it startled me by roaring off with great vim. It may have lost its looks but its muscular body could still propel it, swooping through the air, to wherever it wanted to travel next.

Like any creature, Painted Ladies are driven by an evolutionary desire to see their species survive and maximise the number of offspring they produce. In Britain, the biggest hurdle for every butterfly is to survive the winter. In Africa, and southern Europe, the biggest problem for butterflies is summer, when it is too hot and dry and food plants die off, threatening butterflies and their caterpillars with starvation. Most butterflies deal with extreme heat with a diapause, a form of summer hibernation during which insects stop growing and go into suspended animation. The Painted Lady is more proactive. Just as Wildebeest roam the plains following the rains, it flies across Europe to avoid drought, following the seasons so it can always find relative warmth and plants for its caterpillars to feed on.

During winter, there is enough rain in North Africa for its food plants to grow. Then the rain stops, summer arrives and the plants wither and die. Instead of laying eggs on plants that will be killed by the heat, the new generation of Painted Ladies fly to southern Europe, lay eggs and quickly produce another generation. The spring generation in southern Europe would perish in high summer, so

Painted Ladies move north to the cooler summers of Britain, Germany, Poland and the Netherlands. When they arrive, they get to work, laying eggs on common thistles. As the invasion began, Matthew Oates predicted there could be so many caterpillars on the thistles that many would be defoliated and destroyed by the end of the summer.

In a risk-free laboratory, a female Painted Lady can lay 300 eggs. If in the real world each of the estimated ten million female Painted Ladies arriving in Britain saw the survival of 100 of its eggs there could be an explosion of a new generation of one billion Painted Ladies later in the summer. This butterfly really could swarm. 'From my camel, I noticed that the whole mass of grass seemed violently agitated, although there was no wind,' wrote a nineteenth-century explorer travelling along the Sudanese Red Sea coast. 'On dismounting, I found that the motion was caused by the contortions of pupae of *V. cardui* [the Painted Lady], which were so numerous that almost every blade of grass seemed to bear one . . . Presently the pupae began to burst and the red fluid fell like a rain of blood. Myriads of butterflies, limp and helpless, sprinkled the ground.' Half an hour later, their wings dried, the Painted Ladies flew away to the east.

In Britain, not long after the invasion, a Cornish farmer cast his eye over a couple of fallow fields full of thistles and found them overrun with caterpillars. He called in a friend, who knew about butterflies. Scientific sampling was undertaken and it was calculated that there were 500,000 Painted Lady caterpillars in the two small fields. On some individual thistles, hung twenty very hungry caterpillars. Vast numbers of caterpillars were also reported everywhere from South Wales to Suffolk. In places where they ate all the thistles they moved onto anything they could find, even nettles, which are not a favoured food plant.

On flat, unfarmed fields behind the dunes at Wells, in north Norfolk, there were thousands of thistles. I watched a Painted Lady land on one, hoping to see it lay an egg. If it did, I missed it, and the butterfly thrashed its wings against the thorny spines of the leaves, scarring itself as if in frustration, and making the scratchy noise of a butterfly trapped against a pane of glass.

Flying so far, and in such a fearless manner, the Painted Lady seems a supercharged creature. Its Achilles heel, in Britain, is its dependence on warmth. While I saw Painted Ladies up mountains and in 10°C on Exmoor, captive adults die at 5°C and its caterpillars and pupae are vulnerable to rain, cold and even cloudy weather. Just as this formidable army of caterpillars should have been chomping their way through Britain's thistles in July, the weather changed for the worse. Bad weather brought disease, fungal infections, pests and slow growth, which all threatened the emergence of a billion-strong new generation.

By the second week of the month, there were still some very faded, grey veterans of the great May migration on the wing but walking through the thistle fields behind the dunes at Wells I also found the bright young beauties of the new generation. Several of these newly emerged British Painted Ladies were enormous, far larger than their parents and as big, I was sure, as a Purple Emperor, our second largest native butterfly. They were well-bred, well-fed first-generation immigrants; fatter, bigger and bulkier than their parents who had travelled so far to give them a new life.

This hefty generation would go on to produce a second generation of British Painted Ladies. In the previous good Painted Lady years of 1996 and 2003, there was sunny weather in August and a huge second generation flopped around on garden flowers and gave the impression of being an idle garden butterfly and a severe disappointment to their vigorous grandparents who had flown in from Africa or Spain.

This year, however, the weather turned in July and stayed unsettled into August as big Atlantic depressions ripped in from the west. Despite the less than perfect conditions, in August I heard a story of a biblical swarm on a field on the South Downs near Brighton that had been left fallow and swamped by thistles. By the time I headed over there, the heat had gone from the day and the last of the sun was catching the pink-grey heads of the thistles that spread, chest height, across several acres. At first, I did not see anything much. When I waded into the thistles, however, with every step two or three Painted Ladies rose up, and looped around. Suddenly there were twenty spinning around my head. When one chased another they would be joined by another and then another. Dancing butterflies were strung through the skies like fairy lights. A Large White made the mistake of straying onto the field and soon found itself pursued by a dozen Painted Ladies, which all felt obliged to defend their vast territory. There were pristine bright ginger ones, and faded grey specimens and some with tattered wings ripped to shreds from living among the thistles. Like an overpopulated city, life here looked uncomfortable and exhausting. These swarm dwellers were ageing fast. Food was also running out: everywhere stood thistles without any leaves – just a stem, nibbled to a thin yellow scar and topped with a prematurely grey seed head. Volunteers in the Sussex branch of Butterfly Conservation calculated there were 120,000 Painted Ladies on the wing in this small field. Here was a proper, old-fashioned swarm of butterflies, the sort of spectacular event I read had occurred in Victorian times but never thought I would see.

Great numbers of Painted Ladies have been seen in autumn in the past. Salmon reprinted the enthusiastic account of a lepidopterist who found a small army of Painted Ladies in gardens near Hunstanton, in north Norfolk, in October 1903. 'There were a good many beautiful asters, but bordering all the beds and paths were masses of lavender in full bloom. This lavender was perfectly alive with Painted Ladies; I could not possibly estimate the numbers, but there must have been thousands,' the lepidopterist wrote. 'It was a lovely bright day, and they appeared to be enjoying the sunshine and the flowers, and they sailed about as these butterflies *can* sail.'

What happens next? What is the fate of this large heat-loving butterfly that cannot survive our winters? Logically, the second generation of British Painted Ladies must attempt a reverse migration, and head south again, away from the frost and damp, and back to the distant lands of their forefathers. 'From an evolutionary point of view, it seems absurd that they would not go back,' said Richard Fox of Butterfly Conservation. In laboratory tests, Painted Ladies reared under lights which mimic the lengthening days of spring always fly north when they are released into a flight chamber. These are the 'spring' Painted Ladies that invade our country. When light conditions are changed to mimic autumn, it produces a generation of 'autumnal' Painted Ladies that instinctively fly in a southerly direction.

More evidence supporting the idea of reverse migration comes from butterfly monitoring records in Catalonia, in Spain. These have picked up enormous numbers of Painted Ladies in spring, before the butterfly vanishes from the region all summer. Suddenly, in the autumn, around October, the butterflies have turned up again. Are these the second generation heading back from northern Europe?

It sounds persuasive but there is one problem. Britain has a wealth of observations and records of butterflies over more than three centuries and yet hardly anyone has ever noted Painted Ladies departing from our shores. The migratory Red Admiral is closely related to the Painted Lady. Every autumn, there are plenty of sightings of Red Admirals flying off our southerly cliffs, spotted from ships crossing the Channel, or seen again by birdwatchers on the shores of Brittany, following the coastline to the south, just like migrating birds. And yet these sightings do not include its close relative. 'We expect Painted Ladies to be doing exactly the same as Red Admirals but when people see Red Admirals they don't say they have seen Painted Ladies,' said Fox.

Do Painted Ladies fly all this way for our disappointing summers, breed successfully and then perish? Each year, does another generation attempt to undertake the same epic and utterly futile grand journey? When I spoke to scientists such as Fox over the summer, they just did not know the answer. They hoped more evidence would emerge during the autumn. There was, at least, one possible explanation for the absence of sightings of Ladies leaving our shores. The Spanish lepidopterist Constanti Stefanescu has written of the habit of the Painted Lady flying up several hundred metres – and out of eyesight – so it can take advantage of stronger winds to push it on its way. While Painted Ladies seem to arrive on our shores in a conspicuous fashion, at head height, they might do this simply on arrival, so they can assess the land for suitable places for nectar and to lay eggs. On departure, they could easily sail so high into the skies that we never see them leave.

After an unusually fine autumn and numerous appeals to the public and its members, Butterfly Conservation finally found what it was looking for in October: reliable sightings of Painted Ladies apparently attempting the reverse migration to Europe. Along the Channel coastline of Cornwall, Devon, Sussex and Kent, the butterflies were seen heading straight out to sea, towards continental Europe. Many could have been travelling high in the sky and out of sight but such were the numbers after the great invasion that some were visible. By November, in the Mediterranean and North Africa there were also reports of Painted Ladies arriving again from the north. 'This is exactly the evidence needed to lay this enduring mystery to rest,' said Fox. 'Painted Ladies do return southwards from Britain in the autumn enabling the species to continue its breeding cycle during the winter months.' The children and grandchildren of the grey pilgrims who began this great migration proved as indefatigable as their forebears when instinct tugged their wings and directed them across the ocean before the seasons turned against them.

17. Painted Lady, Start Point, Devon, 9 May

7

The Woodman's Friend and
Lady Glanville

In 1900 a sixteen-year-old boy called Philip Allan took off on his
bicycle and cycled west to Dorset and then Dartmoor to hunt for
butterflies and moths. His expedition began in torrential rain and he
wearily peddled, or paddled, up to a Devon inn 'in much the same
condition as a Persian cat which has been floating off the port of
Basra for a week or two,' he wrote in *Memories of an Old Moth
Collector*, one of several volumes about his butterfly- and moth-collecting days. The 'fat motherly' landlady ordered him to strip, leave
his clothes outside his bedroom door and lie in bed while she dried
his clothes. 'So I lay naked in bed until a pretty young maid came in
with my clothes and told me that dinner would be ready in five minutes. I told her not to be in a hurry to go, so she sat down beside the
bed and put her arms around my neck and kissed me . . . She really

107

was very pretty, and I was very young . . . I thought this was an excellent introduction to Devonshire. However, she was afraid that mistress would come up after her if she didn't hurry, so off she went, and I got into my warm dry clothes.'

Nothing so exciting ever happened to me as a shy teenage butterfly hunter but then I did not have the independence of spirit to get on my bike, let alone seduce a pretty young maid. It never occurred to me to hunt butterflies alone; I enjoyed experiencing them with my dad. It was something we did together. We worked well on these father-and-son trips, we understood each other, moved at the same pace and were moved by the same things, although he could name and understand infinitely more about the flora and fauna than I. Our expeditions had petered out about the time I went to university and although we saw butterflies on walks together when I visited him in Devon, we had only undertaken a special trip to search for a particular species once in the last decade or more.

Just as Allan had written, there was something romantic about travelling westwards in search of butterflies even though my westward journey was on a crowded train from Paddington on a Friday afternoon early in May, in a carriage made up of an uneasy mix of tetchily silent commuters and a stag party of City boys braying noisily. I was heading to meet my dad to go hunting for the first fritillary to emerge in the spring: the rapidly declining Pearl-bordered Fritillary.

Eight fritillaries grace our skies. The word fritillary probably comes from the Latin for a chequered dice-box and early entomologists gave it to butterflies with a chequer-like pattern of gold and black panels and spots and swirls on their wings. These golden decorations match the dappled sunlight in our woodlands and can disguise them in flight and when they rest against last year's dead bracken. Known as the April Fritillary in the time before the Gregorian Calendar, when its May emergence was in April, the Pearl-bordered Fritillary also came to be called the Woodman's Friend because it followed foresters through the trees, quickly colonising the sunny glades they created when they coppiced our ancient woodlands. In 1860, W. S. Coleman called it a 'very common insect'. The twentieth century, however, was a disaster for this grace-ful golden butterfly. The planting of conifers and the cessation of traditional forest management such as coppicing caused the growth of dense, sunless woods that starved it of light and flowers. It was now rare, and still declining fast.

I had already tried and failed to see it once this year. After our suc-cess with the Duke of Burgundy, Matthew Oates and I visited Cirencester Park Woods, a forest privately owned but, luckily, cur-rently managed in a way that favours the fritillary (and qualifies the owner for conservation grants). In decades past, too much conifer was planted but here, at least, the conifers did not prosper and Oates hoped that an emerging market for carbon-neutral wood fuel, pro-viding chips or pellets for wood-based heating systems in schools and hospitals, would see other landowners regularly harvesting our native woodlands again.

As we walked into the wood, a sawmill sounded like a mosquito in the distance. At least it was audible proof that the wood was being harvested. Even so, the Pearl-bordered Fritillary nearly disap-peared from here at the turn of the century. Oates believed its sudden slump was caused by a big cull of deer, which the butterfly also relies on to keep the grass short in the woodland glades. Oates unveiled his equation: violets plus leaf litter minus grass equals Pearl-bordered Fritillaries. Once grass and trees grow up, the butterfly's violet food plant disappears and the ground is too shady and cool for its caterpillars to grow. Large new clearings have to be created every five years; after five or six years, a cleared patch becomes too over-grown for this sensitive butterfly.

We reached a clearing where young oaks rose from protective spirals of plastic. The humped back of a bank vole rapidly retreated as we crunched through last year's bracken. A pair of muntjac deer, resembling dogs with their white tails raised, stole away. It was mid-afternoon and the Pearl-bordered Fritillary was a morning butterfly. 'Most butterflies are,' said Oates. 'The morning emergence of new females stirs them up, gets them looking for crumpet.'

Two cut-glass voices of riders on horseback drifted through the woodland from one of the broad grassy rides created when Alexander Pope landscaped this wood. We patrolled up and down clearings but only saw the odd Peacock, Speckled Wood and Green-veined White. 'That's the wonder of butterflies, they can thwart you like this,' reflected Oates. 'They are very fertile ground for ideas not least because they continuously catch us out. I really thought Pearl-bordered would be starting to emerge. I'm a little bit worried we didn't turn anything up and that these colonies have collapsed.'

After skirting the coastline beyond Exeter, the train deposited me at Newton Abbot, where Dad met me at 4.30 p.m. He lived close by, in Ashburton, a small Devon town tucked into a small valley between two round green hills. It was the kind of place where old people visited the butcher and the baker with a basket tucked in the crook of their arm.

The sun was out but encircled by mocking white cloud which threatened to pluck away the light. Despite the uncertain conditions and cool air of late afternoon, Dad decided to drive straight to Aish Tor on the southern slopes of Dartmoor. He was one of Butterfly Conservation's army of volunteer recorders. Once a week for twenty-six weeks – the half of the year from April to September – he visited this specific area, his transect, and counted the butterflies he saw along a fixed, regular route. His records were sent to Butterfly Conservation and added to its national monitoring data, which then showed how species were declining or expanding.

Five minutes in the car from his home, Dad's transect was not a wood but it was still perfect fritillary country. Every week, he would walk up and down narrow paths on the warm, south-facing slope of Aish Tor. At the bottom, the river that gave the moor its name careered through the woods to begin a more sedate journey through south Devon to the sea. The slope was open, and the bracken, gorse and brambles were trampled and picked over by wild horses and deer, allowing violets and bluebells to flower each spring. The bracken was important because its virulent growth later in the summer stopped grass growing up and shading out the spring violets that are the fritillary's food plant.

This year, walking his transect, Dad had seen Pearl-bordered Fritillaries as early as anyone in the country. He emailed me pictures of the pristine, delicately patterned creatures sunning themselves on last year's dead bracken. There was no tension in this little, local hunt for him, really, and yet we still hurtled around the blind corners of the tiny lanes that led to Dartmoor at 40mph as if chasing a rare species we had never seen before. The scary driving reminded me of stories I heard about his grandfather, a tyrannical Edwardian gentleman so outraged at the introduction of traffic lights that he would drive through every red light that curtailed his divine right of way on the roads.

'Look at that cloud. Bastard cloud,' said my dad with a vehemence that still surprised me. Dad was, for the most part, exceedingly mild-mannered. He was calm and never lost his temper with other people. As we careered around the corners, he was peering up at the moor which was sheathed in dubious black cloud. It was seeping down to Dad's transect, the air was cooling fast and it was nearly 5 p.m., late in the day for these butterflies. We were racing to get there before the black cloud. We juddered to a halt on a rough track. The exact moment we stepped from the car, the sun disappeared. There was a strong breeze and it felt far too cool for even a podgy wild pony, let alone any butterflies. Pearl-bordered Fritillaries could endure low temperatures like this by lurking in warm pockets of air close to the ground. So we headed for the most sheltered corner of the slope. Dad reckoned that as the sun had just gone in, we might still catch sight of a fritillary before it snapped its wings shut and hunkered down in the dead bracken for the night.

He set out, with his characteristically intense walk. I followed and we instantly slipped into the purposeful butterfly-hunting mode we had developed but not practised together for years. Eyes sweeping across the ground, we fanned out. I crunched across the

112

grey-brown skeletons of last year's bracken, hoping to disturb a Pearl-bordered Fritillary that had gone to ground. Dad did not need to disturb anything; like a true expert, he could spot butterflies before they moved. 'There,' he said, quickly. On the narrow pony-trodden path ahead flew up a small, golden-coloured butterfly.

Dad unfurled his net. He was not collecting but, at times, as is often the case in Europe, where there are scores of fritillary species, a net can help identify different but very similar-looking butterflies. Momentarily disabling them in a soft, dark net gave him a chance to look at them more closely. The Pearl-bordered Fritillary was hard to follow in the gloom but it soon settled again on an exposed piece of sun-bleached bracken. Dad dived on it with his net. When he gently untangled it, the soft fritillary compliantly sought out the warmth of my dad's hand and settled there. I peered inside his hand with childish wonder and admired the almost fluorescent yellow tinge to the fur on its body. It bristled in the breeze. On the underside of its wing, Dad pointed out the telltale sign it was a Pearl-bordered rather than Small Pearl-bordered Fritillary: in the middle of the underside of its hindwing was a distinct silvery white cell, whereas the Small Pearl-bordered had a procession of silvery white dots there.

I had not looked so closely at anything as small as this trembling butterfly for months, or maybe years. How often do we as adults study things, really look at them, and pore over every tiny detail? If it is not our job, if we are not jewellers or stamp collectors or seam-stresses, then hardly at all. When we do, most of the time we are checking something out, as suspicious as customs officers studying a passport. Here, I was opening a neglected door into a childhood that was bigger than my boyhood passion for butterflies; I was reaching out and fumbling for the talent we all have as children for observing and taking pleasure in the marvel of small things.

We let the Fritillary fly slowly off and walked on. I saw the flash of a second, smaller butterfly. We closed in on where it too had gone to ground seeking the last pocket of warmth left by the sun earlier in the afternoon. Here was the tiny jewel of a Small Copper. Under grey skies, it looked as bright and out of place as a scrap of rubbish. Although they are common, and very small, it is impossible not to appreciate a Small Copper, even an irritable-looking one who clearly felt she deserved more sunshine for her efforts.

Under grey skies, at 5 p.m. on a Friday, I had seen two butterflies in five minutes and both were new species for the year. The pleasure in these very straightforward sightings came from hunting in tandem and perfect harmony with my dad again; I knew there were plenty of butterflies that would prove far more challenging to see and I would have to find them alone.

The following day, Dad and I visited Start Point on the south Devon coast, where we saw that first definitive Painted Lady of the year. Before it raced by, we walked along the coast path because Dad suspected we might find an early Wall Brown butterfly. Sailing boats leaned into the brisk westerly wind on the water far below. A raven gurgled as it lurked on the headland, as shifty as a hooded teenager in a park. The coast path was punctuated with small clumps of sea pinks and the lemon-yellow flowers of kidney vetch. Dad and I had not seen a Wall together for twenty years, the last time we took a summer holiday at Holme-next-the-Sea, in Norfolk, where it was a regular on our afternoon butterfly counts. This sensible butterfly takes its name from what it is most commonly spotted on. The two Walls we saw a few minutes into our walk had chosen to rest on a sun-warmed rut of dried mud on a field, rather than a wall, although we were leaning on a gritty stone wall when Dad spotted their movement in a field of bluebells below. Once widespread, in recent years the Wall has disappeared alarmingly from inland Britain and tends only to be found roaming the coastline.

Two exotic caterpillars urgently crossed our path: when you see a large, roaming caterpillar it is probably looking for a safe place to pupate. I did not have a clue what these were but Dad identified their comical blue moon faces and spiny, hairy bodies as belonging to a Lackey moth. I could identify the flowers of red campion and the call of a stonechat, a noise like two pebbles being smacked together. I could see the crow mobbing the buzzard high above us and recognise the long black neck of a cormorant flying low across the water but Dad could pick out so much more. He did not babble these facts; he had never been a know-all about wild things but was seldom stumped for an answer if you asked. He showed me the dark pink buds of wild carrot and how to identify a fulmar. I imagined this was a motley old seagull but Dad pointed out its sleek, narrow wings held flat like a balsawood glider. It was not actually a member of the gull family; it was a petrel. From the bushes, Dad identified the churring of the cirl bunting, only found on this coast, and the scratchy song of the whitethroat, which flew steeply into the sky and dropped down again.

After stopping to eat Dad's packed lunch of Marmite sandwiches on the pale cove of Great Mattiscombe Sand, we returned to the coast path heading west towards Lannacombe. A golden orange butterfly skimmed past us at the height of the bluebells. We turned and followed. It was too smart for a Wall and too dainty for a Comma. It settled. I fell to the ground and craned my neck beneath where it was resting to catch a glimpse of its underside. There were many more pale panels than on the Pearl-bordered Fritillary we had seen the previous day. Immaculate, without a scratch on its wings, it was a newly hatched Small Pearl-bordered Fritillary.

Unlike the relief of the previous night, when we beat the cloud to find the last Pearl-bordered of the day, this was an unexpected moment of elation. While the Small Pearl-bordered was more widespread than the rare Pearl-bordered, it usually emerged several weeks later in the spring; we had not expected to see one so soon. If the Pearl-bordered Fritillary was a classic but ageing model of car, the Small Pearl-bordered was the new version: younger, smarter and with more flashy chrome. While the Pearl-bordered was conking out all over our countryside, suffering a catastrophic decline over the past century, the Small Pearl-bordered had showed itself more durable by being less dependent on woodland habitats than its cousin.

Dad didn't have his net and so I decided to capture the second one we saw. I blindly rugby tackled the poor sunbathing insect. Fearing I had been too rough, I slowly parted my cupped hands: it was there, beneath them. I squinted through my fingers. The Small Pearl peered back at me from its prison. I looked again at the underside, and the range of white panels on its hindwing, and then, with the gesture I had not performed since childhood, threw my arms up into the air and opened my palms so it could fly away.

Further on, stuck to the starry white blooms of greater stitchwort, we saw our first Common Blues of the summer. First to show was a bright blue male, a bit tatty after several days braving westerly winds in this exposed spot. In flew the female, a bright brown in colour and most easily distinguishable from a Brown Argus by the blue hairs on her body. This versatile butterfly flies everywhere for long periods of the summer. In 1699, Petiver described the Common Blue as 'the little Blew Argus, common on heaths in August'. It still is. I had seen four new species in one day, one of which – the Small Pearl-bordered Fritillary – was a big surprise and a definite bonus so early in the season.

Of the twenty-two butterflies I had seen so far, only two – the Duke of Burgundy and the Pearl-bordered Fritillary – were rare, although another four – the Grizzled and Dingy Skippers, the Green Hairstreak and Small Pearl-bordered – had certainly required special trips to particular habitats. It was only mid-May, the weather had been unusually sunny, and I had seen all the early spring butterflies I needed to find before they died back like bluebells in a wood and gave way to later summer species. I was finding my rhythm again but I knew the really hard work was still ahead of me. Many butterflies would not emerge until later in June and July, when there would be an explosion of elusive species. Several woodland butterflies would only show up if I lurked under trees in English woodlands, while the most challenging butterflies to find required special trips to Scotland, Northern Ireland and Cumbria.

It was lucky I had seen most of the spring butterflies because for a couple of weeks work commitments prevented me from going anywhere. The weather was glorious and as the days ticked by I became increasingly concerned about the Glanville Fritillary, a spring butterfly I had never seen before which was only found on the Isle of Wight. I would have to go well before midsummer because it was only reliably on the wing in May and early June at the latest, and butterflies appeared to be emerging very early this season, which meant they would disappear early as well.

I then had to remind Lisa I had not been completely lost to butterflies by taking her for the weekend to Wales where the only lepidopteral distraction was a stray Painted Lady on the side of Snowdon. I really had to go and seek out the Glanville Fritillary soon. Luckily, the last weekend of May brought a heatwave. I heaved myself out of bed at 6 a.m. on a Sunday morning, promising Lisa a day by the seaside. Everyone was heading to the coast. The A3 from London to the sea was already busy; in the queue ahead of us was a Range Rover with two pink plastic spades wedged in its rear window. Everyone seemed to be catching the old car ferry from Portsmouth to the Isle of Wight, the last stand of Mrs Glanvil's fritillary.

It seemed appropriate that Lisa was coming with me because no other British butterfly was named after a real person and no other was so closely associated with a woman. 'This Fly took its Name from the ingenious Lady Glanvil, whose Memory had like to have suffered for her Curiosity,' wrote Moses Harris in his famous work of 1766, *The Aurelian*. 'Some Relations that was disappointed by her

Will, attempted to let it aside by Acts of Lunacy, for they suggested that none but those who were deprived of their Senses, would go in Pursuit of Butterflies.'

In the seventeenth and eighteenth centuries, as butterflies were identified and described, many, such as Dandridge's Middling Black Fritillary and Handley's Small Brown Butterfly, were named in honour of those who had discovered them. These clumsy vernacular names rarely endured and Dandridge's discovery is now known as the Marsh Fritillary, while Handley's is the Dingy Skipper. Eleanor Glanville, however, has been immortalised for discovering her Glanville Fritillary in Lincolnshire around 1702. The name's endurance shows that some butterfly collectors had a far more enlightened attitude to women than was suggested by the literature of the time.

Eleanor Glanville – the 'lady' was a printer's error in Harris's text – was a wealthy daughter of a Yorkshire family of apple growers. Aged thirty-one, this independently wealthy, widowed mother-of-two made a fateful decision: she married Richard Glanville. Her new husband was ten years younger and, while handsome, was also a cruel bully and a cheat. After Eleanor bore his child, he lost interest in her and took up with a mistress. Then he threatened his wife with a loaded pistol. Eleanor took refuge from this monstrousness in the pleasures of entomology. She amassed an enviable collection, bred butterflies, wrote about her findings and corresponded with entomological peers, including Petiver, Ray and Dandridge, who spoke admiringly of her work in the nascent – and male-dominated – science of Lepidoptera.

While she became the first to describe the early life stages of the

High Brown Fritillary, her estranged husband schemed against her. He plotted to kidnap one of her sons and persuade him to hand over property he would inherit from his mother to Richard Glanville and his mistress. Sensibly, given the intrigues of her husband, who sought to turn her children against their mother, Eleanor arranged that her estate would be left in the care of trustees after her death.

She had reckoned however, without mainstream society's suspicion of a passion for butterflies. Eleanor Glanville's labours in natural history were used against her in death. Her relatives contested the will and claimed her interest in butterflies was a sign of insanity. Neighbours were called in to attest that she had been seen scampering across the downs dressed 'like a gypsey'. Disputing the will, her eldest son Forest (does the name betray an eccentric veneration of nature?) argued his mother believed her children had been changed into fairies. Only the Aurelians had the decency to stand up for Eleanor. It is believed that one of her fellow lepidopterists, Petiver or Sir Hans Sloane, men of high standing in the world of butterflies, appeared in court in Wells, Somerset, to plead for her good character. The good burghers of Wells were not to be swayed. Chasing butterflies was mad, it was ruled, and Eleanor Glanville's fortune went to the family who had been driven to hate her.

Perhaps this terrible injustice helped ensure that the Aurelians did not replace Glanville with a more functional common name, as was the case with every other butterfly originally named in honour of a notable collector. The years, however, were not kind to Eleanor's fritillary. She had first found this small jewel in Lincolnshire but the butterfly quickly became extinct across most of England. Industrial agriculture was probably the main reason for its disappearance although it may have vanished because it was at the very northerly limit of its natural range. Although repeated reintroductions by butterfly breeders have seen the Glanville Fritillary materialise on sites in Hampshire, Weston-super-Mare and even the Wirral, it has rarely established itself permanently and it is now only reliably found on the southerly coast of the Isle of Wight.

I had never visited the Isle of Wight as a child and only once before as an adult, so this was another of the five species I had never seen before. I had no sense of how difficult it would be to find but Matthew Oates had visited the island a week before and I relied on his advice to head first to the wide sweep of Brook and Compton bays. To the west, the chalk downs of Compton met the coast and pushed the famous Needles into the sea. Before the bright chalk began, the cliffs were as yellow as an old man's teeth, and orange and purple layers of sandstone and sediment slumped and crumbled onto the beach. After every storm, men with rucksacks and geological hammers scoured newly exposed layers that burn red in the setting sun. One palaeontologist discovered forty-eight new prehistoric species in just four years, including crocodiles, lizards, frogs, salamanders and six tiny mammals, by sifting through bright lumps of fossilised charcoal and iron sulphide, fool's gold, for fragments of bone from the Early Cretaceous period, 125 to 130 million years ago. On the beach, ordinary-looking rocks turned out to be perfect casts of dinosaur prints.

This erosion is the reason why so many Glanville Fritillaries take up residence on the rough grassland at the edge of the cliff. As the land falls away, plants are ripped up and new soil is exposed. Among the pioneering plants to colonise the bare earth is ribwort plantain, which is the Glanville caterpillar's food plant (an early name for the Glanville Fritillary was the Plantain Butterfly). This plant rapidly disappears again when the grass gets too thick. So even as its food plants – and, presumably, some of its hibernating caterpillars – are flung into the sea by winter storms, newly suitable ground for the same plant is unearthed.

It was still early and the queues for Mick's ice-cream van were not yet snaking around the cliff-top car park when we arrived. I was tense: this was a long journey to do in a day, for one species I knew nothing about. You can read all you like about a butterfly but until you see it, going about its business in the wild, it is difficult to imagine exactly where you will find it or what it will be doing. I had no idea if this butterfly was an early riser, if it flew in the wind (some don't) or whether it could be seen when it was at rest. I was also worried because butterflies' flight seasons seemed very early this year.

It was breezy but fine. I decided we should start out by walking along the cliff top towards a point where a footpath looped up onto Compton Down. We strolled ten paces from the car park. 'Is that one?' asked Lisa. I was thinking how unlikely this would be as I followed her pointed finger, and there on the scrubby grass between the footpath and the old military road was a faded, windblown Glanville Fritillary, one of the most geographically restricted rare butterflies in Britain, next to hundreds of oblivious day-trippers. It was so simple and lovely – and a bit of an anticlimax.

I had not imagined it would be this easy. We walked a few more paces, stooping to watch another. As it clung to sea pinks that blew in the breeze, the butterfly pulled its forewings over part of its hindwings so that it looked triangular in shape. When the sun went in, it closed its wings and tucked its forewings completely behind its hind-wings, becoming an even smaller triangle. While its top side was a characteristic fritillary chequerboard of golden brown and black, its beauty lay in its striking and unique underside of white and orange bands decorated with black and brown dots and borders.

An elderly couple had paused further along the path, apparently looking at Glanville Fritillaries as well. 'Are you looking at what I'm looking at?' I asked. 'Aren't they fantastic?' said the man. 'Oh, so you are a butterfly widow too,' his wife said, companionably, to Lisa.

The man was called Lee. He had spent some of his childhood in Africa, where everyone seemed to collect butterflies and moths, and when he came to Britain, aged ten, he brought great boxes of insects with him. Later, his biology teacher took him to L. Hugh Newman's butterfly farm, a renowned breeder who fuelled Winston Churchill's secret passion for lepidoptera. For years, Lee had kept records of the butterflies he saw near where he lived, but this quiet man had never joined Butterfly Conservation. He was happy doing his own thing. But perhaps he felt alone in his passion too, because he seemed genuinely delighted to meet someone else who loved butterflies and was seeking what he had just found. He had travelled to the island for a week's holiday with his wife, timing their break to coincide with the Glanville's flight season, and had just seen the butterfly for the first time ever in his life. His modesty made my mission to find all fifty-nine species during the course of one summer seem both frivolous and greedy.

While I talked to Lee, his wife chatted to Lisa about the curious male passion for lepidoptera. It is strange how butterflies are seen both as effeminate and yet, as an obsession, are mostly pursued by men. The first Aurelian societies were male-only affairs and, with the exception of Eleanor Glanville and a few others, such as Miriam Rothschild in the twentieth century, butterflies were collected, dissected and named by men. At best, women played a supporting role. In his history of butterfly collecting, Salmon reprinted an exchange of letters in 1845 between Samuel Stevens, a member of the Entomological Society of London, and James Charles Dale. (Dale was a wealthy Dorset squire who discovered the Lulworth Skipper, kept a meticulous diary of his finds and was so well known as an entomologist that one day when he was sitting as a magistrate a local joker released dozens of butterflies into the court. Dale's last diary entry, shortly before he died aged eighty, recorded the capture of a cockroach.) Stevens wanted to inform Dale of his latest hunt: 'I am on the look-out for an entomological wife,' he wrote. 'I want one that will be useful as well as ornamental.' Elizabeth Harper wrote of the plight of 'an entomologist's wife' in an entomological journal in 1960. 'Entomology is a hobby which is all-absorbing. In some men I have seen it assume proportions almost amounting to mania as the men grow older,' she observed.

The reason butterflies became a male obsession may, of course, have more to do with the male inclination towards mania. The subject of this obsession, whether it is steam trains, racing cars, surfing or guitars, may be incidental, or at least an accident of childhood. But perhaps butterflies exert a particularly strong hold over the male gaze. Great lovers of butterflies, most notably Vladimir Nabokov and John Fowles, have even stuck pins into their fellow enthusiasts in their creative work. The creepy anti-hero of Fowles' *The Collector* is a lepidopterist loner who decides to stalk, trap and collect a young woman instead. Nabokov was a passionate butterfly collector and entomologist of considerable repute and yet the hero of his short story 'The Aurelian' is 'a flabby elderly man with a florid face, lank hair, and a greyish moustache, carelessly clipped'. This grumpy amateur entomologist has a wife and a moth named after him (as Nabokov had in real life) but lacks the gumption to save up for a trip to see the butterflies of the world he lusts after. Finally, he gets hold of the money to pursue his dream – by swindling a vulnerable widow. 'What he craved for, with a fierce, almost morbid intensity, was himself to net the rarest butterflies of distant countries, to see them in flight with his own eyes, to stand waist-deep in lush grass and feel the follow-through of the swishing net and then the furious throbbing of wings through a clutched fold of the gauze.'

In literature, a passion for butterflies has proved an easy metaphor for an alarming attitude to women, who must be pursued, possessed and pinned down. In reality, from the era of Eleanor Glanville until very recently, women seem to have been marginalised in the human history of butterflies. But despite jokes about butterfly widows, things are belatedly changing. Butterfly Conservation's groups and outings almost always attract equal numbers of men and women these days, and the latter are not simply there in deference to their male partner's obsession.

I was not sure how much Lisa wanted to embrace the role of butterfly widow – or butterfly obsessive – and so I was slightly relieved that the search for the Glanville Fritillaries had not turned into a day-long mission. For the next hour, we wandered along the flowery, crumbling cliff edge and counted more than forty Glanvilles. Many were roused to vigorously chase off the invading, and much larger,

Painted Ladies, which were lingering on the south coast after their recent mass migration. The beach and the ocean were calling, and we spent the rest of the day sunbathing and skipping across scalding maroon sand to swim in the cold sea. Most delicious of all, after seeing two men walk past plastered head-to-toe in glutinous green mud, we found a small mud pool that had formed by the crumbling undercliff. It was perfect for wallowing. I was scraping mud from my ears for weeks afterwards.

In the end, it turned out that I could have ticked off the Glanville Fritillary simply by going sunbathing. I don't think I had ever seen a butterfly while on a beach before. This time, as we sunbathed, a Glanville Fritillary drifted past us, a Common Blue perched on the sand ten metres from the gentle surf and Painted Ladies kept heading out into the ocean to the west before turning back to the cliffs again. Even in this perfect spot, full of flowers, sunshine and thistles for their young, their restless patrols seemed to be a constant weighing up of their current situation. In their forays out to sea it was as if the butterflies were asking a perennial human question: was this the best they could get, or should they move on and continue their great journey?

18. Pearl-bordered Fritillary, Aish Tor, Dartmoor, Devon, 8 May
19. Small Copper, Aish Tor, Dartmoor, Devon, 8 May
20. Wall Brown, Start Point, Devon, 9 May
21. Small Pearl-bordered Fritillary, Start Point, Devon, 9 May
22. Common Blue, Start Point, Devon, 9 May
23. The Glanville Fritillary, Brook Bay, Isle of Wight, 31 May

SUMMER

8

A very dark place: Britain's newest butterfly

In 1889 the penultimate 'new' species of British butterfly was discovered in the village of St Osyth in Essex. This tiny, brown moth-like butterfly became the first butterfly to be named after a county. The Essex Skipper was, to the naked eye, identical to the Small Skipper except for the tips of its antennae. These were black, instead of brown. This, surely, was as obscure as the difference between butterfly species could get. For more than a hundred years, butterflies continued to surprise and perplex lepidopterists, inexplicably appearing or disappearing, suddenly booming or going bust, but scientists believed that they at least knew what was under their noses and had compiled a robust list of British species.

They were wrong. In 2001 a former director of a company that sold security blinds in Belfast and an entomologist from Ulster

Museum made a sensational announcement. This unlikely pair of men had discovered a species of butterfly never before identified in Britain: Réal's Wood White.

In the 1960s Pierre Réal, a French scientist working in the Pyrenees, observed that some of the Wood Whites flying there appeared to behave rather differently from others. It was not until 1988 that his observations were found to be the basis of two distinct species: the new butterfly, which became Réal's Wood White, or *Leptidea reali*, was discovered higher up in the mountains; the traditional Wood White, or *Leptidea sinapis* to use its scientific name, was found at lower altitudes. These butterflies were only declared to be different species when they were dissected and their genitalia was examined. Rather than just another variant, or aberration (many of the same species of butterfly appear in different locations with subtly different markings), it was discovered they were distinct species because they could not interbreed. Their genitalia were quite different: Réal's Wood White, it turned out, had an enormous penis.

Over in Ireland, lepidopterists read of the discovery of *reali* with interest. They had long thought there was something puzzling about the descriptions of the Wood White in England compared with Ireland. In England, the Wood White is the daintiest and most delicate of the whites, an elegant drop of pearl, most easily distinguished by the way it weakly stumbles down woodland rides, a vapid, ghostly spirit among more vigorous summer butterflies. 'It is to be seen languidly flying along the roadways and pathways in woods,' wrote Edward Newman, pressing onward 'seemingly bent on the performance of some inexorable duty in which, however, dispatch or hurry was totally out of the question.' The populations of this ineffectual-looking butterfly have drastically declined in recent years as well.

In Ireland, however, it always seemed a more vigorous creature and its populations have thrived. Rather than being confined to woodlands, it is seen flying on roadside verges, by railways and in all kinds of rough grassland. 'Something sparked in me whenever it flew past,' said Brian Nelson, when I met the entomologist from Ulster Museum on a rough strip of parkland once designated for an urban motorway. 'The Wood White is described as weak and fluttery and in woodland. Our butterfly was different. Why was our species doing so well when yours was going down the tube?' That question niggled in the back of lepidopterists' minds for most of the 1990s. Eventually, Nelson decided to test the question. He caught a couple of Wood Whites in Northern Ireland and gave them to Maurice Hughes, a powerful-looking Ulsterman who was Butterfly Conservation's sole full-time official in Northern Ireland, to examine.

'I was dissecting moths at the time and he asked me if I'd be interested in dissecting Wood Whites,' said Hughes. 'He gave me a few specimens and said, "see what they are".' Hughes cut up the butterflies in his kitchen and looked at the specimens under a microscope. He was not expecting any revelations but he quickly saw something that surprised him: they had long penises. These butterflies were not *sinapis* but *reali*.

Nelson dug out some historic Wood White specimens from Ulster Museum's collection. Some had been caught as long ago as 1902 and all were labelled *sinapis*. Every one turned out to be *reali*. Next, they tested specimens from the six or so major Wood White colonies in mainland Britain. These were all *sinapis*. It looked like *sinapis* lived in England and Wales (the Wood White does not occur in Scotland) and *reali* flew in Ireland. But it was not as simple as that. *Sinapis*, they discovered, also occurred in Ireland, but only on the Burren, a unique slice of limestone pavement in the north of county Clare and south-east Galway. *Reali*, meanwhile, was everywhere else.

Like all smart science, this discovery begged dozens of other questions. How long had *reali* been in Ireland? How did it get there? Why did the two species not fly side by side? Why was *reali* thriving and *sinapis* struggling? Were there ways to distinguish the superficially identical two species in the field by their behaviour? And the biggest puzzle of all: if *reali* was so common in Ireland, why was it not found in the neighbouring island – England?

Nelson was amazed no scientists in England had bothered to test for *reali* before and yet he accepted he would not have done so were it not for the endeavours of Pierre Real, who is now dead. What spurred him on to dissect the butterflies in the first place? 'It wouldn't occur to me to think there would be two species but logically when you look at it now it's so obvious,' he reflected. 'It was a very proud moment. To find a new butterfly in Britain and Ireland is not something that happens every day. I wasn't jumping up and down but I was excited.'

The journey to search for Réal's Wood White was one of two potentially difficult trips. Both *reali* in Northern Ireland and the Chequered Skipper in Scotland were butterflies I had never seen before and could easily spend two weeks waiting for the right weather to see. Immediately after finding the Glanville Fritillary, I took a week off work and gambled on a two-day trip to Northern Ireland, followed by a three-day expedition to Scotland with my dad. It was a lot of miles for just two species. We needed exceedingly good fortune with the weather if we were to see these two species in such a short time.

Hughes repeated a saying he was fond of when he picked me up from Belfast City airport. 'The study of Lepidoptera is the study of exceptions, not rules,' he said. We were blessed, at least, with exceptional weather. It was the first day of June and Northern Ireland was enjoying a serious heatwave. At the airport, pale-skinned Irish women sported angry red necks, as if they had been slapped. Tough, small bare-chested men walked the streets of Belfast with unlit cigarettes tucked behind their ears. One was imprinted with a perfect white vest mark and a neck line as red as a Cinnabar moth.

I had met Hughes at Butterfly Conservation's meeting for its butterfly recorders in the spring. He had agreed to show me around some good *reali* sites along with Stephen and Gail Jeffcoate, a couple of keen lepidopterists who happened to be friends with my dad and who were studying how to better conserve the Wood White in mainland Britain. This was a kind offer and it turned out to be a scary one because Hughes drove his sensible-looking Volvo faster than anyone I have ever known. I clung to the cream leather seats as we set off in pursuit of *reali*. This Volvo did not feel normal. Later in the day, I asked Hughes about it and he was delighted to explain. A butterfly and moth enthusiast, Hughes was also a motor-racing buff who was driving a souped-up version of what was already a special high-performance saloon. It must have been the fastest Volvo in Ireland.

Hughes was a man of great surprises and about as far from the image of a butterfly nerd as you could imagine. He had the easy gravitas of a successful businessman, the storytelling ability of a great raconteur and the steeliness of someone who has dealt with a lot of trouble over the years. A fell runner in his youth, he worked his way up through the ranks at a security blinds company. There was a lot of demand for security blinds during the decades when terror held sway in Belfast. But because the company occasionally supplied blinds to government agencies, they became a target. One day, someone tipped off the IRA that the business had supplied decorative blinds to a senior British politician in Northern Ireland. One of the company's managers was killed in a car bomb.

Hughes had bullet-proof glass fitted in the downstairs windows of his family home. He was given equipment to fit on the dashboard of his car to warn him if a car bomb had been stuck underneath it. His workforce was also targeted. Because of where the factory was situated in Belfast, every day, when the employees left, 'the Prods', as Hughes said, would turn right towards their part of the city and 'the Micks' would turn left. Terrorists could tell the allegiance of workers by their route home, so innocent employees were subjected to drive-by shootings. Hughes was scathing about both sides and scathing about the police and the authorities who seemed unable to stop it.

He became interested in moths in middle age. He began trapping them, studying them, and then volunteering for the small Northern Ireland division of Butterfly Conservation. He was encouraged out of early retirement and became their only full-time officer based in the province. With a canny eye for a competitive rental rate, he set up their office in an old asylum that felt like a squat for small charities and NGOs. It was a bizarre place and still had the shiny cream corridors and old waiting-room signs of a hospital. Hughes's lab, where he did his work with *reali* and *sinapis*, was an old kitchen. In the long corridor was a grave sign: 'Please leave this light on. Remember we are in a very dark place.'

It was actually a bright, sharp day. Above our heads, the blue sky was scored with vapour trails from all the flights between Europe and North America that are routed over this corner of Ireland. We drove to Craigavon Lakes. Forty years ago, it was to be a major new city. People were paid to relocate there, away from the horrors of Belfast, but they didn't like it and moved back. The random scraps of new development looked half-hearted. Like lungs, two lakes had been created to control the water table in preparation for the new city. Between these was planned a motorway. Hard core was laid in preparation for the road but it was never built. Instead, this dry, stony ground and poor soil was left to run wild and became a flowery grassland full of oxeye daisies, much loved by butterflies. Walking along the rough track between the lakes now designated a 'City Park', the air smelt of broom, which flowered yellow. The landscape was parched and open, not at all like the English woodlands where you might find the Wood White.

Within five minutes, we saw a white butterfly flapping weakly, but not that weakly, along the path. At first, Stephen and Gail Jeffcoate thought it was a Green-veined White, which can look weak but is also a tenacious flyer. We peered closer. It did not have any green or grey veins. Here, as easy as that, was *reali*, a very different and not at all woody kind of white.

A female, she was laying eggs on the yellow flowers of bird's-foot trefoil. The females are mated as soon as they emerge from the pupa and spend the rest of their lives fending off unwanted male attention and laying eggs. They may lug around as many as a hundred. Eggs, not male admirers. This particular overburdened butterfly clung to the flower and curled her plump white abdomen around, dabbing the tender end against a petal. Unlike many butterflies, she seemed oblivious to us – we could get up close and she did not turn aggressive or skittish. She was preoccupied. After five attempts, she deposited a greeny white, skittle-shaped egg on the underside of a leaf. When I peered closely, I saw the egg glistened like the gobs of cuckoo spit on the plants around it.

Stephen Jeffcoate removed from his pocket a curious device that looked like an iPod. It turned out to be a thermometer with a sensitive probe on the end of a piece of wire. He measured where the egg was laid on a south-facing slope. Tucked next to a rock, the temperature where the egg rested was 29.5°C compared with an ambient temperature of 23.5°C. When I dipped my hand into the grass where *reali* was laying her eggs, I could feel how much warmer it was. This, according to Jeffcoate, may be the key to its reproductive success: both species of Wood White need warm, sheltered places to lay their eggs.

I watched another female dancing along the 5ft chain-link fence of the railway, as if shadow-boxing the fence. It did not look like this butterfly would cross the railway line although it had historically spread along Ireland via roads and railways. Several Irish entomologists had wanted to name it the Railway White, after its love in Ireland not of woods but of railway embankments. As Nelson put it, with what sounded like pride: 'No Irish butterfly would go into the dark places like the Surrey woods where you find the Wood White.'

We moved on to a warm, open meadow close to the shores of Lough Neagh, the biggest inland body of water in the British Isles, the eye in the map of Ireland. There is a legend that two giants were fighting and the Irish giant picked up a rock and threw it at the English giant and it didn't reach him but landed in the Irish Sea. The rock was the Isle of Man, and where it was taken from is now Lough Neagh. The Manx people are not impressed by this story.

In knee-high grass full of meadowsweet, we watched again as a female *reali* struggled through the air. It appeared tipsy, as if it might fall out of the sky at any moment, a strange look for a butterfly. Was it simply overburdened with eggs? The Jeffcoates were examining a new theory of behavioural differences between the two species which had been filmed by a student at Queen's University, Belfast. *Sinapis* has a very distinctive mating ritual. The male rubs his proboscis over the female's shoulders and flicks his wings. But it appears that *reali* men don't flick their wings. That, in Northern Ireland at least, does not impress *reali* women. In the meadow, we crouched and watched a courting couple. The male sat above the female on a stem of grass, uncurled his proboscis and jabbed it at the female, swinging his head from side to side, as if he was trying hypnosis, and waving his white-clubbed antennae. The female tolerated him in a submissive sort of way, flicking her wings as if she was flicking her hair. The male never once flicked his wings in return.

Of all the mysteries that swirl around these two Wood Whites, the most puzzling is why England and Wales lack *reali*. The geographical island of Ireland has fewer species of butterfly than mainland Britain because of its damp climate, lack of chalk grassland and the barrier formed by the Irish Sea. Apart from *reali*, it does not have any butterfly species that Britain lacks. There are other distributional quirks across Europe, but *reali* is present in most other European countries.

'It is a complete riddle. How did they get here and yet aren't in Britain?' asked Trevor Boyd, an engaging, elderly Irish naturalist I met while out looking at *reali*. 'Perhaps they were in Britain at one time but became extinct. But why? You think they might be competing with each other but you'd hardly call it competition. They are not eating each other.'

There are other species of insects and plants which are unique to Ireland, and Boyd suggested that the theory of what is called the Lusitanean element to Irish flora and fauna might explain *reali*'s presence in Ireland. In terms of species, there are mysterious links between Ireland and Spain, but not the rest of Europe. Some of Ireland's indigenous species, including a slug and numerous plants, are found in Spain but not in countries such as England and Wales. Nelson, however, is dubious about this idea. Scientists have shown the Lusitanean theory mostly describes the presence of heather species common to Spain and Ireland, and these were introduced to Ireland many centuries ago through the monasteries.

Would it be far-fetched to think monks might deliberately introduce a white butterfly to Ireland? What if they symbolised the soul? If *reali* were imported from Europe, it was not recently. The oldest *reali* specimen caught in Ireland and tested by Nelson and Hughes dates from 1897; similarly, the oldest *sinapis* specimen from the Burren was caught in 1910. If the monasteries caused the inadvertent introduction of plants, could *reali* also be a freakish accident? The Small and Essex Skippers are both believed to have only recently turned up in Ireland when eggs came across attached to grass in hay for horses imported from mainland Britain.

Among all the speculative answers is also the possibility that *reali* could be hiding in mainland Britain. Lepidopterists say this is unlikely, but to be sure, according to Nelson and Hughes, English and Welsh scientists should test every Wood White population, including specimens from extinct populations in East Anglia and in Cumbria where the meadows, country lanes and rough, mixed grassland are most comparable to parts of Ireland. Scientists have not yet tested all these populations.

Entomologists are still busy uncovering the mysteries of the two Wood Whites, not least the basic differences between them. It is now no longer necessary to kill the species and dissect it to determine what it is. A Wood White can be caught and a small section of its least important middle leg (it has three on each side) can be clipped off and removed as a DNA sample. This is quick and cheap, and from what the scientists have observed of breeding specimens does not subsequently impair their movement or life (although it is kinder to do it to males, who do not bear the burden of a hundred eggs).

The two Wood Whites have been put together to see if they inter-breed, and they don't. Well, this is not quite true: the males are happy to try and mate with both *reali* and *sinapis* females but the women are much more picky and will only accept their own species. 'The males will mate with either,' said Hughes. 'They don't give a damn.' Apart from the microscopic differences in the size of the male appendage, scientists have recently pinpointed another, equally tiny physical difference: a pink stripe on the pupae is fuzzy on one species and more distinct on the other.

While I was in Northern Ireland I hoped to see the Marsh Fritillary, even if it meant more clinging to the seats of Hughes's Volvo. The following day dawned as dazzling as the last. Above Belfast smoke rose from Cave Hill, where youths had started fires. The rocky crag up there used to be good for moths, bemoaned Hughes, but there were now too many glue-sniffers and drug addicts.

At heart, Hughes was a moth man. He seemed less proud of his *reali* discovery than his involvement in the recent unearthing of the White Prominent moth in County Kerry, seventy years after it was declared extinct. This magnificent-looking white moth was so rare its location was officially recorded as in the Atlantic Ocean, such were the fears that moth collectors would wipe it out if they were told where Hughes had hunted it down. Ireland, clearly, was rich in lepidopteral surprises.

Hughes had also discovered and helped document dozens of new sites of the rare and gorgeous Marsh Fritillary. Victorian lepi-dopterists called it the Greasy Fritillary, an unfortunate name redolent of oily spivs with slicked-back hair. The name that caught on is hardly any better. It correctly describes its love of life in boggy grassland but conveys nothing of the beauty of this distinctive little fritillary. Unlike other fritillaries, which show only one hue of golden orange on their wings, the chequers on a Marsh Fritillary are a beautiful variation of ginger and orange; its patterns could be from a classic pair of mid-century modern curtains. This is a retro butterfly.

It is also unusually sociable as a caterpillar. Most caterpillars crawl around alone on plants, eating leaves. The Marsh Fritillary caterpillars are more industrious: when small, they build themselves communal webs on their food plant, devil's bit scabious, in which they live for protection as they grow. After wintering together in a tiny round web, they build a new, larger web, change skins and then split up, feeding singly in the spring before entering their chrysalis. Many butterfly populations boom and bust, and when conditions are right, Marsh Fritillary populations can boom to extraordinary numbers. In 1928, Sir Charles Langham recorded a dark mass of caterpillars in Enniskillen. 'It would be an exaggeration to say the field was black with them but not very far from the truth,' he wrote in a letter to Donovan, who published Langham's account in his book on the lepidoptera of Ireland. Langham, a wealthy butterfly collector, was tipped off about the discovery and when he arrived at the remote field, he found more than twenty-five cars – a rarity in those days – and a hundred local people at the field. Seeing this plague, residents were desperately trying to burn the grass on the field to destroy the larvae. So Langham did what every well-to-do butterfly lover would: he summoned his hired hands. His gardeners collected up 18,000 of the caterpillars and brought them to his home, where he fed them up and bred them.

He observed how a parasitic wasp attacked the caterpillars, which helped explain why this butterfly went through years of boom and then bust. In 1928, 2–3 per cent of the caterpillars were 'stung' – implanted with the eggs of a parasitic wasp – and never hatched into butterflies. Langham released those that did emerge as adults back onto the fields. The following autumn, his dutiful gardeners collected up 10,000 caterpillars. This time, 25 per cent were stung and failed to develop into adult butterflies. In 1930 he could only find a few thousand butterflies where once they had swarmed, and 80 per cent of the caterpillars he scooped up were eventually killed by the parasitic wasp.

So the Marsh Fritillary had its natural enemies. The biggest reason for its rarity now, however, was industrial agriculture and the draining or destruction of boggy grassland. In Northern Ireland, there were still plenty of rough pastures and yet in 2000, there were just eight known Marsh Fritillary sites there, all in the east apart from one in Fermanagh. Then, a few years ago, three conservationists were assessing the biodiversity of private farmland. They were visiting a remote field in Fermanagh in September, around the time when the Marsh Fritillary caterpillar spins its communal webs. They were sufficiently skilled to identify these webs, which was unusual: even lepidopterists struggle to find them until they get their eye in.

Hughes was called and he took bundles of bamboo canes to mark the webs. He stuck 200 canes in the ground. Then he undertook a survey along a spur of land surrounded by bog and estimated there were up to 1000 webs on one spur, half a mile from the nearest road, on private land. Another consultant who was conducting an environmental assessment on farmland in another part of Fermanagh telephoned Hughes about a different sighting. 'Are there any Marsh Fritillary sites in this area?' he asked. 'No,' said Hughes, consulting the distribution data. 'Well,' the consultant replied, 'I'm looking at dozens flying around and, what's more, they are having sex.'

Since then, scores of new colonies of Marsh Fritillaries have been discovered in Fermanagh. This has been the most dramatic discovery of a hitherto unknown population of a rare butterfly in Britain or Ireland for twenty-five years and it has triggered a very modern environmental dilemma. The county has been designated a wind corridor, and there are a sheaf of new applications for wind farms. Which comes first: green energy or a rare and beautiful butterfly? Will the wind farms destroy the butterfly? Must we sacrifice the latter to our insatiable desire for power?

All prospective wind farms must carry out detailed assessments of their impact on the land where they are to be built. A big problem, according to Hughes, is that the trained environmental consultants are often oblivious to the Marsh Fritillary, particularly in areas where it has never been recorded but may secretly live. If a survey is conducted in any month other than May, when they are flying as adults, or September, when you might see their webs (if you know what to look for and where to look), the consultant will have no idea that the butterfly lives there.

Hughes could see a way to save the Marsh Fritillary and build the wind farms. Once the turbines are up, their operation will not affect the butterfly, which flies at much lower levels than the swishing blades. But butterfly populations could easily be wiped out during construction. If by laying hard core and foundations for the wind farms, the water levels of the surrounding pastures were irrevocably changed, this could lead to the disappearance of the Fritillary's food plant.

Hughes, however, hoped the wind farms could actually benefit the butterfly. As 'mitigation', as the legalese goes, for damage to populations during the building work, the wind-farm company could be made to ensure the surrounding land is better managed for the Marsh Fritillaries. This would cost a little money and demand that great care was taken during construction. There would need to be a full hydrology survey to calculate how the new roads, buildings and foundations would disturb the water levels and the marshy, rough pasture. The final danger would be that a wind-farm owner might agree to all of this, including marking webs during construction so existing populations were not damaged by the building work, and then this careful approach would collapse in practice. In these remote areas, compliance with such strict conditions could not realistically be policed. Hughes was a businessman and knew how these things worked. Imagine it was winter, he said, the whole construction site was knee-deep in mud and a contractor could not get his lorry across the field. The contractor might resort to delivering his load of sand onto a vacant patch of ground where a few bamboo canes marked the presence of several thousand hibernating Marsh Fritillaries. No one could stop it happening.

Fermanagh was a long drive away so, after our success with Réal's Wood White, we headed to some boggy meadows on the shores of

Lough Neagh to look for Marsh Fritillaries. Much of this patchwork of small, rough fields was managed by Northern Ireland's Environment and Heritage Service but some meadows were still in private hands. Each one was full of prehistoric-looking horsetails. Hefty dragonflies roared past and we saw a mating pair of Irish damselflies. A green female and blue male, they hovered close to the rank grass, suddenly shifting position like bad computer-generated imagery in a sci-fi film.

A few meadows had run wild and overgrown because no one knew who owned them. These abandoned plots belonged to the families of Irish emigrants to America in the nineteenth and twentieth centuries. They were forgotten and unclaimed. By one field was a pile of fly-tipped rubbish: it looked like the contents of a child's bedroom had been emptied out onto the grass. There was a yellow dumper truck, pink pieces of plastic, odd, small shoes, and a copy of *Closer* magazine with the cover line, 'Tired of being lonely'.

Other boggy fields were being turned over to housing. Ostentatious ranch-style houses, fenced off and bleakly landscaped with brilliant green fertilised grass and nothing else, were springing up everywhere. 'It's amazing what they can do here,' said Hughes, who observed how restricted development was in mainland Britain compared with Northern Ireland where it seemed possible to put up houses on the most precious natural landscapes.

We patrolled several fields but could not find any Marsh Fritillaries. It felt as if they had already been pushed out, so we drove back to Belfast. The following day, Hughes took us to the dunes of Murlough, 700 acres of gorse, bracken, heather and spectacularly large dunes behind the cinematic sweep of an oceanic beach. Owned by the National Trust, these were unusually large, and unusually dry because great storms in medieval times had pushed dune upon dune, doubling their size. This dry ground was not an obvious site for a bog-loving fritillary but, luckily, as in a few other locations in Britain, such as on the chalky hillside in Dorset where the Cerne Abbas giant stands, the Marsh Fritillary had adapted to this habitat as well.

At Murlough, locals called the confluence of three different board-walks in the centre of the dunes 'Spaghetti Junction'. It was almost as busy as a motorway on what was another scorching morning. The boards thudded with feet determined to reach the beach as quickly as possible. On either side of the boardwalk, the song of two stonechats was in perfect stereo.

Sand dune systems are like enormous hotels: they have rooms, discrete dining areas, hollows and dips. Some are huge amphitheatres or ballrooms; others are quiet, secret libraries; each has its own decor, character and butterflies. Each is at a different stage of evolution: from dune to dry grassland and then putative woodland. Each has its own distinctive residents. At Holme in north Norfolk, I had noticed on my childhood butterfly walks that we would always see Red Admirals in one spot, close to the trees and brambles, and the Graylings in another, on dry open dunes and almost out onto the beach.

Diving into the sheltered hollows beneath Murlough's tallest dunes, we scanned the dainty blue flowers of speedwell and the single purple stems of viper's bugloss. We quickly picked up a courting couple of Réal's Wood White. Again, Jeffcoate's theory that the male *reali* did not flick its wings during courting, unlike *sinapis*, was borne out. As I bent down with Jeffcoate to watch the courting, Hughes called out: he had spotted a Marsh Fritillary.

With its wings of dark golden brown, orange and ginger, it landed on a stalk of marram grass and sat still, in the sun. When resting with its wings open, it had a habit of letting its forewings fold over part of its hindwings. This made it look floppy and round-shouldered. When I got too close, this impression of laziness was confounded: it flew off surprisingly fast.

For the next hour, I roamed the dunes in the sunshine, getting lost in its rooms and reorienting myself by running in the pale, soft sand to the highest point, and looking out enviously on the glittering Irish Sea. To the south-west, the mountains of Mourne rose up from the coast, with Slieve Donard, the tallest mountain in Northern Ireland, an imperious triangle of black and blue.

In one hot pocket of dune there was a huge white puffball, as strange as an alien spaceship. In another, three Marsh Fritillaries spiralled up into the sky in pursuit of each other. A cuckoo began calling, at first in the distance, and then close and loud. It was the first I had heard all year and I finally caught sight of it, skulking between two stunted sycamore trees. There were day-flying moths too, a bright red Cinnabar moth and another of those deceptive Lattice Heath moths (which I had mistaken for a Dingy Skipper earlier in the spring), but the dunes were dominated by the Marsh Fritillary. They basked on the last of the wilting bluebells and buzzed busily between marram and flower, zipping over hillocks of sand faster than I could run as they patrolled the different rooms of Murlough.

To finish off, Hughes drove down tiny lanes to a marsh at Ballykilbeg, to try and see the Marsh Fritillary in its 'proper' boggy habitat. By an old corrugated-iron animal shed was a fenced-off meadow. I ducked under the fence and waded through shoulder-high stinging nettles. They soon stung their way through my trousers. Further on, the nettles gave way to open, hummocky grass-land. I jumped over a barbed-wire fence and into an open field. There was a glorious strong wet smell of water mint, and meadow-sweet. I stood on my own in the late-afternoon sunshine and instantly a Marsh Fritillary flew into view, older and more faded than the perfect brown and orange specimens I had photographed on the dunes. Several dozens went about their business on this field.

I wondered how long they would be allowed to continue. Any butterfly that lives on farmland must always be watching its back. One plough or a bag of pesticides could finish it off. So could doing nothing. This field had not been grazed for a couple of years. If that neglect continued it would not be long before it was too overgrown for the Marsh Fritillary. Working on his own, Hughes was virtually a lone voice for butterflies in Northern Ireland. With its fine old farmland, the province had a wealth of butterfly habitats but many appeared to be in a perilous state. One man and his exceedingly fast car could not protect it all.

24. Réal's Wood White, Craigavon Lakes, Northern Ireland, 1 June
25. The Marsh Fritillary, Murlough Dunes, Northern Ireland, 2 June

9

The Highland ruler

The classic Georgian or Victorian butterfly collector was a rector with an undemanding rural parish and a love of nature. 'A taste for Natural History in a clergyman has great advantages, both as respects himself and others,' noted J. C. Loudon in *The Magazine of Natural History* in 1835. If fox hunting was too brutal for a respectable rector, went the argument, then pursuing butterflies was good for the health and got the rector out of his rectory, 'affording ample opportunity for frequent intercourse with his parishioners', as Loudon put it.

Charles Abbot appeared typical of the tireless spirit of enquiry of the day. The good Reverend made the final great lepidopteral discovery of the eighteenth century when he captured a Chequered Skipper in 1798 at Clapham Park Wood near his home in Bedford in his 'first season' as an Aurelian. This little butterfly had never been documented before, but flew in discrete colonies in middle England. Abbot, who shunned the fashionable entomological societies of London for the pleasures of rural Bedfordshire, then blotted his copybook in the eyes of right-thinking Aurelians. In the same wood, he discovered a Scarce Swallowtail, an incredibly rare migrant, and two foreign skippers. He also claimed to have collected two more rare migrants, a Bath White and a Queen of Spain Fritillary, nearby. This was too good a run of beginner's luck to be true.

Collecting butterflies was an increasingly profitable passion. There was a thriving market for rare specimens and, later, for freakish aberrations of common species. Chequebook collectors would pay particularly big money for butterflies if they were caught in Britain. In 1921, the great collector Walter Rothschild – uncle of Miriam – paid £65, a fortune in those days, for an extremely unusual black version of a Swallowtail butterfly caught by a fisherman in Norfolk.

Where obsession and money led, so fraud followed, and the first criminal Aurelians were born. One ruse was to advertise rarities it was claimed were captured in Britain when they were simply imported from overseas. Many old rarities in 'British' collections turned out to be butterflies caught on the Continent, imported as dead insects and re-arranged and 'set' in the British style. A cleverer trick was to import live specimens from abroad, alert rich Aurelians that a certain rare specimen had been spotted at a secret location and release them close to credulous collectors who would then 'discover' them. This had many advantages, not least that respectable collectors could verify that they had indeed seen with their own eyes this butterfly flying freely in Britain.

Unless the Reverend Charles Abbot nursed a distinctly unchristian attitude towards the truth he probably fell victim to this scam. According to Salmon, the exotic butterflies Abbot believed he found were almost certainly planted by a butterfly dealer called Plastead, who, Salmon notes drily, 'seems to have specialised in planting exotic butterflies and moths on honest, unsuspecting lepidopterists'. Abbot's gullibility was treated witheringly elsewhere. James Charles Dale recorded in his journal that the Reverend 'had cracked his skull and had a piece of silver plate let in and fancied odd things'.

The disappearance of the Chequered Skipper from England was as swift and mysterious as its arrival. Abbot was not duped about its discovery for it was later found living in woodlands across central England, with a particular stronghold in the old hunting forests of the East Midlands. As recently as 1961, R. E. M. Pilcher wrote that the Chequered Skipper although less common than it had been was at least in 'no apparent danger of extinction' at its headquarters close to Peterborough. Within fifteen years, however, it had vanished. Its extinction took lepidopterists completely by surprise. It was last seen in 1975 in a wood in Rutland. Every summer afterwards, people searched for it in woods around the East Midlands but it had gone, another butterfly to join the Large Blue, Large Tortoiseshell and Black-veined White on the sad list of species lost to England in the twentieth century.

Fortunately, and equally inexplicably, around the time of the outbreak of the Second World War an incredible discovery was made in woods in north-west Scotland. About three hundred miles north of the nearest known colony, the Scottish Chequered Skipper was found and announced to the world in 1942, breeding on a type of grass that does not grow in the old English localities.

The Scottish and English Chequered Skippers looked the same and belonged to the same species but, over hundreds of years, like the humans of each country, had developed distinct characters. In England, the Chequered Skippers were sedentary; in Scotland, the males were quick to kick off, buzzing after rival males and fighting any other insects that strayed into their keenly held territories. Was this aggression the key to their survival? Were their English brethren too passive?

It is fascinating to wonder how these tiny butterflies ended up as a relic population, completely isolated in a chilly outpost too cold and wet for most butterflies and hundreds of miles from the nearest colonies of their own species. The story of the Scottish Chequered Skipper is far older than a simple decline linked to intensive agriculture and the neglect of our forests. Perhaps they spread north throughout the British Isles during the warm Bronze Age, vanishing when the centuries turned colder again except in sheltered, south-facing bogs close to Fort William where they adapted to the climate, laid eggs on purple moor grass and clung on.

This robust, relic population had certainly adapted to the inhospitable climate in a number of ingenious ways. The Chequered Skipper has one of the slowest-growing caterpillars, taking until October, after more than a hundred days of feeding, to become fully grown. It feeds on purple moor grass, which is widespread across Scotland and the north. Why, then, was the butterfly so rare?

Relatively recent studies suggest the Chequered Skipper is particularly picky about the tussock of grass it chooses, and has to be, for its caterpillar to survive. The grass must be in a warm and sheltered spot, where it is also wet, sunny, but not in direct sunlight, and with leaves that contain high concentrations of nitrogen.

Seeing a Chequered Skipper was the biggest and most exciting challenge of the year. It was another of the five British butterflies I had never seen before. For Dad, it was the final species – the only one he had never laid eyes on. It was nice we were doing this trip together; it was one we had often talked about when I was a boy but we were thwarted by the distance and the fact that the Chequered Skipper was another of those exam-term butterflies. To see one of these small butterflies is not easy if you live in Scotland, let alone in southern England. For thirty years after it was discovered in the Highlands, it was confined to just two colonies around Fort William. When more sites were belatedly discovered closer to Oban, conservationists began to conduct more thorough surveys of little-walked land. They turned up another forty or so small colonies on sheltered Scottish hillsides close to woodland. There are almost certainly further colonies still to discover. But these skippers are very difficult to spot. The weather in the Highlands is unpredictable. In rain, or drizzle, the butterflies go to ground, tucked deep in tussocks of grass. You could easily travel to Scotland during their brief flight season in late May or early June and spend a week holed up while it rained.

I flew straight from seeing Réal's Wood White and the Marsh

Fritillary in Northern Ireland to Glasgow, where I met Dad, who had undertaken an epic drive from Devon. The weather forecast was not terribly promising but the skies were bright. Even though we were both tired, we decided we should drive straight to Glasdrum Wood on the banks of Loch Creran, a small loch not far from the main road between Oban and Fort William. It might be the only chance we had.

The weather stayed implausibly sunny on the drive north and as we pulled off the main road for Glasdrum Wood we saw a small man with an extremely large camera ferreting around in the undergrowth. We stopped and wound down the window. He was virtually dancing with delight. He had travelled north from West Yorkshire and had just photographed four Chequered Skippers on the roadside. He had seen a Small Pearl-bordered Fritillary as well but had hoped – and so far failed – to see a Marsh Fritillary here too. 'Still, you don't want to see all the butterflies in one summer, do you?' he said philosophically. 'There's always next summer.' I kept silent about my extravagant mission.

Gaelic for 'grey ridge', Glasdrum was made up of stooped birch and oak trees which sprouted grey lichen like unkempt beards. Under these clear skies, however, the landscape was not grey but a vivid spring green and yellow. It smelt glorious. The sweet scent of sunshine on thick moss and woodland that has been wet for centuries was a bit like the suburban smell of freshly cut grass, only earthier and much, much older. This straggly and damp wood was ancient and yet had long been sculpted by human hands. In the past, Highland cattle were grazed in glades between its mix of old hazel coppice, pale ashes, birch and stockier oaks. By the 1700s, the local laird sold charcoal from the wood to the Lorn Furnace on Loch Etive, where pig iron was smelted. The furnace was now a tourist attraction.

The year after the Chequered Skipper vanished from England, Glasdrum was made a nature reserve and small clearings were cut out to encourage the butterfly. A gravel path for visitors now climbed through the wood from the loch in a modest loop. On the footpath was a small curl of dark poo that looked as if it could have come from a small cat. Perhaps it was a pine marten. Stationed along the path were idiotic fingerposts that some communications director had been paid to dream up. These signs did not tell you anything in themselves. 'Natural powerpoint', read one by a cleared strip of woodland below a line of telegraph poles. 'Looking to Europe', said another, higher up the slope. I later discovered that the signs were linked to an explanatory leaflet in a wooden box by the reserve entrance, but their effect was to have the voice of a metropolitan marketing man on an away-day brainstorm ringing out through the woods.

This intrusion made me more determined to do something vaguely transgressive like not stick to the path. We turned onto the rough, boggy grassland beneath the power lines and picked our way through the bracken, Dad in the lead. We moved in tandem, not needing to talk; we knew the drill and understood what each of us was looking for and how we would find it. Underfoot were layers of young bilberry shoots, tiny sprigs of heather, unusually creamy spotted orchids and a tangle of honeysuckle. Bluebells were still in flower here and foxgloves were showing columns of pink. Dad identified hummocks of purple moor grass, the Chequered Skipper's food plant. There was nothing purple about it: it resembled ordinary wild grass although it came in clumps and looked a bit spikier.

Dandelion seeds drifted on a delicate breeze across the clearing beneath the telegraph wires. Midges began munching on my forearms. We agreed, without having to say anything, that this was the most sheltered and most promising place for a butterfly. Dad paused, just before a minute stream. Inevitably, he had seen it first. On a small sapling of alder was a Chequered Skipper, basking in the sunshine on top of a leaf. He had spotted this tiny insect without it even moving. Like feeling yourself become fitter, I felt my spotting skills were sharpening up again during this year of intensive butterflying but I would have never seen this creature until it flitted off. It was similar in size and disposition to a Duke of Burgundy except the boldly coloured checks on its four small wings were yellow and brown rather than golden. And it seemed a formidable personality: it had big clubs on the ends of its antennae and, like other skippers it had a chunky, furry body far larger in proportion to its wings than most butterflies. So very relaxed and so very sure of itself, the skipper allowed us very close to admire it. We inched nearer, taking pictures until it almost filled our viewfinders, and watched it for ages. Showing no desire to move out of the way, eventually I had to flick the bottom of the leaf to make it fly off.

The second Chequered Skipper we saw looked bigger and kept meandering into the bottom of the grassy tussocks. Dad thought it might be a female laying an egg. I managed to follow it for a few minutes. On the south-facing slope, it ducked into a tussock, landed on the side of a stem of grass and curled its abdomen around. Three seconds later, it was off again. I leaned in, and took the grass stem in my hand. The blade had two surfaces, forming a v-shape, and tucked inside the v, halfway up the stem was a tiny greenish egg, securely glued to the leaf. It was not as minuscule as I imagined.

Climbing into the wood, and up the hill, Dad found a couple engaged in courtship, flicking and batting their wings. The male fell about the female. Desire made him as clumsy as a moth bewitched by a light. The female had her wings snapped shut. It didn't look good for the male. Conceding defeat, he hopped off his blade of grass and whizzed backwards, perfectly reversing in mid-air. I had read that the Chequered Skipper could do this but I never really believed it could be so agile.

We watched these skippers for several hours in the wood as they visited the small pink flowers of herb Robert, greedily dipped their proboscis in and out as they systematically worked their way around a purple thistle flower, and even jabbed around the inaccessible flutes of foxgloves like hummingbirds, trying to dive in and extract nectar. Like a rural sheriff, one male chased another to the edge of a small stream. Once the rival had retreated beyond this county line, the sheriff returned to the satisfying business of feasting on flowers in his own personal dell.

With their solidity and robust bearing, these Scottish skippers looked like they had a right to be here, and knew it. I felt sorry for the Small Pearl-bordered Fritillaries which glided along at bracken height. Every time they passed, a Chequered Skipper would heave itself from its flower and buzz after them, showing no deference to the bigger, more beautiful butterflies as it vigorously shooed them away. Two more skippers attacked each other with such a rapid cut-and-thrust that they appeared to be shape-shifters. At full pelt, these feisty little creatures just disappeared, as quickly and strangely as they had vanished from England.

My twenty-sixth and most challenging species of the year so far had been spotted in a day. The following morning, Dad and I treated ourselves to a walk up Ben Nevis, followed by a quick trip to another beautifully remote butterfly site on the banks of Loch Arkaig, an unspoilt loch to the north of Fort William. The Chequered Skippers here were less plentiful as the weather turned cool and cloudy. It made us wonder again how a butterfly that so meekly vanished from the warmth of middle England could survive in a chilly landscape where so few other butterflies flew.

The next day we drove from Fort William to Devon in a day. I have never deliberately killed a butterfly although on this busy, Friday slog down south at least two Green-veined Whites dashed their wings on the radiator of my car. I judged collecting to be cruel and yet I had probably slaughtered a mahogany drawer's worth of butterflies during my adult life behind the wheel of a car. There may be an element of double standards in my contemporary distaste for catching a rare butterfly in a net, squeezing its small body between finger and thumb until it is lifeless, poisoning it to make sure, pinning its body to a cork board and shutting it in a drawer. We may inadvertently slaughter far more butterflies than the collectors of old. But some of the ways in which butterflies were killed and preserved in the golden age of butterfly collecting were downright creepy.

In an 1827 instruction manual on collecting and preserving insects, Abel Ingpen (a solicitor's clerk by day) advised on dipping a pin in nitric acid and piercing its thorax – the equivalent of a poison-tipped dagger to the throat. Victorian advances in chemistry and the use of poisons like chloroform led to the deployment of a sophisti-cated 'killing bottle'. Once caught, a butterfly would be tipped from the net into a wide glass jar and the lid screwed firmly back on. Beneath a zinc mesh at the bottom of the jar lay a sponge soaked in chloroform or, later, potassium cyanide. Schoolboy collectors impro-vised with crushed laurel leaves which also released toxic fumes that gassed the butterfly to death but they could also purchase cyanide until the 1950s. Many chemists would willingly assemble a cyanide jar for small boys, with the poison secured under a layer of plaster of Paris. The Aurelians of old were amusingly oblivious to the health and safety concerns of our more risk-averse times. Writing in 1916, W. Furneaux urged 'young readers' to follow his advice on slaugh-tering butterflies. He responsibly warned that the collector's 'cyanide bottle' contained 'a very poisonous substance called cyanide of potas-sium' but the blithe assumptions in the following sentence are delicious: 'If you are old enough to be trusted with deadly poisons, you may buy the "cyanide" of a chemist who knows you well and is satisfied as to your intentions.' Imagine a boy (in short trousers) attempting to do the same today.

When we pulled off the M5 for a rest in Gloucestershire, it was mid-afternoon and we were tiring after an early start. We drove through Stroud to Rodborough Common, where I had seen the Duke of Burgundies with Matthew Oates. Somehow I found my way again to the amorphous lane so loved by Oates and yet when I burst up through the dark beech wood I thought I had taken a wrong turning. I scarcely recognised the steep hillside, so tall was the grass and thick the scrub, six weeks on. 'Summer, June summer, with the green back on earth and the whole world unlocked and seething – like winter, it came suddenly and one knew it in bed, almost before waking up; with cuckoos and pigeons hollowing the woods since daylight and the chipping of tits in the pear-blossom,' wrote Laurie Lee of this land around Stroud in *Cider With Rosie*. 'The grass was June high and had come up with a rush, a massed entanglement of species, crested with flowers and spears of wild wheat, and coiled with clambering vetches, the whole of it humming with blundering bees and flickering with scarlet butterflies.'

On this afternoon, a storm was brewing and the only butterfly in sight was pale. Up flapped the first Marbled White of the year, looking more like a spectacular European species you might chase in an Alpine meadow than the curiosity that it was: a white butterfly which was a member of the brown subfamily Satyrinae. I wondered if this unmistakable butterfly with a chequerboard of black and white markings on its wings appeared larger than it actually is because it flaps its wings unusually slowly. This, as my Jeremy Thomas guidebook told me, makes it easily identifiable in flight as well as at rest. Relatively common in midsummer woodland edges and rides in south-west England but rarely occurring in the east and north of the country, this was an unexpected surprise and very early in the season for one. The Marbled White was one of those butterflies that would be feted for its beauty if only it were rarer.

Dad and I slumped to the turf, stupefied by miles of motorway driving, and ate tomatoes and boiled egg stuffed between stale bread.

With his abhorrence of waste and unnecessary purchases from garages, Dad had, typically, made enough packed lunches to last the entire trip before he started out. The reason we had called in at Rodborough was to see if we could snatch sight of a Small Blue, Britain's smallest butterfly and a species I was slightly worried about seeing because I had already tried and failed to find it in several locations.

It was cool, almost 4 p.m. and billows of blue-grey cloud gathered over Stroud, threatening rain. After the ease with which we had seen the Chequered Skipper, I felt like my luck was due to run out. When I looked around the combe where Matthew Oates and I had seen the Duke of Burgundies – all dead and gone by this stage of the year – all I could find moving in the grass were pathetic beige moths. They were enough to grab my attention for a second before I realised they were far too mothy to be Small Blues. I was exhausted and irritated from the drive. Forlornly, I told Dad I would just check the bottom of the combe before the skies opened. I staggered down the slope as single spots of rain, as if aimed with precision from the clouds, began to make the grass dance.

Dad looked down the slope towards me at the sound of manic laughter. 'It's here,' I called out, hopping around with an odd excitement. I had disturbed dainty little *Cupido minimus* in the grass, it had flown up and was now clinging to a grass stem by my knee. The dusky Small Blue was the colour of the grey clouds overhead, its tiny wings – typically with a span of 25mm or less – snapped shut. A little gem and an overlooked beauty, like most British butterflies it is much rarer than it once was. With its modest demands for shelter, kidney vetch for its caterpillars and some tall grass and shrubs to roost and perch in, the Small Blue has colonised abandoned quarries, brownfield sites and even motorway cuttings since it disappeared from abandoned or overgrazed grassland where kidney vetch was crowded out. But, in the round, it has still suffered a massive decline. As the rain began to fall in earnest, this little butterfly looked like a courageous survivor, clinging on, against the odds.

The great Victorian naturalist and collector Alfred Russel Wallace famously described how the excitement of discovering the world's biggest butterfly, Queen Alexandra's Birdwing, in the tropical forests of Malaysia caused him to retire with a headache for the rest of the day. In his 1869 book, *The Malay Archipelago*, he wrote: 'My heart began to beat violently, the blood rushed to my head, and I felt much more like fainting than I have done when in apprehension of immediate death. I had a headache for the rest of the day.'

I had just become tremendously excited about seeing the smallest butterfly in Britain and I too had a splitting headache, if not quite the apprehension of immediate death. I was not a mad Aurelian, I hoped, and so I blamed feeling slightly unhinged on the traffic and the long drive home.

There were more early summer fritillaries to see before the trees established the thick canopies of midsummer, and the woods still offered a chiascuro of light and shade. Back in Devon and staying with Dad for the couple of days, the heatwave had broken. After a day of torrential rain, the kind that killed butterflies, Sunday dawned unexpectedly fine and we rose early to go back to Aish Tor – where I had seen the Pearl-bordered Fritillary – so that Dad could undertake his regular transect, counting butterflies for Butterfly Conservation. Dad had heard reports from fellow butterfly recorders in the county that the first two of the big fritillaries of midsummer, the virtually indistinguishable High Brown and the Dark Green, had already been spotted, even though it was still the first week in June.

Once again, Dad cursed the clouds that were already building up on the edge of Dartmoor and seemed to permanently enclose his butterfly slopes in shade. The bracken was spring-green and slender in its youth, although it now curled up to chest height. Stands of pink foxgloves stretched above. The Pearl-bordered Fritillaries had disappeared now and only a few tired Small Pearl-bordered remained. Droplets of rain hung from each flower; the earth was sodden, the air cool. Dad saw hope in the first bramble flowers that usually coincided with the emergence of the High Brown and the Dark Green Fritillaries. So he dived down the hill for the warm hollows where new butterflies might be emerging as I dawdled to admire a battered Green Hairstreak, its luminous green scales flaking off with age as it tilted its closed wings towards the sun.

A few paces on, up flew a large golden butterfly. To mere mortals, the High Brown and Dark Green are indistinguishable in flight. At rest, if you can see their underwings, it is relatively easy to tell them apart: on the hindwing of the High Brown are an extra row of silver eye-like dots with pupils of reddish brown, while the Dark Green tends to have washes of green around its silver markings. In summer, however, these two butterflies both roar around in the sunshine and are not inclined to show you their underwings.

I could not tell what this particular butterfly was although it helpfully closed its wings for a photograph. When I inspected it later, it was no use. My picture showed the extra reddish brown dots of a High Brown but they weren't encased in silver as they should be. Every illustration of a High Brown I could find in butterfly books had those dots with silver around them. This butterfly had the extra reddish brown dots but no silver; yet if it was a Dark Green it had far less green on it than any of the guidebooks showed.

For nearly two hours, we patrolled the hillside, stalking these majestic fritillaries. Walking through bracken is like wading through water. You create ripples and tremors far beyond your body. These alarmed the resting fritillaries, and three more flew up when I approached, avoiding a definitive identification, and Dad's butterfly net. We eventually spotted several which were certainly the more common Dark Green Fritillary.

As is often the way, it was only when we gave up on the High Browns and plodded back to the car that we spotted another possible candidate. This time, it obligingly closed its wings and showed the reddish brown dots surrounded by silver on its underside that unmistakably belonged to a High Brown Fritillary. The dynamism of this big, powerful butterfly was deceptive; its population was in free fall and it now rivalled the Duke of Burgundy as the most endangered species in Britain. It was also my thirtieth species of the summer. I was halfway there.

26. Chequered Skipper, Glasdrum Wood, Scotland, 3 June
27. Marbled White, Rodborough Common, Gloucestershire, 5 June
28. Small Blue, Rodborough Common, Gloucestershire, 5 June
29. Dark Green Fritillary, Aish Tor, Devon, 6 June
30. High Brown Fritillary, Aish Tor, Devon, 6 June

10

Singing with the Large Blue

The Large Blue was declared extinct in 1979. It is now merely one of Britain's rarest butterflies. This strange and miraculous reversal was masterminded by a modest, scholarly entomologist, Jeremy Thomas, who picked up his personal napkin from a wooden box in his Oxford college dining hall and told me one of the saddest and most compelling stories of death and rebirth in modern conservation.

I had chosen a gloomy day with no prospect of seeing any butterflies to travel to Oxford to meet Thomas, Professor of Ecology at Oxford University, and talk about the Large Blue. When we met, I did not immediately tell him I had carried his old guidebook in my pocket on every butterfly trip I had undertaken since 1988 and it was hard not to be a little star-struck when Thomas's tale was also witnessed by Richard Dawkins, another fellow of New College, who pulled up a chair next to Thomas and, between spoonfuls of soup, discussed Greenpeace with the Emeritus Professor of Philosophy opposite.

Thomas is a hugely respected figure among lepidopterists. Unlike many, he is not visibly eccentric but rather a reliable, middle-aged professor whose precise, academic gravity is leavened with good humour, particularly when asked to describe the biological complexities of insect life. If one person could ever be credited with the resurrection of a species of butterfly it is Thomas, and he began by failing. He would never claim it himself but since then, as well as bringing the Large Blue back from the dead, he probably saved four or five other British butterflies from certain extinction.

Some species of butterfly disappeared from Britain before we even realised they existed. As we have discovered and named our precious species, so we have steadily lost them as well. At least five species have vanished from Britain in the past 150 years. The attractive and intriguingly named Mazarine Blue (was it named after Cardinal Mazarin, a seventeenth-century French statesman or the Duchesse de Mazarin who died in 1699 and walked the streets of Chelsea in a blue hooded gown?) vanished in the nineteenth century. So too did the stunning, bright orange Large Copper, around the same time. Both were probably victims of more intensive farming; in the case of the Large Copper it vanished soon after the widespread draining of the East Anglian Fens. In the 1920s, the almost translucent Black-veined White slipped out of our orchards for ever; the

1950s saw the last reliable sightings of native Large Tortoiseshells. There are theories which account for all these disappearances, from parasites to psychotic collectors, and yet we remain in the dark about precisely why they were lost to our land. They may have been on the very northerly edge of their European range, they may have suffered from subtle, completely natural warmings or coolings of our climate, or fallen victim to new strains of disease or predation. We may have a guilty hunch that our urbanisation is responsible. But it is changing patterns of forestry and, most of all, farming, that are most culpable. In the twentieth century, intensive, industrial farming was responsible for more species' catastrophic declines than any other single factor. In the twenty-first century, we may yet exterminate many more by fiddling with the climate.

The decline of the Large Blue perfectly captures our ignorance, greed and inability to comprehend our impact on fellow creatures. This striking blue butterfly, which flew in a jaunty, jinking manner quite unlike its smaller blue relatives, was always rare. During the 1770s, Henry Seymer annotated his copy of *The Aurelian* by commenting about the Large Blue: 'very rarely met with, & in few Collections'. In those days, it flew in corners of Northamptonshire, the Cotswolds, the Polden hills in Somerset, on the south coast of Devon and near Dartmoor and in north Cornwall, although it was so discreet it was never known in all these locations at one time and was only latterly discovered in many of its West Country haunts.

A Large Blue was a great prize for butterfly hunters not merely for its beauty and rarity but because no collector could work out how to breed it in captivity. (Most collections of other species were augmented by perfect specimens bred in greenhouses and killed when fresh out of the pupae.) Its life cycle was a complete mystery to the most expert of lepidopterists. In 1886 William Buckler wrote how he enticed Large Blues to lay eggs on potted thyme but then could not see any caterpillars emerge. Other entomologists noticed that caterpillars reared on thyme didn't grow very big. In the preface to Buckler's book, Stainton noted the Large Blue caterpillar's failure to develop in captivity despite devouring thyme flowers when young: 'It seems at a certain stage of its growth to require something else.'

That something else was ant grubs. After years of study and numerous failed attempts to breed it, three great entomologists of their era, Chapman, Frohawk and Purefoy pieced together the secret life of the Large Blue after Chapman made the crucial breakthrough: he spotted the remains of ant grubs in a Large Blue larva he had accidentally killed.

As the lepidopterists explained in meticulous research published between 1915 and 1953, the caterpillar at first fed on thyme. When it reached its final instar, or stage of growth, it was still tiny. Waiting until the end of the day, it threw itself from the thyme flower to the ground and secreted a seductive fluid to attract the attention of a red ant. Upon finding the caterpillar, the ant tapped it. There ensued a frenzied 'milking' of the creature as other ants clustered around it. Eventually the caterpillar reared up into an 'S' shape and, at this inscrutable command, the ant became agitated, grabbed the Large Blue in its jaw and took it to the safety of its nest.

Having entered the nest, the caterpillar turned tyrant, tricking the ants into believing it was the grub of a queen ant and so required their loyalty and protection. It rested on a silk pad set apart from the ant brood, rising only to gorge itself on ant eggs, larvae or prepupae.

There it stayed, underground, for ten months of the year, acquiring 99 per cent of its final body weight from its time as a 'social' parasite in the ants' nest. Perhaps most creepily of all, it sang softly to the ants all the time, mimicking the sounds of adult ants in an impressive impersonation of the most important individual in the entire ant colony: the queen.

Although this seems a terrific con, the caterpillar also suffered a high mortality rate in the ant nest. If there were too many caterpillars brought into a nest, they would starve because there were not enough ant grubs to go around. On other occasions, this cuckoo would be rumbled. The disadvantage of mimicking a queen ant is that the queen does not like it and in ant colonies with a high number of queens they will lead the workers to turn on the impostor, attack and kill it. Sometimes the parasite itself can be parasitised. Explaining this incredible, natural twist of events, Thomas revealed his unsentimental delight for the complexities of biology. Even more exotic than a Continental species of Large Blue was a rare parasitic wasp which could enter the ants' nest, disable opposition by spraying a chemical around the nest that turned the ants against each other and, while they were fighting, inject the Large Blue caterpillars with its eggs. So the ants would still be duped into feeding the caterpillar, thereby providing food for the wasp grub growing monstrously inside it. Eventually, the wasp would burst out of the butterfly-chrysalis-pretending-to-be-an-ant-grub. By then, the parasitic Large Blue caterpillar would have been completely devoured by another parasite and, once again, the ants would be sprayed again with a disabling chemical so the newborn wasp could crawl out of the nest.

If the Large Blue survived all these hazards, rather than sneak out of the nest to avoid an army of angry ants, it would make a clicking sound which encouraged the ever-willing workers to help unzip it from its pupae. Then, reassuring the ants with chemicals and soothing sounds, it would keep its wings soft and flexible for longer than most butterflies so it could safely crawl up the ants' tunnel and out into the sunshine.

Jeremy Thomas has helped study some of the four other species of Large Blue found across Europe. The Rebel's Large Blue has an even more sophisticated relationship with its friendly ants. Once inside the nest, rather than snatch food for itself, the butterfly's caterpillar induced worker ants to serve it their own regurgitated food. This helped it feed up more quickly and efficiently. If food was short inside the ants' nest, the Large Blue grub would become a target. 'Like all societies, like human societies, when things get scarce they blame the foreigners. In the case of ants, they kill the foreigner,' said Thomas wrily. Ant societies are intensely hierarchical and will do everything to protect the queen. But such was the skill of the Rebel's caterpillar in impersonating a queen ant grub, it could even persuade the workers to feed it their own ant grubs in times of scarcity.

Bit by bit, the elements of this remarkable life cycle were pieced together as Large Blue numbers in Britain were in free fall in the wild. Entomologists still did not really understand what this complex butterfly needed in terms of habitat to survive. Populations collapsed. At Speke's Mill, in Devon, there were more than 10,000 individuals in one valley in 1954. By the end of the decade, there were none. The Large Blue had already vanished from Northamptonshire and the Cotswolds. It disappeared from the

Poldens in the 1950s. By the 1960s, it was reduced to a handful of colonies in north Cornwall and Devon.

'There had been real efforts to conserve it since the 1920s and they had all failed,' said Thomas. 'Unfortunately, without our modern knowledge of the ecology of this butterfly, these well meaning people used the most logical explanation of decline. The best guess was butterfly collectors. Large Blues were this great prize because they were mysterious, because they were beautiful and because of their weird life – it gave them a great cachet for collectors.'

Realising this butterfly was slipping inexorably towards extinction, lepidopterists blamed butterfly collectors. In 1860 W. S. Coleman wrote how the Large Blue flew at Barnwell Wold in Northampton 'but it is less abundant there than formerly, from the repeated attacks of collectors, who catch all they can find'. The year he published his book, one dealer alone snatched 200 adults from that colony. As quickly as new sites were discovered, they were stripped bare. In 1896, it was estimated that collectors took more than 2660 Large Blues from a colony in Cornwall soon after it was discovered. When Baron J. Bouck's butterflies were auctioned in 1939, they included more than 900 specimens of Large Blue. Salmon dug out this piece of 1950s doggerel from Air Marshal Sir Robert Saundby, who found some humour in the decline of the Large Blue (*Maculinea arion*):

A chap who had scores of *arion*
Found some more on the links at Polzyon,
While trying, no doubt,
To wipe the lot out,
He was clubbed on the head with an iron.

In response to the threat from obsessive collectors, nature reserves were created. One site was completely sealed off with high fencing to protect the butterfly from the ravages of collectors; here, however, the butterfly disappeared even more quickly than from the surrounding area. In 1972, Thomas was a young biologist working on his PhD, studying the needs of the rare Black Hairstreak at the research station by Monks Wood, where it was first found. Rather unusually, officials at the Nature Conservancy, which later evolved into the government's conservation body Natural England, asked Thomas to break off from his studies and conduct emergency research to prevent the extinction of the Large Blue. He was chosen because there was almost no one else bothering to study butterfly conservation in the world.

His was a lonely mission. It also appeared hopeless. There was not one example where conservation or the new science of ecology had successfully saved butterflies from extinction. The Large Copper had been reintroduced into Fenland nature reserves, where populations had stumbled on, requiring regular top-ups from foreign species, before becoming extinct again. Attempts to bring Swallowtails back to life in the Fens failed, and smaller-scale attempts to re-establish the Black-veined White also foundered. Perhaps the only moderately successful introduction programme was pioneered by Charles and Walter Rothschild, who released the Black Hairstreak into new woodland sites during the First World War.

By the time Thomas was given his mission, there were two small colonies of Large Blues left in Britain. One, in north Cornwall, was down to twenty individuals. This died out as soon as he started work. The other was a tiny, rough field on the edge of Dartmoor in Devon. It was known only as Site X – its location kept a secret to foil butterfly collectors.

For six summers, Thomas lived by Site X, trying to solve the puzzle of the Large Blue's decline. He knew there was a piece of this butterfly's life cycle, and its relationship with other plants and creatures, which lepidopterists did not fully understand. But he had no idea what this missing fact was. So he spent almost every daylight hour 'measuring everything'. He crumbled multi-coloured Battenberg cake and laid trails of pink, white and yellow crumbs across the field. He followed ants when they dragged this bounty to their nests; the different colours helped him identify exactly where the ants lived. 'It was a quick way and it still took forever,' he said, describing this work as 'incredibly tedious' before hurriedly correcting himself: 'Time-consuming, is better.' It was an heroic endeavour. He listened to *Test Match Special* on the radio and counted butterfly eggs. He looked at emigration of adults, studied the effects of the climate, examined whether some plants were more attractive to the butterfly than others and studied a different parasitic wasp that stung the butterfly eggs.

In this way, he systematically identified twenty-eight different factors that could affect whether the Large Blue lived or died. The key factor, recalled Thomas with a glimmer of a smile, 'took a lot of unearthing'. The solution to the puzzle lay in the ants' nests. By 1975, he had worked out that although the Large Blue lived near, and entered, five different species of red ant, its caterpillar only regularly survived in the nest of one species of ant, *Myrmica sabuleti*.

The Large Blue was completely dependent on this little ant for its survival. The trouble was, this sun-loving ant was even more fussy than the most neurotic of butterflies.

Thomas painstakingly deduced that *Myrmica sabuleti* needed the grass in the meadows where it lived to be very short. Longer grass shaded the earth and stopped it heating up enough for the ant. Turf at 1cm was good; 3cm was too long. This was subtle; we would struggle to tell the difference with our naked eye in a rough field; but the temperature for the ants could drop by 4°C if the grass was a couple of centimetres too long. That, in effect, was the difference between *Myrmica sabuleti* and the Large Blue basking in France or rapidly dying out in Scotland.

With this knowledge, the reason for the Large Blue's decline across Europe was obvious. Agriculture had become more intensive and farmers had abandoned grazing steep and rough meadows. For a while, rabbits kept the turf short in these fields where the ant, and the Large Blue, thrived. Then myxomatosis struck in the 1950s, and the grass became rank, shading the earth and driving *Myrmica sabuleti* and the Large Blue to extinction. The nature reserve fenced off from collectors had also been fenced off from livestock, so its colony of Large Blues and ants were killed by kindness, dying out even more quickly than unprotected areas. The abandonment of traditional grazing explained why the Large Blue was in serious decline across Europe.

Thomas had statistical proof for his theory by 1976. There was one site left, and no margin for bad luck. 'When you are down to almost nothing, you then get into chance. They are called stochastic events in ecology,' said Thomas. 'We weren't very lucky in the last decade.'

In 1973, the Large Blues did too well. There was such a high density of caterpillars inside the ants' nests that many starved or were turned on by the ants. The next year, the population was less than half the size, down to 100 butterflies. In 1975 and 1976, Britain experienced two severe summer droughts, which were devastating for the Large Blue. 'After the 1976 drought it did nothing but rain, which didn't help either,' said Thomas. 'You get into such low numbers it is like a whirlpool, sucking you down.' In 1977, about sixteen adults emerged. Of these, six or seven were females. One or two failed to mate because the feeble, shorter-lived males had emerged earlier and had already died. Captive breeding programmes and extra introductions of caterpillars into the wild also failed. In 1978, the last ever summer of the British Large Blue, five butterflies crawled out of ants' nests. Unluckily, only two were females. As with many butterfly species, the males emerged before the females. This is so they are active and ready to find the females as soon as they hatch. On Site X, however, two of the last three males were dead by the time the first female emerged. By the time the second, and last Large Blue in Britain hatched out, there were no males left alive with whom she could breed.

The Large Blue was extinct in Britain. Thomas was devastated. 'It was bitterly disappointing and quite emotionally draining. I knew the odds were stacked against us on the day I started because no one knew the explanation for the decline or whether it was within our powers to revive it. You felt you had failed,' he paused, 'because you had. When we trumpet this now as the most successful, largest-scale conservation project for an insect in the world you do have to temper that with the memory that actually it started off as a failure.'

175

If he had started five years earlier, Thomas said as we continued to talk over lunch in his Oxford college, he believed he could have stopped its extinction. Faced by this failure, but convinced he had armed himself with the knowledge of what this butterfly required to succeed, he became determined to use what he had learned to establish a new colony. As he put it, if the 1970s were the Enlightenment he began the 1980s determined to initiate the Restoration.

He enlisted the help of David Simcox, an ecologist who looks more like a magician with his impish smile behind a pointy white beard. Assisted by wardens from the Nature Conservancy and the National Trust, they prepared the heathland so that Site X would be a perfect habitat for Large Blues: ensuring it was heavily grazed so the turf was kept short enough on warm, south-facing slopes, with a mosaic of thyme and longer grass around it. In these conditions, populations of *Myrmica sabuleti* built up. Next they scoured Europe for a suitable colony of Large Blues from which they could take eggs for its reintroduction. Simcox spent his summer holidays in his camper van, driving around Sweden where the same species of Large Blue flew. Eventually, he found a colony on Öland, a long, narrow island in the Baltic Sea. With the blessing of the Swedish authorities, he brought eggs back to Britain. In the autumn of 1983, 98 larvae were released on Site X. Seven butterflies emerged in 1984. At least one female paired and laid eggs. In 1985 around four adults emerged and in 1986 there were up to a dozen. Thomas and Simcox scattered 200 young caterpillars around the site and the breakthrough came in 1987 when 75 Large Blues emerged, and laid more than 2000 eggs. The following year, adults were removed to establish a second colony nearby. The Large Blue had been resuscitated in Britain.

176

Over the next two decades, Thomas and Simcox continued to devote their working lives to the Large Blue. They oversaw seven introductions, including one in north Cornwall and four in different localities on the Polden Hills, in Somerset. The butterfly is still rare but from those seven introductions it has expanded to form thirty-three distinct colonies, most of which are in the Poldens, where landowners have been chivvied and persuaded into managing their land to help the butterfly. Up to 6000 of the butterflies fly at the largest site, where Thomas and Simcox have counted 150,000 eggs. This, Thomas believes, is the largest known colony of Large Blues in the world.

The sites are all on private land or on nature reserves which are closed off for the duration of the Large Blue's flight season, except one, Collard Hill, which is National Trust land and open to members of the public who want to see the Large Blue flying again in the wild. It had more than a thousand visitors in the summer of 2009. Passengers catching a train to Cornwall can also see them on the embankment if they have the good fortune to get delayed just west of Castle Cary. The butterfly flies on five different railway embankments, which are so steep, sheltered and hot they have created a mini-Dordogne for the insect. When engineers had to rebuild an unstable embankment nearby, Network Rail agreed to allow the Large Blue scientists to design a butterfly-friendly embankment with thin topsoil and local wildflower seeds. 'David Simcox said can we design it for the Large Blue's idea of heaven and to their enormous credit they said yes,' said Thomas. The Large Blue heaven was actually cheaper to build than Network Rail's original scheme.

Climate change should, in theory, help the Large Blue in Britain.

As it gets warmer, however, the butterfly and its ant won't need the grass to be kept quite so short. It will be a challenge for the Large Blue – and conservation management – to adjust. Many of the butterfly's current sites are hot south-facing slopes that could become too hot. The cooler, flatter areas that the butterfly could fly to nearby are too intensively farmed and very butterfly-unfriendly. 'It will be difficult for some of them to move if it gets warmer,' said Thomas. He and other Large Blue scientists are looking at how to help them. One railway embankment has been designed and rebuilt as a Large Blue site for the future, with cooler areas which the butterfly and its ant can migrate to as the earth warms up.

A week after I visited Thomas in Oxford, his achievements were hailed with a party celebrating the approximate twenty-fifth anniversary of the Large Blue's reintroduction. Although he would never entertain the idea, it was also a celebration for him. Over four decades, he had become the most respected butterfly scientist in Britain and an internationally renowned biologist.

As part of the celebrations, Thomas and Simcox published an academic paper in the leading journal *Science*, summarising their life's work, and luminaries from the world of conservation, including Sir David Attenborough, made public their praise. Somewhat surprisingly, the Large Blue appeared in the newspapers, and on the radio. Friends mentioned to me they had heard all about the amazing Big Blue or the Great Blue or the British Blue. It was really Jeremy Thomas's Blue.

Hesperiidae (Skippers)

Chequered Skipper

Small Skipper

Essex Skipper

Lulworth Skipper

Silver-spotted
Skipper

Large Skipper

Dingy Skipper

Grizzled Skipper

Papilionidae (Swallowtails)

Swallowtail

The left-hand wing of the butterfly is its upper side; the right-hand wing is its underside, which is visible when a butterfly closes its wings. In some species, males and females differ in appearance.

Pieridae (Whites)

Wood White

Réal's Wood White

Clouded Yellow

Brimstone ♂

Large White

Small White

Green-veined White

Orange Tip ♂

Lycaenidae (Hairstreaks, Coppers, Blues)

Green Hairstreak

Brown Hairstreak ♀

Purple Hairstreak

White-letter Hairstreak

Black Hairstreak

Small Copper

Small Blue

Silver-studded Blue

Lycaenidae (Hairstreaks, Coppers, Blues)

Brown Argus

Northern
Brown Argus

Common Blue ♂

Chalkhill Blue ♂

Adonis Blue ♂

Holly Blue

Large Blue

Duke of Burgundy

Nymphalidae (Nymphalids, Fritillaries, Browns)

White Admiral

Purple Emperor ♂

Red Admiral

Painted Lady

Small Tortoiseshell

Camberwell Beauty

Nymphalidae (Nymphalids, Fritillaries, Browns)

Peacock

Comma

Small Pearl-bordered
Fritillary

Pearl-bordered Fritillary

Queen of Spain Fritillary

High Brown Fritillary

Dark Green Fritillary

Nymphalidae (Nymphalids, Fritillaries, Browns)

Silver-washed Fritillary

Marsh Fritillary

Glanville Fritillary

Heath Fritillary

Speckled Wood

Wall

Mountain Ringlet

Nymphalidae (Nymphalids, Fritillaries, Browns)

Scotch Argus

Marbled White

Grayling

Gatekeeper/Hedge
Brown

Meadow Brown

Small Heath

Large Heath

Ringlet

The swarm of Heath Fritillaries at Blean Woods: every bramble leaf, every blade of grass was taken

My third species of the year: this Comma surprised me in my
dad's Devon garden

On my first butterfly expedition of the year I flukily caught this
Small White in flight

A brilliant – and toxic – male Orange
Tip

I liked this meeting of a fly and a
Green-veined White

The Duke of Burgundy, the most
endangered butterfly in Britain

An old and tatty – but still brilliantly
coloured – Green Hairstreak

I watched this Swallowtail imperiously chase off a swallow

This was the first time I had seen a Purple Emperor close up. Iris had descended to feed on Shito, an evil-smelling fish paste from Ghana

A Marsh Fritillary at Murlough
Dunes in Northern Ireland

A feisty Scottish Chequered Skipper

A Peacock caterpillar

The Scotch Argus: proof that brown
butterflies can be beautiful

It wasn't until I waded into this thistle field close to Brighton that I saw thousands of Painted Ladies

The Blues brothers: an Adonis, Chalkhill and Common Blue feasting on a tasty dog turd

Living in the Painted Lady city near Brighton looked uncomfortable: many had their wings ripped to shreds from combat and thistles

Britain's cutest butterfly: the teddy bear-faced Silver-spotted Skipper

An unexpected sighting of a Brown Argus was the perfect cure for butterfly burnout

I eventually found this delicate Wood White, in near darkness, in the pouring rain

I never before noticed the impressive veins on the Clouded Yellow's wings
which show how this muscular migrant crosses oceans to reach us

The final surprise of the summer: two incredibly rare Queen of Spain
Fritillaries mating, in the October sunshine, near Chichester

For the experts who knew it as *Maculinea arion,* its scientific name, there were talks and a buffet lunch at Montacute House, an Elizabethan mansion owned by the National Trust in the impeccably feudal Somerset village of Montacute. The backslapping was followed by a trip to see the Large Blue at one of its secret sites in the Poldens. This was my motivation for crashing the party.

I did not admit it to anyone present but I had seen the Large Blue once before, in 1993, when Dad had wheedled the secret location of Site X out of a retired conservationist friend of his. I have the letter sent to my dad. (It was still in the era when genteel lepidopterists communicated by post.) In a thick blue scrawl, it began with a grid reference for Site X. 'It doesn't look a very prepossessing area, with much gorse and brambles and very little wild thyme in evidence,' my dad's friend wrote. 'It was also overgrazed when I saw it last year. However, I understand that Large Blues are still present there.' The friend went on to 'strongly recommend' that Dad spoke to local conservationists first about Site X. Reading between the lines, the friend thought Dad should take the diplomatic approach.

Despite this good advice, Dad never did talk to local environmentalists. We arrived at this tiny, scruffy-looking little meadow on the edge of Dartmoor without asking permission or smoothing the way with anyone in authority. We had been there for half an hour and had just seen a couple of Large Blues when a warden strolled purposefully across the field. I felt that stomach lurch of someone about to get told off. We were just looking at Large Blues, we said, guiltily. We hoped it was obvious we were not collectors. The warden pretended he had no idea what we were talking about. He was not impressed by Dad's conservation credentials or name-dropping. He would not confirm whether we had seen Large Blues or not and we were marched off the premises with a stern lecture. Mercifully, my dad did not have his butterfly net with him.

Sixteen years on, I was returning to see the Large Blue again with as much security clearance as it was possible to get. I was travelling in a fleet of minibuses with Jeremy Thomas and a hundred other conservation VIPs through the lanes to Green Down, a Somerset Wildlife Trust nature reserve in the Poldens which was closed to the public during the Large Blue flight season.

I knew the Poldens. They had always been a magical set of hills to me. When I stayed with my granny when I was small, I learned the names of all the hills around her house in Somerset: the Quantocks to the north-west, the Brendans beyond, the Blackdowns to the south-west, the Mendips to the east, and the distant volcano of Glastonbury, visible on a clear day from the moor below Granny's cottage. Then there were the Poldens. I can still see the map on Granny's wall that they were marked on, but I could never find them in the landscape at all, they were so small. It was only much later that I realised that you zipped right through the middle of the Poldens on the train to Cornwall. In my twenties, the Glastonbury festival became a vivid part of every summer and I associated this area of Somerset with sleep-deprived exits from the festival and the relief of falling into the calm green folds of the Poldens after the weird city-in-a-field chaos of Glastonbury. The Poldens are a perfect island of English countryside: the kind of unobtrusive, unshowy landscape also found in places like Northamptonshire and Leicestershire. These landscapes lie unruffled and undisturbed because we pass through them in a hurry to get somewhere more spectacular.

When we stepped onto Green Down, immediately below it we could hear the railway line carrying trainloads of people east to London and west to Exeter. Helicopters regularly flew overhead, en route to the naval base at Yeovil. Even horses and their jockeys sped past on a gallops that, crazily, had been cut through the middle of this steep, precious meadow in the 1980s. The only thing that did not rush past was the River Cary in the flat valley bottom. It meandered and gurgled.

The sun had disappeared and the breeze was strong, and conditions were not promising. To an untrained eye, Green Down looked neglected, with its ruts of short turf and random patches of longer grass. Tangles of sheep's wool hung like litter from sloe thickets. The field was not neat and not obviously flowery either, although pink heads of thyme were dotted across the grass and in a shady corner of the nature reserve were three pale-cream greater butterfly orchids, standing like guardians over this precious butterfly landscape.

Cropping the grass short with intensive grazing every spring had encouraged the spread of *Myrmica sabuleti* nests. There was now an incredible density: two nests of the Large Blue ant in every square metre of downland. Even when the sun disappeared, you could feel the heat radiating from the short turf. The site had been managed to perfection for Large Blues.

There were Large Whites and Large Skippers, Speckled Woods and Small Heaths. A smart new generation of Small Tortoiseshells also flew for the first time since the spring. When I asked Thomas about the Large Blue's personality as an adult butterfly, he shot me the pained glance of a scientist who does not like anthropomorphising his subjects. 'It is the floppiest of all the butterflies. It gently flaps from place to place,' he grimaced, and that was as far as he would go. Its personality was not relevant.

After ten minutes of speculative wandering, trying to escape the largest crowds of VIPs also looking for an unusually floppy blue butterfly, a Large Blue bounced past, more animated than I expected, given that one butterfly book described it as 'generally slow and fluttering'. It was not a big butterfly but was significantly larger than any other blue, and the bold dark blue of its wings were framed by firm black borders and a sharp outer edge of white. A second Large Blue was resting, on a bent grass stem, in a similar pose to the Small Blue I had seen at Rodborough. A group gathered to watch a third Large Blue briefly land on thyme. It did not seem to curl its abdomen around to lay an egg but when we inspected the flower after its departure, we could see a microscopic egg, the smallest I had yet seen, pasted inside one tiny bell-like flower of thyme. It had perhaps a one-in-a-hundred chance of surviving the next ten months, mostly in darkness below ground, before creeping out of its underground lair and stretching and drying its blue wings in the sunshine for an all-too-brief flight around Green Down.

Assisted by the efforts of graziers and a broad coalition of local landowners, from the National Trust to the family which owns Clarks Shoes, long based in the small town of Street, close to the Poldens, the Large Blue is likely to expand to fifty separate sites in the West Country. Thomas and Simcox have identified 100 areas in total in Britain where it could return if the correct grazing regime was established for its friendly ant. The scientists hope to establish what they call metapopulations, clusters of loosely connected colonies, such as there are now in the Poldens, so the Large Blue can expand freely, without further human intervention, through the Cotswolds and along the coasts of north Cornwall and south Devon.

People sometimes ask Thomas why he plays God and what is the point of saving 'a dinosaur' like the Large Blue? Extinction is a natural process, as well as a man-made one. The Large Blue is disappearing across Europe. Why put so much effort into an attractive but apparently trivial insect? Thomas was reluctant to celebrate his role in reviving the Large Blue not merely because of his modesty but because he felt it was not the most important part of his life's work. Far more significant, he has argued, is what that success showed: one of the first examples of insect conservation, it proved that we could save an insect only if we truly understood its ecology, the way it interacted with other species and what it needed. His triumph was also energising. It triggered a conservation boom. For most of two decades he worked alone; now there are more than a hundred people in sixteen countries studying the biology and conservation of the five subtly different species of Large Blue.

Thomas did not realise it at first but in reviving the Large Blue, he was actually restoring a type of habitat lost to much of Europe. By discovering the importance of traditional, well-grazed and unfertilised grassland, he was helping a suite of other rare species – not just butterflies but plants such as the pale heath violet. The success of the

Large Blue project almost certainly saved three other British butterflies from extinction in the 1980s. When we met at Oxford, Thomas said he feared the Adonis Blue, the Silver Spotted Skipper and the Heath Fritillary would have all become extinct within a decade of the Large Blue. Armed with the knowledge of the Large Blue's needs, a new generation of young butterfly ecologists including Thomas and Martin Warren worked much more quickly on plans to revive these three other species. Since these ideas were put into action in the 1980s, populations of all three have stabilised and flourished. The success in bringing back the Large Blue cemented knowledge of how best to manage grasslands for the needs not only of the adult butterflies but for the caterpillars as well.

But is it really viable to save every endangered British species in this costly, time-consuming and labour-intensive way? 'Yes, I think is the answer,' said Thomas. 'The initial problem with the Large Blue was not a lack of resources or willpower but a lack of knowledge. With increased knowledge, we can do the same for all these other endangered species through woodland management and grassland management. That doesn't necessarily cost more, it is just doing things differently.'

Science, for Thomas, does not know all the answers. He found it 'lovely', he said, that there was still so much more to discover about the secret miracles of the Large Blue's life cycle. Nevertheless, science could guide the practical conservation work that saves rare butterflies from extinction, even when we are beset by climate change. 'I'm more optimistic than most, at least about the practicalities. Whether it will happen or not, the scientists like me did the easy bit. It's how the land managers put it into practice that matters. It's certainly not a ridiculous idea to turn all our species around, and not just on nature reserves.' The success of the Large Blue on railway embankments is one example of butterflies adapting to improbable brownfield habitats. In this way, insects are more rational creatures than we might imagine. Beautiful butterflies do not necessarily need beauty spots to survive.

31. Large Blue, Green Down, Somerset, 16 June

11

The swarm at Blean Woods

Once there were swarms of butterflies in our skies. Victorian collectors would rave about clouds of butterflies in the New Forest or on the South Downs. Mr Banning, a farmer on the Isle of Man, encountered a flock of Small Tortoiseshells in 1855 – on Boxing Day. 'Whilst standing in my farmyard on the day following Christmas day, it being unusually fine and warm, I was suddenly astonished by the fall of more than a hundred of the accompanying butterflies [Small Tortoiseshells]. I commenced at once collecting them, and succeeded in securing more than sixty,' he recalled. In 1892, S. G. Castle Russell took a walk through the New Forest. 'Butterflies alarmed by my approach arose in immense numbers to take refuge in the trees above,' he wrote. 'They were so thick that I could hardly see ahead and indeed resembled a fall of brown leaves.' Five years later, in woods near Aldershot, Castle

Russell captured a hundred Purple Hairstreaks with two sweeps of his net.

Those days are definitely over. Mention butterflies to anyone and they will say they used to see far more when they were children. Some of this may be nostalgia. Some of the Victorians may have had hyperbolic imaginations. But I had certainly never seen a swarm of butterflies in my life. In this year, so far, despite the Painted Lady invasion, nearly all my trips to find butterflies ended with the sighting of ones and twos of species, or a dozen or two dozen at most. Now it was midsummer. Late June was sultry. After two years of washouts, the country baked in what the Met Office and the papers prematurely christened 'a barbecue summer'. Everywhere I went in the city and the suburbs 'the same almost embarrassingly familiar breath of sweetness' wafted out of gardens, as Michael Frayn put it in *Spies*. Reeking and intimate, privet 'has a kind of sexual urgency to it' wrote Frayn. The countryside had its own sickly and unsettling version of privet: the fecund flowers of sweet chestnut trees wafted their own coarse scent through the woods as butterflies tugged and pulled their way out of chrysalises in hidden spots all over the land. And slowly, concealed in a small clearing in the heart of Blean Woods in Kent, a swarm began to build.

My first trip in search of the Heath Fritillary in early June ended in the most perfunctory of successes. This was a technical victory, a win on points, and there was not much satisfaction in it. By the end of a very cold day, I had seen one and a quarter. And neither the one nor the quarter moved.

The Large Blue was the last British butterfly to become extinct. When it was declared lost in 1979, the Heath Fritillary, a fragile woodland butterfly with a pretty scientific name, *athalia*, was expected to follow. At this point, conservationists had yet to save any endangered butterflies. Collecting was in decline and the Wildlife and Countryside Act of 1981 gave the Heath Fritillary legal protection, but this butterfly was fast disappearing from our woodlands. The Heath Fritillary, so called because of its predilection for dry, heathy woodlands, seemed a curiously passive butterfly. According to Edward Newman, Victorian collectors found it would play dead when caught 'falling into the collector's net in an apparently inanimate state, closing its wings and contracting its legs'.

In the early 1980s, Blean Woods near Canterbury was its last significant stronghold and even here its population appeared to be dying out. Several hundred miles to the west, there was a tiny colony in the Tamar Valley in Cornwall, where I had seen it once with Dad. There were also a few, random claims that it had been sighted on Exmoor in Somerset, which were given short shrift by lepidopterists: it was not officially listed as having flown there for decades and was assumed to be extinct here. This made its rediscovery on Exmoor almost as dramatic as the sudden appearance of the Chequered Skipper in the Highlands of Scotland had been forty years earlier.

Faced by the Heath Fritillary's inexorable decline, scientists conducted the first survey of Exmoor in 1984 after a local farmer insisted he had seen the butterfly there the previous summer. 'Quite frankly, we didn't believe him but he was a good enough recorder for us to check it out,' said Martin Warren, who was then a rangy young entomologist and is now chief executive of Butterfly Conservation. Warren found the butterfly in several different places on Exmoor. For a few years, these colonies were kept secret: the old survey papers have 'strictly confidential' marked on their covers in red pen. Lepidopterists struggled to get their heads around the fact that this butterfly of dry woodlands had completely confounded their theories by thriving on a different kind of habitat: moorland. A few years later, in the hot summer of 1989, on the sheltered bracken-rich slopes just below the high tops of Exmoor, Warren found thousands of butterflies. Here, unnoticed by landowners including the National Trust, and without anyone doing anything to preserve them, were large, vibrant colonies of Heath Fritillaries.

'It turned out that bracken had been the big overlooked habitat and that lower moorland edges were really important for butterflies in Britain,' explained Matthew Oates as we drove through low cloud on the Brendan Hills on our way to Exmoor. 'It was an amazing discovery, it really was.' There was not, however, a happy ending for the Heath Fritillary.

I had persuaded Oates to help me find the Heath Fritillary – another butterfly I knew very little about – and I got the impression he was only too happy to avoid the office for another day. This time, the weather was not on our side. The day was dark and cool and wet, as if nature had grown tired of all this hot weather and flicked a switch. He picked me up from Taunton railway station and we drove through lanes thickly lined with beech hedges which met in the middle, creating perfect dark green tunnels. When we stopped at an old-fashioned service station to get lunch supplies, the air inside the shop was a fug of pasties.

On the flat rainswept top of Exmoor close to Dunkery Beacon, we pulled over by a lonely hawthorn, still in bloom, above Bin Combe, historically the best Heath Fritillary site on Exmoor. This small valley sprang up from nothing, steep and short. Walking down it, the combe quickly closed in and swallowed us up. Once inside it, all we could hear was water from its tiny stream, which quickly gathered momentum and slipped down as a diminutive waterfall at times. Through a gap in the hills, we could see the Bristol Channel topped by the faded grey line of Wales beyond. 'If we'd had the weather the Met Office had forecast we would have seen a hundred Heath Fritillaries by now,' said Oates. Instead, we saw one bright-yellow frog, several brilliant salmon-coloured grasshoppers with arresting green Mohicans and dozens of treacly black slugs, tasting the cool drizzle. I ate a rainwater-flavoured bilberry. It was June and my hands were almost numb.

Below us, a large red deer kicked up in alarm and bounced beyond a ridge on the horizon, over what looked like an enormous precipice. I approached the ridge more sedately, half expecting to see the deer on the ground clutching its ankle and gazing up at me beseechingly. Of course it had landed perfectly, found its feet and was long gone.

We drove a short distance to Halse Combe, another, broader valley nearby. Bracken was forcing its way up the slope. The off-spring of trees from the ancient woodland below were marching up the hill too. Left alone, ungrazed, this landscape would become a thick forest (fatal for a Heath Fritillary, which needs coppiced woodland) in a couple of decades. The National Trust was managing this area, and beating back the bracken so that the Fritillary's food plant, common cow wheat, could prosper. In places, however, the cleared bracken had become a carpet of brambles. 'So often when you control bracken you get brambles,' said Oates. 'Nature conservation is like that. You swap one set of problems for another. Quite often you don't know which ones you are going to get instead.'

The miraculous discovery of Heath Fritillaries on Exmoor was followed by disaster, for which well-meaning conservation strategies were largely to blame. During the 1990s a new conservation-minded farming plan was introduced on Exmoor. The authorities wanted to encourage the purple heather on the moor and discourage excessive winter grazing, which was damaging areas of the moor. Separately, commercial pressures were encouraging Exmoor's farmers to swap traditional breeds of sheep and cattle for less fatty breeds, which were not grazed on Exmoor. The traditional burning of the moor was discouraged and, in many parts, grazing almost ceased.

The Heath Fritillary's needs – or rather the needs of its incredibly neurotic food plant, common cow wheat – were still not fully understood. What conservationists did not realise was that the butterfly had thrived by living on the edge of moorland that had been fairly intensively exploited by commoners and graziers. When these new conservation plans discouraged established grazing, Heath Fritillary populations collapsed on Exmoor. Oates admitted his organisation, the National Trust, was among those who were culpable. 'There was a massive decline on National Trust land within ten years of it being discovered and all being hunky-dory,' he said. 'It was egg on face and panic.' By the turn of this century, it looked like the Heath Fritillary was heading for extinction on Exmoor.

The biggest problem was the virulent growth of bracken and gorse, unchecked now there was less grazing. Within a few years of being hacked back, bracken and gorse returned so rampantly that the cow wheat was crowded out. So Butterfly Conservation teamed up with the National Trust to conduct experiments on stretches of moor. As we strolled across Halse Combe, we compared the results: patches of ground the conservationists had left alone, or cut back by hand or treated with a chemical herbicide called Asulox, which kills off bracken but little else and does not harm cow wheat.

Oates enjoyed the knotty paradoxes of conservation and it was almost with delight that he pointed out the patch that remained more clear of bracken, and more filled with the Heath Fritillary's food plant, than any other. It had been cleared with the chemicals, an anathema to most conservationists. Where the bracken had been simply cut back, and not treated, it was growing so thickly it looked like it had never been cleared. Just like an iceberg, most of a bracken plant is underground: it always sprouts back.

'Ideally we don't want to use herbicides at all,' said Oates. 'We don't want that butterfly to become dependent on a chemical. We always regarded it as a stopgap measure but for what? Cutting back bracken does not produce anything like the right results. What do we do now? The key thing is "do nothing" is not an option. We've tried that and do nothing equals extinction.'

There was no one else in Halse Combe as we trudged across the soggy brambles. It was 10°C. Oates paused. 'There,' he pointed. Delicate and silvery, a female Heath Fritillary was sitting low down on a cream bramble flower, visibly wrestling with the cold wind, struggling to keep her wings tightly closed against it. She was smaller than I expected, and the underside of her hindwings, the only bit visible, was decorated with the finest tracings of silver, black and gold. She wisely did not move and we left her in peace; I wondered whether she would survive this miserable day.

Without Oates, I would never have seen it; only the real experts can find butterflies in bad weather. A few minutes later, however, I found the only other trace of a Heath Fritillary we would see that day: a pristine forewing of a male, detached from a butterfly and deposited on the damp earth. He was probably struck down by the previous night's torrential rain. I put the quarter in the pocket of my waterproof and later slipped it between the pages of a butterfly book. When I next opened the pages, the wing was as bright as the day I had found it.

Oates suggested that I could not count a butterfly as successfully spotted if I had not seen it fly. (I argued I had at least seen it move, as it trembled in the cold.) Whenever I visited my nieces, Carla and Amelie, in Chelmsford, I took them to Tropical Wings, a slightly scruffy butterfly sanctuary in Essex that had gradually expanded its sheds over the years and now housed all kinds of owls, ravens, otters, wallabies and giant tortoises.

I had discovered that a couple of miles from Tropical Wings was Thrift Wood, a modest square of ancient woodland owned by the Essex Wildlife Trust. The Heath Fritillary had been successfully reintroduced here in recent decades and, when I visited Carla and Amelie later in June, I thought they would enjoy seeing a real rare butterfly in the wild rather than a fat foreign thing flapping around a hothouse. They grudgingly agreed to a quick detour on the way to Tropical Wings.

With a tiny entrance and no obvious place to park, Thrift Wood did not seem to have many visitors compared with other woods close to Chelmsford, which thronged with families and small children. We had the wood to ourselves, which was nice, but I was sceptical about the Heath Fritillary flying here simply because this nature reserve was so very small. Blean Woods in Kent is huge and the Heath Fritillary requires a very active regime of coppicing, with large clearings, to maintain generous supplies of cow wheat for its caterpillars.

We quickly reached a clearing in the middle of the wood that had been coppiced a couple of years ago. The grass was busy with common species of butterfly and there, buzzing through them and looking much smaller on the wing than I imagined, were four frail-looking Heath Fritillaries. This colony seemed so small, and therefore so precarious, I wondered how it was viable. There did not seem to be enough wood to coppice. I felt sorry for the Heath Fritillary, isolated in this tiny patch of woodland, although several other colonies re-established in Essex woodlands were proving more successful.

I followed them on their low, looping flight paths but they struggled to gain Carla and Amelie's attention. The Heath Fritillaries here would not let them get close when they rested on flowers, unlike the butterflies at Tropical Wings. Then the girls were distracted by the massed ranks of wood ants marching around their feet and threatening to jump onto their sandals. I showed them a large, rustling ants' nest. Scared, they demanded the sanctuary of tame nature. When we reached Tropical Wings, the greenhouse full of foreign butterflies was a culture shock: the exotic Owl butterflies were so large and clumsy compared with the slender grace of the Heath Fritillaries. It was like munching a fat, flavourless strawberry from the supermarket after feasting on tiny, sharp berries plucked from the wild.

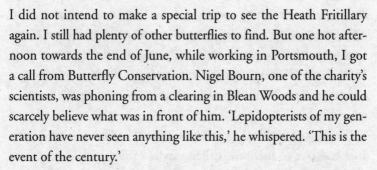

I did not intend to make a special trip to see the Heath Fritillary again. I still had plenty of other butterflies to find. But one hot afternoon towards the end of June, while working in Portsmouth, I got a call from Butterfly Conservation. Nigel Bourn, one of the charity's scientists, was phoning from a clearing in Blean Woods and he could scarcely believe what was in front of him. 'Lepidopterists of my generation have never seen anything like this,' he whispered. 'This is the event of the century.'

Bourn was not given to hyperbole, so I hurriedly finished off my work and drove there as fast as I could. I arrived at Rough Common, part of the Blean Woods complex, at 3.30 p.m. It was hot and dry. After a few moments struggling to get reception on my phone, I got hold of Michael Walter, the warden of this RSPB reserve, who told me to open the wooden gate and take the dirt track into the wood. I bounced through the trees in my car, throwing up a thick cloud of dust behind me. Coming the other way was a television van; the local news had got there first. Two miles into the forest, in North

Bishopden Wood, there was a small clearing. It was off the main forest rides and not on the way to anywhere. Few people walked this far. I pulled over with a crunch on the rough ground and jumped out.

I found Walter and Nigel Bourn standing in an ordinary rough square of open ground. The clearing was interspersed with a few oak standards – big trees which were not cut down when the rest of the wood was coppiced – and surrounded by hornbeam and sweet chestnut. The clearing was carpeted with cow wheat, poking between bramble patches and self-seeded birch and hornbeam. Looking around, at first I only saw one or two Heath Fritillaries. Then I saw another couple, then dozens, then scores, then hundreds. It was a dizzying, disorientating spectacle, a music festival for insects: an uncomfortable, heavy, heaving mass of butterflies. In this ordinary-looking patch of recently coppiced woodland there were at least 1300 Heath Fritillaries flying. Half the entire British population of one of our rarest butterflies currently on the wing were in this quarter of a hectare.

I stood and watched, gormless with shock. These Heath Fritillaries had one of the most striking styles of flight I had ever seen. They would move through the air like moths, blown in the breeze like a leaf and every bit as feeble as those Heath Fritillaries that would play dead in the nets of Victorian collectors. Then they would buzz more purposefully, with a very flat flight, dipping and swerving with fast wingbeats, before finishing off with a lazy little float.

They must have felt claustrophobic in this clearing. There was no space. Every perch – every blade of grass, every bramble leaf and certainly every bramble flower – was taken. A few were sunning themselves in pairs and looked peaceful enough. People often see two butterflies together in a garden and believe they are a couple. But butterflies do not pair off for peaceful companionship; their adult lives, their existence as butterflies, is all about mating. These pairs of Heaths were invariably a male hassling a female, who was then molested again by other males. Two-thirds of this swarm were estimated to be men. Poor things. They were not going to get much satisfaction. The females looked tired and harassed, subject to constant gropings and probings by desperate male butterflies. One female had a broken wing from fending off so many advances. Another landed on a slender head of grass. One by one, four males joined her, and the grass stem bowed lower and lower, finally touching the ground. The female flapped her wings, as if to shoo the men away. Then she deployed what Bourn explained was a mating-avoidance posture. To me it looked like a provocative come-on, but then I was not a Heath Fritillary: she stuck her abdomen in the air, and peeled back the end, showing a bright orange tip. It looked obscene but it told the men she had already mated. It seemed to work, until the next desperate male cruised past.

Blean had long been the headquarters, as Victorian Aurelians would say, of the Heath Fritillary. Even within this last major site, however, by the start of the 1980s, the butterfly only clung on in tiny colonies in clearings, mainly in East Blean. It looked doomed, particularly when a disastrous population crash was triggered by the eighties recession. The wood had always been coppiced for pulp for a paper mill in Sittingbourne. When the mill closed in the recession, suddenly there was no local market for wood from Blean. Coppicing was halted and sunny glades filled with cow wheat were quickly swamped by a tangle of new trees.

Michael Walter, the RSPB warden, arrived at Blean Woods nature reserve, a western section of the forest that had long been church land, when the RSPB bought it in 1982. Church Wood, as this area was traditionally known, was noted for its Heath Fritillaries in the 1950s. According to R. E. Stockley, thousands were found there in 1951 but when he visited in 1959 there were only 'a handful'. It was not surprising, Stockley wrote, because 'the woodcutter' was no longer active and the forest had quickly become overgrown. 'Little or no attempt had been made to keep the undergrowth in check; and in consequence the cow wheat, the food plant of *athalia*, had almost died out.' By the time Walter arrived, one small colony remained in the wood. On a good day, he might see ten of the butterflies. After several decades of good woodland management, the number of Heath Fritillary colonies has increased to between thirty and forty in the reserve (which has expanded to 509 hectares). Even so, less than 2 per cent of the wood holds colonies of Heath Fritillaries. These tiny, fragmentary populations do not seem very capable of flying through dense woodland to expand their range. They need tracks or forest rides between clearings so they can move around the forest, and find the latest clearing where cow wheat has seeded.

What had caused this swarm? After almost thirty years managing the wood, Walter had created the perfect habitat with heavy coppicing every season. Because it was a mile from the nearest colony, and Heath Fritillaries are notoriously feeble about moving through the woods in search of new and suitable habitat, he reintroduced this colony himself, bringing forty butterflies from another site. For a few summers it did well, but by 2006 it had declined and Walter thought it would become extinct. 'In 2007 something happened and the population began to build up again. In 2008 it was better still and this year it has shot through the roof,' he said. The next biggest colony in the wood holds about 130 butterflies.

Despite all his experience and all his years in the wood, Walter said he had no inkling what, precisely, brought about this population explosion. 'We know next to nothing about cow wheat,' he said. He noticed it sprang up very well for a couple of summers after he coppiced an area but he also knew it was not that simple. Because he had been on the reserve so long, he was now coppicing areas he had originally coppiced twenty-five years ago. After the second coppicing of an area, the cow wheat did not seem to come back. Even when he had worked the land for a quarter of a century, he did not have all the answers. Conservation was more challenging than it looked. I could understand if the Heath Fritillary tried Walter's patience. 'I don't personally know what the key is. I coppice a bit and the following year or two there is a nice patch of cow wheat,' he said and shrugged. 'It's a rod for their own back really. They've chosen to specialise in cow wheat – it's no wonder most years they struggle to do well.'

So fussy and fragile, the Heath Fritillary was the last butterfly I would have expected to see in a swarm. Witnessing such an extraordinary gathering of rare butterflies was a stunning event, but it was less glorious than I imagined. It did not fill me with rapture; rather, it was stressful to look at these butterflies and watch their will to power, their urge to find a mate and lay eggs in such a crowded, competitive environment. It was sad to think how this great, excessive population explosion actually jeopardised each individual's urge to perpetuate its species.

As the sun withdrew beyond the wood, the butterflies sank, exhausted, into the grass to roost. I counted eighty-six on a square metre of bramble. They hung off small birch seedlings like Christmas decorations. They looked so fragile and, in this number, they were. As I picked my way carefully across the clearing, I trod on several. Others looked like they were dying, as they dropped to the ground. I found one trussed up in a grateful spider's web and another fresh-looking couple dead together, as if they had undertaken a gruesome pact to escape this world.

32. Heath Fritillary, Halse Combe, Exmoor, Somerset, 8 June

12

Urban butterflies and the problem with binoculars

Coldharbour Lane is dirty and noisy even on the quietest days. Its only lane-like quality is the interminable slowness with which it takes you through south London. Red buses with busted engines throttle up the slight incline from Brixton to the bus garage in Camberwell. The road is saddled with a bad reputation. Unfairly or not, play a word-association game with a Londoner and they are likely to pair Coldharbour Lane with riots, crack dens or stabbings. It would be harder to find a more uncompromising urban setting.

In August 1748, the leafy lane that twisted its way towards the marshy village of Camberwell was known as Cool Arbour Lane. Here, the first Camberwell Beauty was caught by a curious butterfly collector. Soon afterwards, another was taken in St George's Fields, a series of low-lying meadows south of the Thames close to the village of Newington, now dominated by brutal 1960s tower blocks and the monstrously scary roundabout at Elephant & Castle. In those days, the only thing looming over the water meadows of the Thames Valley were willow trees, and the Camberwell Beauty was prosaically named the Willow Butterfly because it was thought its caterpillars fed on the willow it was found amongst.

In his 1860 guidebook, W. S. Coleman reminisced about the days when Camberwell was a village rather than a London suburb and the Camberwell Beauty, an impressively large dark-brown butterfly with borders of lemon yellow, could be collected there. Now, he added sleazily, 'though it has its "Beauties" still, they are not of the lepi-dopterous order, nor game for any net that the entomologist usually carries'. Eighty-five years later, Camberwell was even less salubrious and E. B. Ford wrote that those early pinned specimens of Camberwell Beauties caught there were 'perhaps the last memento of "the village" long ago engulfed by the catastrophic growth of modern London'.

It is easy to see the rise of the modern city as a catastrophe for but-terflies. The accounts of the early collectors are exotic and utterly implausible in today's world. The Camberwell Beauty is not the only butterfly named after what became a London suburb: the Speckled Wood was originally called the Enfield Eye, such was its popularity in the woods that bowed to the frenetic development of north London. On Enfield Chase, Dru Drury, a wealthy entomolo-gist, recorded 'Black veind white Butterfly plentiful and fine' in the 1760s; 150 years later, the Black-veined White would be extinct across the whole of the country. These suburban locations were once unimaginably blessed with butterfly life, as were the inner cities.

Imagine strolling through St James's Park and seeing a Swallowtail. In 1699, Petiver wrote of one being caught in the royal garden at St James's.

One urban location is more important than any other in our butterfly history. Hampstead, in north London, is still an attractive village, albeit one overrun with millionaires, and the Heath remains a leafy sanctuary, blessed with fine trees and birds you would expect to encounter only in proper countryside. Three hundred years ago, it was a butterfly hotspot and a favourite haunt of the first collectors. Scores of early specimens and new species were first captured here by the likes of Ray and Petiver. I would love to wander the Heath of 1696, when Petiver first identified the Grizzled Skipper, or when the Marsh Fritillary could be found flying there, an impossible fantasy today. Hampstead Heath was also the scene of the capture of Albin's Hampstead Eye, a mysterious creature which the butterfly illustrator Eleazar Albin believed he had caught on Hampstead in the early 1700s. For years, this exotic butterfly was unidentified apart from Albin's specimen, until it was found to be a species common to Indonesia, called *Junonia villida*. How had it got to Hampstead? The most likely explanation was simply that someone got their labels mixed up in their butterfly collection and an insect brought back from Indonesia was accidentally listed as being found on the Heath.

Butterflies vanished from our cities earlier and more quickly than from the countryside. Woods became houses, marshes turned into industrial estates, meadows gave way to motorway junctions. As butterfly collecting grew in popularity, locations close to towns were within easy reach and vulnerable to over-collecting. The Northern Brown Argus was found on Arthur's Seat in Edinburgh but by 1870 it had disappeared. Salmon reproduced an 1857 letter from R. F. Logan. '*I* have not diminished their numbers, having always a wholesome dread of exterminating species,' Logan wrote. 'But I believe a *dealer* has, and a host of small boys who come out of Edinburgh, with *orange*-coloured nets, and bottle them up wholesale, *five or six together, alive,* in the same receptacle, generally a match-box.'

Tales of butterflies in cities appear to be wild fantasies today. Stoke Newington, in London, is a leafy urban village prized by the middle-classes for its farmers' market, fashionable bakeries and yoga classes. When it was a more traditional rural village, in the 1720s, the butterfly collector Joseph Dandridge went to live there for health reasons – for its clean air. One day, a farm labourer spotted him lunging wildly at thin air. Suspecting him to be a deranged lunatic, the labourer wrestled the entomologist to the ground, whereupon his suspicions seemed confirmed by Dandridge's wail: 'The Purple Emperor's gone! The Purple Emperor's gone!'

A Purple Emperor sighted in Stoke Newington these days really would be a hallucination, although this species has a talent for the preposterous: one was found, squashed, on the steps of the High Court a few years ago. What it had been found guilty of was not clear. So I ruled out the possibility of seeing exciting butterflies in the city too readily. While I was making steady progress spotting butterflies in my trips into the countryside, whenever I was stuck at work in the city I felt trapped, in the wrong place and unable to stumble on any. I was sure it was no coincidence that whenever I was staying in London I seemed to dream of improbable sightings of Purple Emperors and Camberwell Beauties.

I feared the Purple Emperor held some kind of curse over me but the Camberwell Beauty was a more simple, and impossible, dream. Contemplating one felt like a lament for a lost London. Siegfried Sassoon, the poet, once wrote of stumbling across a butterfly in the attic of his home in Kent. 'By standing on a chair – which I placed on a table – I could just get my hand between the gauze and the glass. The butterfly was ungratefully elusive, and more than once the chair almost toppled over. Successful at last, I climbed down, and was about to put the butterfly out of the window when I observed between my fingers that it wasn't the Small Tortoiseshell or Cabbage White that I had assumed it to be. Its dark wings had yellowish borders with blue spots on them. It was more than seven years since I had entomologically squeezed the thorax of a "specimen". Doing so now, I discovered that one of the loftiest ambitions of my childhood had been belatedly realised. I had caught a Camberwell Beauty.'

In 1766 Moses Harris wrote in *The Aurelian*: 'This is one of the scarcest flies known in England.' He called it his 'Grand Surprize'. Harris and Sassoon perfectly capture one truth about the Camberwell Beauty: like many ambitions, you cannot go looking for it; you can only hope that it will find you. As a rare migrant, the Camberwell Beauty was not one of the fifty-nine British butterflies on my list; I would be lucky if a sighting of it was bestowed on me once in my lifetime. Searching for one of these rarities was like recognising a long-lost lover in the face of a stranger you passed on the street. I thought I saw a Beauty in the flash of every large dark butterfly, and yet a heartbeat and a second glance later it was always revealed to be a Peacock or a Red Admiral.

Some years there would be sightings of Camberwell Beauties all over England – called *Antiopa* Years, after its Greek name – and then it was hardly seen for a decade. In the hot summer of 1976 about 300 were recorded and some 350 were recorded in 1995, the greatest immigration since 1872, when more than 400 were recorded. Using meteorological data, it was thought to have flown in from the south of Norway and Sweden and Denmark, with the first arrivals hitting the most easterly point in the country, around Great Yarmouth and Lowestoft, in late June. Contrasting two of the great immigrations shows the decline in collecting butterflies: in 1872, more than one-third of the Camberwell Beauties recorded were captured, killed and pinned by excited Aurelians; in 1976 the proportion slaughtered was mercifully reduced to about 8 per cent.

I was, however, about as likely to see a Camberwell Beauty in London as anywhere. The Painted Ladies had already demonstrated this year that a city is no obstacle to strong-flying migrants. They had danced around Stoke Newington in their dozens in May and I had seen them in the dirtiest quarter of King's Cross too. Rare and random foreigners continued to find their way into town. A Camberwell Beauty was captured in Dulwich in the twentieth century, very close to its spiritual home in Camberwell but long after the Surrey village had succumbed to the concrete, brick and tarmac of inner London. More recently, the Long-tailed Blue, a rare and exotic migrant, took up residence in a scruffy park in north London for some unfathomable reason. During four weeks of the hot summer of 1990, a dozen adults appeared to lay eggs on the dry edge of

Gillespie Park, a community park next to the east-coast mainline railway shooting out of King's Cross and now overshadowed by the bombast of Arsenal's Emirates stadium. Was it a rogue release by a butterfly breeder? Perhaps not, as another colony was found in Kensal Green cemetery in north-west London and the butterflies were also seen at Kew Gardens in the south-west and in Petts Wood, Kent.

My first butterfly expedition of the year had been an urban one. The day out in Ham Lands and on the banks of the Thames in Twickenham had proved very successful for seeing spring species like the Orange Tip and Holly Blue. In truth, however, since then I had avoided taking my rucksack, binoculars and packed lunch on another urban expedition to somewhere like Hampstead Heath for fear of being mistaken for an oddball stalker. Perhaps even more inhibiting was my enduring terror of wielding my binoculars in public. I whipped them out in the privacy of Blean Woods happily enough, but being outed as a butterfly geek in London? I was still not ready for that.

Towards the end of June, there was no escape. I was stuck in the office in London during the hottest two weeks of the year so far. Time was ticking by, and I really needed to get out while the weather was good and find more butterflies.

Eventually, one fine Monday morning, desperation won out over self-consciousness. I managed to get off work and headed to Ponders End. This is a lugubrious name for a lugubrious place. Negotiating the torrid North Circular or trundling on the supposed express train to Stansted airport, you pass its four signature tower blocks in north London. Tarted up in pastel shades of blue, green, yellow and red, they look like they were built by children from primary-coloured building blocks. Beyond the towers are miles of industrial sheds and warehouses, barricading this part of north London from the reservoirs trimmed by the lush green of the Lea Valley.

I drove to the semi-detached suburban home of Andrew Middleton. It was easy to guess which house belonged to the butterfly lover. Most gardens had been paved over for extra parking; Middleton's front lawn was a miniature wild-flower meadow. A slight, boyish man who I guessed was probably in his early forties, Middleton was deceptively determined, uncompromising and unapologetic about his passion for butterflies. I could probably learn a lot from him.

He had grown up in Ponders End, became interested in butterflies through his father and, as an adult, nursed a quiet passion for the most overlooked butterfly in Britain. I telephoned him to arrange a visit because he and a friend had, in their spare time, discovered probably more new colonies of one species of butterfly than any other amateur butterfly enthusiasts in the country.

This butterfly was the White-letter Hairstreak and, apart from Middleton and a few other devotees, even Aurelians seem to have been oblivious to it from the very beginning. For most of the nineteenth century the White-letter Hairstreak suffered the indignity of having its name muddled up with the similar-looking Black Hairstreak. The two butterflies are a similar size, shape and colour but have very different habits. The White-letter Hairstreak was once called the Dark Hairstreak. Its name was then changed to the Black Hairstreak. A year after the real Black Hairstreak was discovered, a lepidopterist inadvertently transferred the White-letter Hairstreak's common and scientific names to the Black Hairstreak. The White-letter Hairstreak was now nameless. Then Victorians decided to rename the Black Hairstreak as the Dark Hairstreak, and return the name Black Hairsteak to the White-letter Hairstreak. Luckily for everyone, the name White-w Hairstreak, or White-letter Hairstreak took hold, inspired by the spidery white scrawl on its dark hindwing. By the end of the nineteenth century, all was settled and the dark business was done away with. The more recently discovered Black Hairstreak was able to keep its name and the White-letter Hairstreak, which had, after all, the clearest white letter on its wings, was now, irrefutably, the White-letter Hairstreak.

Like its fellow hairstreaks, the White-letter is not a butterfly of flowers and grasslands. It is a butterfly of trees. A butterfly that dislikes flowers seems an oxymoron. A small insect spinning around the tops of big trees is also pretty inaccessible. Because they were so rarely spotted, for decades it was assumed that the White-letter Hairstreak was a rare and even endangered butterfly, particularly when the tree it lived and fed on, the elm, was struck by Dutch elm disease, a fatal fungal infection spread by the elm bark beetle which massacred elms in the 1970s.

It turned out, however, that the White-letter Hairstreak could get on perfectly well without our adoration or assistance. Virtually unnoticed, this modest butterfly was far more mobile and successful than we ever imagined. When elm trees died off, local authorities planted up parks and schools with a hybrid elm called Sapporo

Autumn Gold. Purists might resent this introduced cultivar but the White-letters quickly adapted to it. Dozens of other, more disease-resistant strains of elm were planted as well, and the butterflies were also able to survive on wych elm, which fared better than English elm, and on the regrowth of diseased elm, which laboured on in our hedges, sprouting up to a few metres, dying off with fresh bouts of the disease and then coming back again.

I had only ever seen a White-letter Hairstreak twice in my life, once when by fluke I found one resting on a summer flower in our garden in Norfolk, and then on another occasion with my dad in Somerset when we went butterflying together more than twenty years ago. Without knowing it, I had missed this butterfly more than any other. Within a few minutes of meeting him, Middleton reeled off squares and parks across north and south London where he discovered they lived; I had passed through these parks and under these trees, oblivious, unseeing, dozens of times in the past decade.

Unless you got very lucky and caught sight of a White-letter Hairstreak on a rare foray to the ground, there was only one way to satisfactorily spot this high-flying butterfly: with binoculars. Or, preferably, a telescope. It was not just my pathetic teenage self-consciousness that was an obstacle here; the paranoia of society was not helpful either. Using his telescope to scan the hybrid elms planted in school playing fields was, confessed Middleton, a bit of a problem.

It was muggy and overcast when I arrived at Middleton's house. He put his telescope on his shoulder and we walked around the corner to Durant's Park, a big, flat and exceedingly well-mown public space, bordered by schools, a cemetery, a bowling green and tennis courts, and then housing estates and more tower blocks. The park was silent but for the grizzle of a white van in a nearby street. On the far side was a scruffy wood where a series of tatty young elms were about to succumb to Dutch elm disease again. The scars on their small trunks were not caused by the elm bark beetle but by people inducing their pitbulls to attack the trunks in training for dog fights. 'This is the psycholand we live in,' sighed Middleton.

Close to the park entrance was a pair of slightly scruffy, middle-aged trees that looked like cherries or hornbeams. These were actually a variety of hybrid elm and Middleton pointed out a useful distinguishing feature: rather than their leaves being round and neat where they joined the stem, they were asymmetrical. These two odd elms were next to a few lime trees and the White-letters apparently enjoyed taking nectar from lime flowers. Most insects seemed to appreciate limes; only the motorists below dislike them for raining sticky honeydew – from the aphids living on their leaves – onto car windscreens and metallic paint.

Almost everything in the textbooks was wrong about White-letters, according to Middleton. He was qualified to offer this view because he had discovered colonies in more than twenty of the 10km squares in which butterfly populations are recorded by the Butterflies for the New Millennium Scheme run by Butterfly Conservation, where no White-letters had ever been recorded before. 'Scientists say it's sedentary, not mobile. That's complete garbage. White-letters are not demanding, and they are mobile,' he said firmly, plonking his telescope down in the park.

I got out my binoculars. At least they were small compared with the telescope, although we did look a right pair, standing side by side with our equipment trained on a random park tree. In the gentle breeze, the crown of the tree looked like a cow's head trying to shake off the bees and hoverflies buzzing around it. Through my binoculars, everything looked like a bee but Middleton quickly picked up a butterfly. Sitting on a leaf, a triangle of black with its wings closed, the White-letter Hairstreak spun off and headed for the lime flowers. Another then returned and sat, its wings snapped shut but tilted, like a Green Hairstreak, towards the direction of the sun. Borrowing Middleton's telescope, I could make out the jagged white line that formed the white letter on its underside.

White-letters could be confused with the treetop-loving Purple Hairstreaks except that White-letter males spiral up into the sky in dogfights, whereas Purple Hairstreaks just tumble in the air around their trees. White-letters, which are generally a butterfly of June, also prefer mornings whereas Purple Hairstreaks, which are more a July butterfly, tend to enjoy being out in the evening sunshine. This butterfly required appreciation from afar, something Middleton believed most modern Aurelians were not prepared to tolerate. Even if we do not collect butterflies these days, most of us demand the satisfaction of getting in close and collecting our own photographs. It is not enough to lie under a tree, and look up at a tiny insect far above, feeding and mating and fighting in the branches. I think Middleton viewed his butterfly as one for the purists. 'If you like observing butterfly behaviour, this is a species for you,' he said.

At least Nabokov appreciated these elusive creatures even if he too could not get close enough to them. 'I remember one day when I warily brought my net closer and closer to an uncommon Hairstreak that had daintily settled on a sprig,' he wrote in *Speak, Memory*. 'I could clearly see the white W on its chocolate-brown underside. Its wings were closed and the inferior ones were rubbing against each other in a curious circular motion – possibly producing some small, blithe crepitation pitched too high for a human ear to catch. I had long wanted that particular species, and, when near enough, I struck. You have heard champion tennis players moan after muffing an easy shot . . . But that day nobody (except my older self) could see me shake out a piece of twig from an otherwise empty net and stare at a hole in the tarlatan.'

I was squinting into the telescope when two park wardens lazily motored up in a vehicle and eyed us – and our equipment – suspiciously. 'Can we have a picture taken?' asked one. 'They're birdwatchers, not photographers,' said the other. 'Come on park boys, stop abusing the residents,' replied Middleton. 'We're butterfly watchers.'

He sighed. I admired his robustness. I wished I didn't feel so embarrassed by butterfly watching, particularly in the city. Pointing his big telescope at unprepossessing trees in unprepossessing places, Middleton was used to the curiosity, and scorn. 'You do get bibbed at by cars and abused,' he said. We continued to scan the treetops.

'Have you ever . . .?' began Middleton, tailing off as we squinted at another White-letter. The conversation drifted on, and then Middleton returned to his question. 'You know, honeydew. That sweet stuff deposited by aphids on leaves. Have you ever licked a leaf?' he asked. 'People talk about it – honeydew, honeydew, honeydew – but have they taken it themselves?' I had not.

213

We walked over to the lime tree and felt each leaf until we found a sticky one. Middleton broke one off and licked it. Like a naughty schoolboy, I followed his lead. The sticky leaf tasted sugary. If White-letter-Hairstreak-watching invited ridicule and suspicion, I wondered where leaf-licking left you in the eyes of sensible society.

Big cities are famously tolerant of differences and yet it still felt to me that butterfly watching was a perilous activity in an urban environment. As if to emphasise the unforgiving nature of city living, the cloud closed in and the day ended on an ugly note of aggression. Attracted by sliced loaves dumped on the grass for the birds, a gang of crows set upon a baby green woodpecker as it fed beneath a willow tree. We raced over, shouting at the gang. The young woodpecker stood, stunned, its head bleeding from the hard pecks of crow beaks, while its parents squawked and dithered in the branches above. I picked up the immature woodpecker and took it over to the cemetery, not to die, but to place it in a bushy hedge that would give it more cover from the crows. We hoped it would call out for its parents, who we could still hear, broadcasting their impotent distress from the willow tree in the middle of the desolate park at Ponders End.

33. White-letter Hairstreak, Ponders End, London, 22 June

13

Midsummer: butterflies of water, woods and down

Weak and skinny are not adjectives you would expect to see applied to our biggest and most spectacular butterfly. Early on, the Swallowtail was named 'the Queen'. It is certainly a diva and, with its lemon yellow and black markings and spectacular tails bordered by dabs of dark blue and red, looks more like an exotic escapee from a butterfly farm than a native butterfly. Despite its size and flashy foreign appearance, our rare Swallowtail is uniquely English.

On the Continent, the Swallowtail, *Papilio machaon*, is a mobile, versatile butterfly of dry, flowery meadows. When the seas rose and the land bridge between Britain and France was flooded 8000 years ago, the Swallowtails that were left behind in Britain slowly developed their own style and distinct habits. They became smaller, weedier and more introverted. They decided they preferred boggy marshland above all else. And as this marshland was drained and ploughed up, so the Swallowtail became rarer and more enfeebled and, eventually, confined to the Norfolk Broads, a flat land of reeds and slowly silting-up lakes created by old peat diggings. The British Swallowtail changed so much over the centuries, and chose to breed on a different plant, that it is now considered a distinct subspecies (*britannicus*), although migratory Swallowtails (subspecies: *gorganus*) from the Continent also occasionally touch down on our shores.

As Jeremy Thomas, the scientist who brought the Large Blue back from the dead, explained when I visited him at his Oxford college, there is a curious evolutionary jitter when a butterfly's habitat becomes fragmented, as is the case for many species in Britain. Because it is a gamble for a butterfly to leave its isolated site, natural selection rewards the least risky butterflies. The cautious sons and daughters of the most cautious survive. In this way, certain species of butterfly become more sedentary, more set in their ways, and less likely than ever to break out of the small pockets of land where they cling on. This process, however, can reverse in just a few generations if conditions are favourable, and Thomas had seen it with the Large Blue and its sudden and successful natural dispersal over the Polden Hills in Somerset.

Jack Dempster, Thomas's mentor, had studied *britannicus*. He would breed the butterflies and release them at one end of the large room where he worked. A young Thomas would take a stopwatch and time how long it took before they were hurling themselves at the window at the far end to escape. It turned out that the British subspecies had a narrower thorax, which was where the muscles to beat the wings are located. *Britannicus* was skinnier and not as strong a flyer as its Continental cousins, weakened by centuries of confinement to ever-smaller parts of East Anglia.

Growing up in Norfolk, a trip to see the Swallowtails was almost an annual event. This was a charismatic, rare creature and other butterfly enthusiasts would travel across the country to see it. Because it was on my doorstep I probably took it for granted, and had not bothered to seek it out for more than a decade. But there was something else, something wrong about my relationship with this stunning butterfly that I could not put my finger on.

They are a June butterfly, and it was a sunny Sunday laced with big cottony clouds when I travelled to Hickling Broad with Lisa and a gang of her mates, for whom butterfly watching was definitely a novelty.

The wind made a scratchy rustle in the reeds, which was not good news. Swallowtails do not like wind. In fact, they do not like much really. This high-maintenance butterfly will only lay its eggs on the new leaves of milk parsley, a pretty, delicate plant that grows on the edge of the Norfolk Broads. Any fresh leaf will not do: it has to be on a plant that is exposed, and taller than surrounding reeds and vegetation. It also requires open broad: when the broads clog up and revert to swampy woodland, the Swallowtail disappears. Like many great beauties, it has a steely side too. When the caterpillar goes into its pupa, usually low down on the stem of a reed, it can survive several months completely submerged in water if the Broads flood in the winter months.

The Swallowtail has always been an uncommon, and therefore a treasured, sight. It was distinctive enough to be depicted in the first British butterfly book, *Theatrum Insectorum*, which was published in 1634. In past centuries, its strongholds were marshy undrained meadows such as those beside the Thames and the Lea before London grew up. By the nineteenth century, it was restricted to the Fens and the Broads in East Anglia but it became extinct in the former area by the early twentieth century. Like the Large Copper, it fell victim to the massive programme to drain this low-lying swath of East Anglia and turn it into the bleak but productive arable prairie it is today. Its numbers were also hit by the hundreds of enthusiastic '*Machaon* hunters' who would alight from a train at Ely and catch dozens of these fine insects.

Imagine if the most admired political hard man of his day visited a butterfly farm and inquired about ordering butterflies by the dozen so he could release them in his garden, when his country was on the brink of war? He would be derided in parliament and mocked in the press. Questions might be asked of his judgment and his sanity.

Fanciful schemes to release and breed Swallowtails, however, were just what Winston Churchill dabbled in. In 1939, when he had a few larger problems on his mind, Churchill paid his first visit to L. Hugh Newman's butterfly farm in Kent. He wanted to increase the butterfly population in his grounds at Chartwell, his nearby manor house, and asked Newman's father how to do it. To be fair to Churchill, he did not follow up his inquiries and Newman waited until the Second World War was over before writing to him again. This time, the young butterfly farmer was invited to stroll with Churchill around his gardens. 'I shall never know if he was serious when he suggested laying on "fountains of honey and water" in the rose garden to feed the butterflies,' Newman wrote in 1953. Nevertheless, Churchill employed Newman to turn his old summerhouse into a miniature butterfly farm. The farmer released a number of adult Small Tortoiseshells and Peacocks so that one of Churchill's garden parties would be adorned by butterflies.

What Churchill really wanted, however, were Swallowtails gliding around the grounds of Chartwell. This was ambitious. Swallowtails probably once prospered in the Thames Estuary but would not have regularly flown in Churchill's part of Kent for centuries. Britain's great prime minister could fight them on the beaches, defeat Nazism and rebuild nations but he could not play God with butterflies. Newman struggled manfully to introduce Swallowtails with specimens from his farm but they all disappeared and Churchill's labourers accidentally cut the fennel, which had been planted by the water for Swallowtail caterpillars to feed on. Churchill's butterfly schemes were an abject failure.

Apart from Churchill, the Swallowtail picked up other admirers over the years who were more threatening. Reed buntings, sedge warblers and bearded tits all developed a taste for Swallowtail caterpillars, which are large and showy. In 1922 the naturalist Frederick William Frohawk related the observations of Fergus Ogilvie about the 'insatiable' appetite of the cuckoo for the impressive and juicy Swallowtail caterpillar: 'One young cuckoo, obtained July 27th, contained a considerable number of the larvae of the Swallowtail butterfly . . . Cuckoos are exceedingly plentiful here. They are distributed in greater numbers over the Broad district than in any other locality with which I am acquainted.' I wondered whether the scarcity of cuckoos in modern times might explain why the Swallowtail is prospering in its Broad-land headquarters, although conservationists judge this unlikely; far more crucial is the maintenance of reed beds and open fen on nature reserves.

We walked slowly along the boardwalks that took visitors around Hickling Broad nature reserve. It may be sacrilegious for someone born and bred in Norfolk to say so but I have never really loved the Broads. I adore the flat marshes of north Norfolk but at Hickling it seemed as if we were below sea level. It felt oppressive. I could not see a horizon for the tall reeds and their wavy beige heads. I could not see water either. So it was a surprise when white triangles of sailing boats sped past, behind the reeds. It looked like they were sailing in the sky.

One of Lisa's friends spotted a bittern overhead and we saw a dozen Painted Ladies and a couple of Red Admirals, but for forty-five minutes there was no sign of a Swallowtail. Several dozen other people, all retired couples bearing sophisticated camera gear, were also looking for Swallowtails. Everyone said they had seen at least one. Lisa's friends were getting restless. I climbed into an elevated hide for birdwatchers and scanned the horizon. Nothing.

We walked on along the grassy path through the reed beds and then, directly over our shoulders, sailed a large yellow-and-black butterfly. The effect of the black and yellow blurring together made the Swallowtail in flight the colour of weak tea. It veered left and looped back behind us, settling on a prominent twig in the middle of a patch of sallow.

It clearly felt proprietorial about this spot. First it roused itself to chase off a big dragonfly. Then it settled back down in the same position. I rummaged clumsily in the undergrowth below, shaking sallow branches to encourage it to move to a lower branch, where we could photograph it, though I was not sure this was acceptable behaviour in a Norfolk Wildlife Trust reserve. Finally, it moved off, not because of my flounderings, but to chase off a swallow. A butterfly chasing a bird! The Swallowtail really did tear after the tail of the swallow.

Then it landed closer to us, clinging to the top of a prominent reed and swaying in the wind. A perfect specimen, the red spot down by its tail was very prominent. It had the flashy familiarity of a famous person in the flesh – the Swallowtail, like a celebrity, was somehow more glossy, perfect and compact in real life. We all inched closer, gawping and taking photographs. Lisa's friends were entertained. 'Nothing like a Swallowtail to get a bunch of people staring into space,' said Sam. 'Except perhaps Ecstasy,' said Alan.

It was impressive. But something about the experience of watching Swallowtails on the Broads failed to move me. I think it always had. Was it the order of the nature reserve, with its boardwalks and regular trudge of stunned visitors, where leaving the path and plunging into the reeds – the delicious bit, the embrace of nature – was forbidden? Are Swallowtails showy but shallow? Or inbred and unfriendly?

I was still focused on the twitch of every insect in the breeze but Lisa's and her friends' minds were wandering. They had seen a Swallowtail and that was enough. No matter how normal I felt, my interest in butterflies obviously exceeded the norm. It made me realise how well attuned I was to my dad when we went on trips together; we moved in pursuit of butterflies at the same rhythm and seemed to become satisfied and fulfilled at the same time. I did not feel I had finished with the Swallowtail, but the others were done. So we jumped in the car and drove to Sea Palling, part of a crumbling coastline that would probably give way within a century and cause the Broads to be inundated with salt water. If this happened, new habitat would have to be found for the Swallowtail or it would become extinct.

After we had swum in the surprisingly blue North Sea and thrown a ball around on the beach, Alan returned to pondering Swallowtails. 'Are they very inbred, a bit like Norfolk people?' he asked. (He was from Sussex.) I did not even begin telling Alan about the idea that butterflies could be the souls of the dead before he was imagining that the Swallowtails might be a race of tiny country people. These folk had grown wings and taken to flying around, eating milk parsley and digging peat. Maybe they were the souls of old reed-cutters. If so, what strange bewitchment had taken place on the Norfolk Broads to have them reborn as such an exotic and spectacular insect?

That week in Norfolk I saw my first Meadow Brown of the year, sleek and chocolatey, quite unlike the faded specimens I would see on grass verges and on parkland everywhere later in the summer. The most satisfying butterfly sightings are always those where the insect pirouettes into view when you are least expecting it, and so it was with the Dark Green Fritillary that materialised on the sea bank by the lifeboat station at Wells-next-the-Sea. Despite spending all my childhood in Norfolk and much of the last five years at Wells, I had only ever seen one Dark Green in north Norfolk before and this was when I waded across the channel to a virtual island of pine trees and sand dunes called East Hills.

Despite the excellent weather, June had been a slow butterfly month for me. The successes in Scotland and Northern Ireland had only seen my tally creep up one by one. Then I had been stuck working in the city for two weeks of perfect butterfly weather. By midsummer, I had left it a bit late to see the butterfly with the shortest flight season of all: the Black Hairstreak.

I was out with Lisa and her brother on Friday night and set out alone on Saturday morning, feeling inexplicably lonely, to drive to Oxfordshire to hunt down the rarest of our little hairstreaks. The air had the chill of October, the sky was dark and on the A40 south of Oxford three badgers lay twisted by the roadside within a few hundred metres of each other, a whole family massacred by the motor car.

Growing up in the 1980s, two of the most vivid intrusions from the wider world were the threat of nuclear war and the great programme of road-building. In that decade, new roads materialised as naturally as breathing. Every year, if we drove to granny's in Somerset or grandma and grandpa's in the Lake District, I expected to cruise along a shiny new bypass somewhere which shaved another minute off our journey time. I remember stories of the protests too: tales of tunnels, Swampy, Winchester and Oxleas, an ancient wood in southeast London. It was vivid and yet ancient history. When I travelled along those new roads now they were worn and battered: concrete bridges were tattooed with cracks, crash barriers were rusting and rank with weeds and the roads had sunk into the landscape. Nature had hit back, a bit.

I could distantly remember some fuss about the construction of the M40 and the Oxfordshire countryside it cut through. Just east of Oxford, maybe in response to environmental concerns or perhaps it was just cheaper not to chop down all those trees, the planners flicked their pens and drew in a curve so the M40 snaked around Bernwood Forest and kept east of the smaller oblong of Whitecross Green Wood to the north.

I was going to start by visiting Whitecross Green Wood. Looking at a map, I imagined that it was ruined, a scruffy copse right by the motorway, filled with noise and fumes and rubbish from the road. But it was still a shock when I arrived, to stand at the eastern edge of the wood and see an incessant silver river of cars, slipping across the landscape at speed, just a small field away. With the breeze from the north-east, wherever I walked in the wood I was followed by the white noise of the motorway. There were chiff-chaffs and pigeons and the delicate calls of different warblers. In the background, implacable, was the motorway. We accepted it now it was there. We had to. But imagining the landscape without it was to see what a colossal act of vandalism it was, even skirting around the wood. Of course, without the M40 and other motorways, my journey to find every butterfly would be considerably more arduous.

The entrance to the wood, by a tiny thatched cottage, was unsigned. Visitors also had to open and close two gates. This was enough of a barrier to most and on a Saturday morning only one vehicle stood in the small car park. It was midsummer, in a wood, in England, and I was alone.

Ten strides into Whitecross and I had fallen in love. A wide grassy ride stretched out ahead. In the middle, the summer grasses were in full flower with their seed heads of subtle greens, golds and purples. Below them were pale mauve common spotted orchids and ragged robin. On either side, tangled sweet banks of honeysuckle, bramble and sallow eventually bowed to a dark conifer plantation beyond. Everything was still, and dripping wet. Like so many English woods, 60 per cent of Whitecross had been felled in the 1960s and planted up with conifers. Slowly, these were being removed by the conservationists who now managed the wood. Despite the conifers and the motorway, an essence of Whitecross had survived. The air still smelt sweet, the birds still sang and a tawny owl made me start when it swooped low along the path towards me.

On the western side of the wood, away from the M40, a small path twisted along the boundary underneath thickets of hawthorn and blackthorn. Two wrens hopped through the undergrowth. Cows lowed in the field beyond. This was Black Hairstreak territory.

The Black Hairstreak is an odd little butterfly. It lives on one of the most common, weed-like scrubby trees you can find, blackthorn, and yet for some unfathomable reason, in the two hundred years we have known it, has never moved beyond a small sliver of central England between Oxford and Peterborough. It kept so quiet and still, so sedentary, that it was the last distinct butterfly of southern England to be discovered (the Essex Skipper was found later but it was almost identical to the Small Skipper so for years was assumed to be the same species). First found in 1828 in Monks Wood, for decades the Black Hairstreak's name and identity was mixed up with the White-letter Hairstreak. If not exactly indolent, this butterfly displayed no urge to expand its range or do anything other than conservatively stick to its favourite twigs. After its eggs are laid towards the end of June, the embryo develops into a fully formed larva after three weeks inside the egg. But it does not hatch until the following spring and then it takes an almighty effort: up to seventy-two hours of labour before the caterpillar breaks out of the thick eggshell. Jeremy Thomas found that Black Hairstreak caterpillars move, on average, just 23cm away from the egg by the time they are ready to pupate.

Unsurprisingly, the adult butterfly is similarly unadventurous, sticking to the low-lying clays between Peterborough and Oxford, in unobtrusive wooded colonies. These woods have romantic names: Bernwood, Grendon Underwood, Whaddon Chase, Whittlewood, Salcey, Yardley Chase, Rockingham. Why did the Black Hairstreak stay in the East Midlands? Scientists believe it is because of the history of woodland management. In the past, this area, uniquely, had coppice cycles that were long enough to sustain colonies, which died out in more regularly disrupted, felled woodlands. While the decline in coppicing means that there are now probably hundreds of suitably undisturbed woods across the country, because the Black Hairstreak is so unadventurous it has been unable to discover them.

It was always rare, became rarer and is now stable, but still rare, in its small overlooked colonies, thanks to conservation efforts once again informed by the studies of Jeremy Thomas, who undertook his PhD on the Black Hairstreak and counts it as his greatest conservation success (and when you have almost single-handedly brought the Large Blue back to life that is saying something). It was grey and cool and after an hour in the wood I had only kicked up three Meadow Browns. Even these rose reluctantly from their invisible perches in the long wet grass. There was a notebook in a waterproofed wooden cupboard at the entrance to the reserve where, sweetly, visitors could record the wildlife they had seen. The previous day, someone had spotted three Black Hairstreaks but noted they were 'rather worn'. The Black Hairstreak has one of the shortest flight seasons of any British butterfly, sometimes barely two weeks, and I was worried that this year's could already be at an end.

I had seen the Black Hairstreak just once before in my life, at the start of the first big butterfly expedition my dad and I had undertaken in 1988, just when the motorway was being built around Whitecross. Driving from East Anglia to Oxford, we had stopped in a wood near Peterborough. I only remember that the Black Hairstreak was easy to see but high up, out of reach of a small boy on its bank of blackthorn and bramble. I did not have an instinctive feel for the behaviour of this butterfly. That only comes when you have a regular relationship with it.

As I trudged through the wood I was becoming seriously concerned and yet, with every step, this magical place gave up more gifts: deer, stooging through the trees like dogs, squirrels and the tantalising blink of a mysterious butterfly that might have been a Purple Emperor. It was there and then it was gone. There were so many times when I had tried and failed to see one that I shut this possibility out of my mind. My luck seemed cursed when it came to the Emperor.

One of Whitecross Green Wood's wide grassy rides ended on the western side with a large patch of young blackthorn. Jeremy Thomas, tucked in my rucksack as usual, said the Black Hairstreak preferred big old bushes with trunks covered in lichens and moss, but this young thicket instinctively felt good. It was the warmest spot in the wood and there were plenty of bramble flowers. There was also a small patch of grass that had been trampled by human feet. Perhaps other people had watched Black Hairstreaks here.

I stopped and stood still and waited in the wood, alone, my feet soaking wet and grey sky above my head. A constellation of tiny blue holes in the cloud appeared. They were slowly arranged and rearranged, the holes gradually shifting to where the sun might be. I listened to blue tits and the crashings of wood pigeons and the rest of the world flying past on the motorway beyond, oblivious to this small marvel in middle England. To be alone in a wood, on an overcast summer's day, was a perfect, everyday miracle.

It would seem the most obvious of narrative devices to write that at this moment a Black Hairstreak flitted past. It didn't. I started at something high on the bramble patch but it was a Meadow Brown. I twitched at another movement but it was a fly. This wood and this day seemed a work of fiction, however, and the constellations of cloud shifted above, sending a shaft of hazy sunshine onto the scene. The second the sun appeared, as if in slow motion, a Black Hairstreak picked a path through the air right in front of my eyes.

I felt the most delighted rush of excitement so far that year. This discreet dark butterfly was bigger than I remembered and it landed on a bramble leaf right in front of my nose. The guidebooks said it was an obliging insect and it sat, still and calm, on the leaf and allowed me to creep in until my face was a big moon peering over it from less than a metre away. I studied its dark, dusty body and the blobs of orange on the underside of its wings. One wing had a faint nick in it and the spidery white tracings across its underwing were almost rubbed out, like a faint line of pencil.

There was something deeply restful about this small butterfly with its trim little tails. For the first time, I saw it had snazzy white-and-black-striped legs and its antennae were finished in brilliant yellow with black dots on the very end. While a small spider busied itself at the other end of the leaf, the Black Hairstreak slowly tilted its closed wings towards where the sun would be if it had not disappeared behind the cloud again. It sat for a while. Then it walked to the edge of the leaf and, antennae waving, peered over the edge. And finally it sat some more.

I savoured our time together. For the period our paths crossed, in Whitecross, both of us, man and butterfly, were perfectly in the moment, two living things mysteriously bound together. Butterflies always did live in the moment, of course, unlike foolish humans, and one little hairstreak helped me lose track of the tyrannical ticking of the clock, for a few minutes at least. As I watched it, I understood why this butterfly had failed to move beyond its modest headquarters in the Midlands. Its pace of life was that of old England. It pottered about on the warmest patch of blackthorn it could find and that was good enough. Why fly off to see the world, why take on the winds and the oceans, why cross streams or rivers of cars when all you needed could be found by being still, in a small calm spot in the centre of our countryside?

The sun did find a small window in the cloud and the woodland rides were suddenly, capriciously, animated with dozens of indefatigable Meadow Browns, warring Large Skippers, beautiful Marbled Whites, bejewelled Common Blues and a couple of pristine, velvety Ringlets, the first of the year. But that modest, slightly tatty insect was the only Black Hairstreak I saw.

Leaving it to its woodland contemplation, I turned and jumped again. Twenty metres behind me was a sleek biscuit-brown roe deer, nibbling at a fallen branch. It looked at me and carried on its work, unafraid. When it sized me up, it must have seen a fellow creature of the woods, the biggest compliment it could pay me.

The sky was beginning to bruise, so I started out for home. On a whim, I called in at Bernwood Forest. Not far from Whitecross, this wood was bigger and its rides were broad and less homely. Shorn of wild grasses by being already mown at the edges, it was bereft of butterflies compared with Whitecross although it, too, was a place where the Black Hairstreak flew. Tired of the well-trimmed rides, I turned right at random and struggled through some brambles into a rough clearing. There, in the centre, coiled, its fangs set in the snarling rictus of death, was a dead grass snake. It was a strange omen. It felt I had been taken to this random spot and not merely stumbled across it. I saw the fat blue flies poring over its body and hurried home.

The Black Hairstreak sighting helped me edge closer to forty species. Once again, however, I was confined to London, working, during some perfect weather. It was the first weekend in July, when I had booked two weeks to go on holiday alone and attend to butterflies, before I could search for anything again. I began in Norfolk and headed to Marsham Heath, part of a nondescript band of coniferous woodland ten miles north of Norwich. We used to walk our dog, Bella, here; she would dance with joy when the car hit the bumpy, sandy track that signified a walk. This dry and heathery heath was a stronghold for the Silver-studded Blue. Dad and I had seen them here years ago.

There was a nice sense of drama entering the heath, created by a narrow path between towering spirals of old gorse bushes, which nearly met overhead. The bramble flowers were thick with Ringlets and freshly emerged Commas. On the path, a winged black ant carried an enormous lifeless caterpillar – far bigger than itself – in the opposite direction. It did not heave this great green lump onto its shoulders but rode the caterpillar, holding it between its long legs, like a child clinging to a banana boat.

The heath was far more grown up than I remembered. It was now managed by the Norfolk Wildlife Trust and someone had gone to great efforts to clear areas, but even where the gorse and brambles had been removed they were still springing back far more quickly than any heather. The habitat did not look good for Silver-studded Blues, a tiny silvery-blue butterfly which favoured fresh heather and bare earth.

There was no one about. Normally that would be lovely. Today it was just dull. The place did not light any spark in me. I tried the sit-down-and-let-them-come-to-you approach. Nothing came. Except there was a large yellow butterfly that sped through the heath far quicker than I could run. I chased it, and didn't stand a chance. It could only be that other great migrant, a Clouded Yellow, but it was such a blink of a sighting I was not sure it should count.

The excitement of a probable Clouded Yellow should have been energising but I felt depressed by the sorry state of Marsham Heath. I had a vague recollection that Silver-studded Blues had been re-established on Kelling Heath, close to my mum's home in Sheringham, so I called her, quickly arranged a late-afternoon walk and sped over. The ridge of dry, heathy high ground that stretches from Holt to Cromer close to the Norfolk coast makes up the most impressive hills in the county. That is not saying much, but they still surprise people who think Norfolk is unremittingly flat. They are an old glacial outwash plain, from when a vast ice-sheet spread out and then retreated, depositing sandy, gravely heaps of poor soil.

As soon as we arrived, we heard the scraping call of a stonechat, which in Norfolk dialect is called a 'furze chuck', a wonderful name. Like Marsham, this heath too did not look ideal for the Silver-studded Blue. There was not much heather and immediately by the car park someone must have once dumped garden waste because now the dry ground was covered in evening primrose flowers and the nasty piripiri burr. On a flower was a skipper. I moved closer to investigate whether it was a Small Skipper or an Essex Skipper.

The Essex Skipper was first found in 1889, making it the 'newest' butterfly species in England and Wales. To mere mortals, it looks just like the Small Skipper. The differences that explain they are distinct species, and can't interbreed, are highly technical. Put away any sexist jokes about the Essex Skipper: the genitalia of female Essex Skippers are very demure in comparison to the female Small Skipper who is, to put it delicately, much larger and hairier in certain microscopic attributes. Thankfully, there is one obvious and perfectly respectable way to distinguish Small from Essex in the field: an Essex Skipper's clubby antennae are black, while the Small Skipper's are tipped with golden brown.

The antennae on this skipper appeared to be both golden brown and black. I decided it was a Small Skipper. A few minutes further on, by the brambles, sat another skipper. I could deny it no longer: I was now finding the binoculars that Dad had given me extremely useful. At last, and about time, I was more relaxed about using them as well. These skippers required the binoculars. This second one was a paler golden brown, and waved very distinct, much darker antennae: an Essex Skipper. As in most cases, as soon as you see two similar butterflies together, or at least on the same day, the differences are obvious.

In another couple of seconds, I saw my third new species on Kelling Heath. Stretched out on a bramble flower was a Hedge Brown, also called the Gatekeeper for its habit of lurking in the grasses by farm gates. This was a cheerful and common brown insect that vied with the Small Tortoiseshell for the title of Britain's friendliest butterfly. Like many butterflies, its eye spots, visible on both sides of its forewings, may have been designed to scare off potential predators but they gave it a cheerful look, especially when set on bright orange panels. This butterfly's behaviour also seemed friendly; it was not nervous or flighty but appeared to enjoy bumbling around people.

Mum and I meandered through the heath looking for heather. I was fretting about the absence of the Silver-studded Blue. I wondered if I had got its flight season wrong – butterflies were emerging very early this summer – and somehow already missed it. We came to a halt where the ground sloped steeply down and the woods began. A butterfly landed on mum's back, right in front of me. A

Grayling. Another new species for the year, an underrated grey butterfly with subtle and beautiful patterning on its underside. Confined
mostly to the coastline, and much rarer than it once was, the Grayling
is superbly camouflaged when it rests on stone or dry grass and is most
easily distinguished by its habit of always landing with its wings closed.

In a blink of an eye later, a gorgeous black-and-white butterfly
glided flatly out of the shady woods. It was a White Admiral, an
exciting and completely unexpected sighting. The White Admiral's
scientific name is *Limentis camilla*. We often come to associate butterflies with certain moods or even people, and the White Admiral
makes me think of a beautiful friend called Camilla, who possesses
the grace of this butterfly and also shares its love of woodland. The
early Aurelians thought the same because they gave the prettiest
feminine names to the popular, striking butterflies of the Nymphalidae family: the Red Admiral is *Vanessa atalanta*, the Painted Lady
is *Cynthia cardui*. Nabokov was clearly an admirer of the White
Admiral's beauty: in his novel *Ada*, he named the birthplace of his
heroine's mother Ladoga, after an earlier scientific name for the
White Admiral. His fiction is full of sly tributes to his favourite
lepidoptera. The White Admiral may be understated, but many
quieter Aurelians believe it is the leading contender for the most
beautiful butterfly in Britain. A shy butterfly of shady woods in July,
it is far scarcer than a Red Admiral and sometimes mistaken for a
female Purple Emperor. The White Admiral may be only black and
white in colour but it has the most elegant of flights, holding its
wings horizontal as it sails through dappled sunlight, pausing in the
spotlights that shine into dark woods to feast on curls of honeysuckle
or the cream flowers of bramble.

While the decline of coppicing pushed many of our woodland fritillaries to the brink of extinction, the White Admiral has prospered. It is one of relatively few species that has extended its range over the last century. Confined to southern England and particularly Hampshire at the start of the twentieth century, it expanded rapidly in the 1930s and 1940s, spurred on by a series of good summers. The White Admiral also benefited from the neglect of our woodlands, because it enjoyed a tangle of honeysuckle, its food plant, in relatively shaded woods. Abandoned coppices were perfect for it even as they spelled death for many fritillaries. Now, curiously, it is continuing to expand its range, moving north, east and west, helped by climate change, but has been declining in overall number, probably because the country's burgeoning deer population has nibbled away at the honeysuckle in our woods.

Without expecting to, I had seen five new species at Kelling Heath but not the one butterfly I was searching for. It was nearly 5 p.m., the sun was weakening and I was giving up hope of seeing any Silver-studded Blues, and contemplating a swim in the sea. Mum insisted there was a better patch of heather on the east side of the steam railway line, so we trudged on. When we got there, on the footpath ahead was a man with an immaculate padded camera bag and expensive walking boots. His trousers were tucked pedantically into his socks. Even his T-shirt looked expensive. He had a flash camera with an extremely flashy flash – 'The macro functions are brilliant,' he said gravely. Despite all this, somehow, he appeared too successful and self-assured to be a geek. He was looking for Silver-studded Blues and had just seen one.

It turned out he was a doctor. In his minimal spare time, he had somehow acquired an encyclopaedic knowledge of plants, birds and butterflies. He was handsome, distant and seemed reluctant to chat. Like me, I guessed he probably enjoyed a solitary communion with nature. Eventually, mum got him talking before he was saved from conversation because a male Silver-studded Blue popped up right in front of us. This silver-and-blue jewel was almost as tiny as a Small Blue. It glittered and posed for a minute, and then disappeared over the purple heather and out of sight. The sun went in, and that was that. Six new species for the year in an hour on an unpromising patch of heath in north Norfolk. It was the height of summer and the butterflies had really come alive.

34. Meadow Brown, Wells-next-the-Sea, Norfolk, 10 June
35. Swallowtail, Hickling Broad, Norfolk, 13 June
36. Black Hairstreak, Whitecross Green Wood, Oxfordshire, 20 June
37. Ringlet, Whitecross Green Wood, Oxfordshire, 20 June
38. Clouded Yellow, Marsham Heath, Norfolk, 4 July
39. Small Skipper, Kelling Heath, Norfolk, 4 July
40. Essex Skipper, Kelling Heath, Norfolk, 4 July
41. Hedge Brown, Kelling Heath, Norfolk, 4 July
42. Grayling, Kelling Heath, Norfolk, 4 July
43. White Admiral, Kelling Heath, Norfolk, 4 July
44. Silver-studded Blue, Kelling Heath, Norfolk, 4 July

14

The curse of the Purple Emperor

In the glade of an ancient royal hunting forest, dressed in the deep green of midsummer, stood five tables covered in white cloth. These were laid for breakfast, with a fat candle in the middle. On each of twenty paper plates was a different dollop of food. On one dish, two king prawns sweated in the sunshine. On another sprawled dozens of tiny pickled mudfish. There were crushed grapes, a blackened rotten banana, honey water, horse manure, fox scat and plenty of servings of stinking shrimp: shrimp curry, sautéed shrimp fry, Thai Boy shrimp paste and Big Cock shrimp paste. One brand had been banned from Britain the previous year after it was deemed unfit for human consumption.

This elegantly presented and utterly rancid repast was not for human consumption. It was for the Purple Emperor.

No other butterfly in Britain can compete with the charisma of

His Imperial Majesty. The Purple Emperor has entranced entomologists and bewitched butterfly lovers for centuries. It has fired imaginations and driven its pursuers to the edge of insanity. This is understandable. We desire things that disdain us, and this soaring winged messenger scorns and tantalises us. It is a muscular, swooping, gliding black beauty, and the male shimmers iridescent purple when caught in the sunlight. Despite its size and power, it is one of our most elusive insects. Considered a creature of ancient English woodlands in July, it is rarely seen because it lives in the tops of trees and haughtily refuses to descend from its kingdom to feed, like an ordinary butterfly, on mere flowers.

Like most butterfly lovers, I nursed a long, unrequited passion for the Purple Emperor. It captured my imagination as a child, when its striking looks leapt out of the pages of my Jeremy Thomas guidebook. Populations had once lived in Foxley Wood, the ancient forest four miles from my door, but it had been driven to extinction in Norfolk. Every summer, Dad and I would search for it there, just in case. Most years, with a lurch of the heart, we would see a dark butterfly sailing along a ride, only to realise, seconds later, that it was a White Admiral. For a number of years, the highlight of our summer butterfly expeditions would be a trip to seek out the Emperor in his headquarters in Surrey and Sussex. In perfect July conditions, we repeatedly traipsed the rides of Tugley Wood, where they were known to fly. We never saw anything. Season upon season of failure only strengthened the pull of the Emperor. It felt like a curse.

Even in my twenties, when I was mostly too busy living to contemplate old unrequited loves, I found the time to seek out this purple beauty. Finally, in the hot summer of 2003, I accompanied Dad and his butterfly friends, Stephen and Gail Jeffcoate, to Tugley Wood again. The weather was glorious, we strolled through the trees in shorts and, finally, we saw our Emperor. For two seconds, a dark triangular shape was silhouetted against the sky like a kite. It danced down the ride, twenty metres above my head, and disappeared. I saw no flash of purple. Even though it was hardly a rewarding sighting, we chalked it up as a belated success. For many butterfly lovers, this is all they ever see of an Emperor.

If this butterfly cast a strange spell over me, however, it was not lifted. The next day, I noticed a small spot on my thigh. I thought nothing of it. A few days later, I pinched it absent-mindedly. Over the coming days, the squeezed spot mutated into a furious red boil the size of a fifty pence piece. After a week, I went to the doctor. He said I had a small infection and dispensed a round of antibiotics. Despite these, the boil became painful to touch and the inflammation spread wider. I felt sick and weak. I staggered back to the surgery and was sent straight to A&E. The doctors looked alarmed. I had a serious case of blood poisoning. I was given a bed, instantly, and the next morning underwent a general anaesthetic. The surgeons carved a large hole into my thigh and cut out the mysterious infection. For several days, I lay in a stupor in hospital and then, slowly, recovered. The surgeons decided there was less risk of the infection recurring if I was not sewn up, so for weeks afterwards I had a hole in my thigh into which I could have slid a strawberry. The doctors did not know what had caused the infection but we theorised it probably began as a bite from a tick that had leapt onto my leg in the wood when I was hunting Purple Emperors. It could have killed me.

Two seconds watching a Purple Emperor had led to this physical pain. I called it the Curse of the Purple Emperor, and I was not sure how much I wanted to see one again. The lure was too great, however: His Imperial Majesty still flew through my dreams, he offered a vision of elusive beauty and lovers of nature had made pilgrimages and paid homage to him for centuries. I was excited. I was not prepared for how easy it would be, or for the pain the Purple Emperor, once again, would herald.

No other butterfly has attracted so many names, tributes and epithets. Petiver named it Mr Dale's Purple Eye, in honour of a fellow collector, in 1704. By the middle of the eighteenth century, it was known as the Purple Highflier. In 1795 Lewin called it the Purple Shades, which was rather cool, but Harris had already hit upon a winning blend when he had named Britain's premier butterfly the Purple Emperor in 1766. To Germans it is the Large Shimmer Butterfly; to the French, the Greater Flashing Mars, after the Roman warrior god. For scientists it has long been *Apatura iris*, an apt, and carefully chosen, classical name. Iris was a Greek demi-goddess, a winged messenger who appeared in the guise of a rainbow, showing colours not unlike the Emperor's iridescence. Iris, as the Emperor was called by devotees, was also hailed as the Emperor of Morocco, the Emperor of the Woods and His Imperial Majesty, or simply H.I.M.

'By universal suffrage, the place of highest rank among the butterflies of Britain has been accorded to this splendid insect, who merits his imperial title by reason of his robe of royal purple, the lofty throne he assumes, and the boldness and elevation of his flight,' wrote W. S. Coleman of the Purple Emperor in 1860. While scientists scorn the anthropomorphising of butterflies, the Emperor is undoubtedly possessed of great personality and tends always to be a he, not least because the Empress is exceedingly retiring and a plain black and white; she does not glitter with purple in the sunshine.

Like all great things, the Purple Emperor has long reached beyond the converted, shimmering into popular consciousness and moving poets to pay tribute. Writing in the eighteenth century and inspired by a passage in Virgil's *Aeneid*, Alexander Pope's paean to the colour of butterflies must have been directed at iridescent Iris:

Dipt in the richest tincture of the skies,
Where light disports in ever-mingling dyes,
While ev'ry beam new transient colour flings,
Colours that change whene'er they wave their wings.

Later, John Masefield wrote of 'that dark prince, the oakwood haunting thing / Dyed with blue burnish like the mallard's wing'. And the Purple Emperor was an almost mystical presence in *Brendon Chase*, a wonderful novel about three boys who run away and live in the woods and which inspired a love of wildlife in a generation of boys like Matthew Oates. The author, Denys Watkins-Pitchford, writing as 'BB', was an acolyte of the Emperor and the Whiting, the foolish village vicar in his story, is more desperate to see the Emperor than find the runaway boys. Eventually, he chances upon 'the glorious regal insect of his dreams' in Brendon Chase. 'It was flying towards him down the ride and it settled for a moment on a leaf. Then, as he advanced, trembling with excitement, it soared heavenwards to the top of an oak. There he watched it, flitting round one of the topmost sprays far out of reach, mocking him, the Unattainable, the Jewel, the King of butterflies!' The Whiting can only watch from the ground, 'looking up at it like a fox watching a pheasant in a tree'.

Another novel to obliquely mention the Emperor was *Three Men on the Bummel,* by Jerome K. Jerome in 1900, which described the morning rush hour of 'stout City gentlemen' at Ealing station, where an onlooker shouted, 'even money on the Purple Emperor!' It was a mocking term attached to retired military men 'liable to colour under exercise' and also the nickname given to Ian Robert Penicuick Heslop, the most devoted acolyte of the Emperor in the twentieth century.

For collectors, the Large Blue may have been a great catch because of its rarity but the Emperor was the greatest prize of all. For Heslop, a fastidious and rather pompous colonial official turned Latin schoolmaster, it was the grand passion of his life. He defined this butterfly as 'big game' because 'one could recollect every particular' of the chase. 'I have caught exactly as many Purple Emperors as I have shot Elephants, viz. four in each case; but I think I would rather have one of the former than all four of the latter: and nothing in all my sporting or collecting career has ever given me so much joy as the seeing of my first Emperor safely in the net,' he wrote in 1953.

The closest equivalent to a contemporary Emperor obsessive, Matthew Oates, has written about Heslop, who was a fascinating and complex man. A Cambridge classicist with a blue in rifle shooting, Heslop spent much of his life as an administrator in Nigeria, where he took charge of Owerri province, an area the size of Wales, discovered a subspecies of pygmy hippopotamus which is named in his honour and dispensed wisdom such as: 'The Nkalus are on the whole not likeable people. Their extraordinary deceitfulness and lack of good faith towards each other is their most repulsive characteristic.' When he returned to Somerset with his young family – his three children all captured Purple Emperors at a precocious age – he found no suitable quarantine facilities for Tabitha, his three-legged tabby cat, so he had some built in memory of her. He was that kind of man.

The Emperor's loyal Victorian and Edwardian subjects were most fascinated by his dark side. 'I have watched the Purple Emperor soaring above the oaks at Darenth,' wrote Edward Newman of his days hunting H.I.M. in a Kentish valley, 'and have wondered why he should seek realms unknown to his lady-love, his empress-queen; and I have wondered still more why a creature so gloriously refulgent with purple, should condescend to feed on filth and putrefaction, instead of feasting on ambrosial pollen and quaffing nectar.'

Victorian Aurelians saw it as a great paradox that a creature so aristocratic should only be tempted from his treetop throne when he could plunge his proboscis into muddy puddles and the carcasses of dead animals. They observed these degraded moments with a morbid fascination. 'His majesty had been caught regaling himself upon the imperial delicacies of dead stoats, weasels, etc, hanging upon some low bushes as a terror to evil-doers,' reported one lepidopterist and Newman, regretfully, pronounced it was true. 'I would gladly have depicted the Emperor of our insect world as banqueting on ambrosia,' he wrote, 'or quaffing the nectar of flowers, but this would not be truthful.' Rather, he would only observe in the case of this 'depraved' appetite '*de gustibus non est disputandum*' – in effect, there is no accounting for taste. For the Emperor, it is not, however, a question of taste. It is thought that the males replenish themselves after mating, with sodium and other chemicals from the rotting matter.

The butterfly collector who penned a rhyme called 'How to Catch an Emperor' concluded:

> But sinful sweets subdued him,
> And filthy lust o'ercame,
> Try muddy pools and sugar,
> And thou shalt find the same.

When much of southern England was swathed in hunting forests the Purple Emperor may have been more common, but it has always been hard to spot. Unlike other rare butterflies which can be found in great numbers when conditions are favourable, *iris* lives at a very low density. To catch a rare, treetop butterfly stretched collectors to the limits of their ingenuity. Some built enormous nets on unwieldy poles, up to fifteen metres in length, to scoop them from the tops of oaks. Heslop eventually devised a net set on bamboo poles. 'My high net, with maximum extension, now considerably exceeds thirty feet in length: so that, with my own height and reach, I can strike at and secure specimens up to forty feet from the ground,' he wrote with pride.

The Victorian lepidopterist Henry Guard Knaggs recommended shooting the butterfly at rest with dust shot, the smallest gunshot, or a charge of water, which was a technique used by hunters to bag humming birds in South America. He also suggested ensnaring the Emperor by throwing up pieces of tin or stones with pieces of white paper attached. When the Emperor's dignity is wounded, he wrote, the butterfly would sometimes 'chase the offending object to the ground'.

Most of all, however, entomologists tried to catch the Emperor with bait. Knaggs once deployed a dead cat as bait. 'Although we let the cat out of the bag, and H.I.M. evidently smelt our game, we could not induce him to come within reach – perhaps the game wasn't high enough,' he wrote in 1869. In the same era, another entomologist noted that Purple Emperors could become so preoccupied with 'swine droppings' they would 'permit me to take them between my finger and thumb'.

By the 1960s, Heslop, who once took a trailer-load of manure from 'Brigadier Fanshawe's pig farm' into the woods to bait the butterfly, theorised that the Emperor was losing his taste for dead rabbit. The Victorian tactic of luring them with rotting carcases no longer worked and he linked the butterfly's new reluctance to descend to bait to its predation by 'vermin' such as magpies and jays, which had increased in number with the decline of gamekeepers in the twentieth century. 'A Purple Emperor imbibing of its traditional repast and oblivious to any outside influence . . . is a sitting target for air attack,' he wrote. In a characteristically idiosyncratic experiment, Heslop positioned a dead, dried Emperor from his collection (he could spare one; he caught 185 Emperors during his lifetime) on a forest ride, hid, and watched until a jay descended and pecked it to pieces.

When not advising the National Trust, Oates runs a website in his spare time with fellow devotees called thepurpleempire.com. He has noticed a further evolution in its tastes during the four decades he has been in love with the insect. The males, he believes, are once again descending to forest rides because of the relatively new attraction of dog faeces. 'The big thing now is what I call canine deposits,' he said. In previous eras, woods were dominated by game and forestry; nowadays, they are places of leisure and well penetrated by dog walkers. Generations on, *iris* has rediscovered its love for picking over disgusting things on forest tracks.

Emperors also seem attracted to car parks. The winged messenger's relationship with the chariot of our times is another curious kink in its character. As soon as motor cars drove into our countryside, the Emperor developed a penchant for them. 'I now know of an open car-shed in Sussex which is an almost certain draw for at least one Purple Emperor during the season, provided the car is in it,' wrote Heslop in 1961. For a time, it was believed Emperors were attracted to petrol fumes; more likely, they were inquisitively drawn to examine the sparkling glass and bright metal of cars. And in the days of less traffic, roads through woodlands were as attractive as forest rides. Heslop caught his first Emperor in Sussex 'on the very banks of the A272: which has remained for me the highway of the Emperor's world'. Oates, who routinely smears shrimp paste and other disgusting baits on his rear windscreen, has been known to drive away from woods with Emperors following his vehicle as if he were their Pied Piper.

A breakthrough in the baiting of Purple Emperors came in the Philippines. Yasutaka Murata, a Japanese businessman who has been known to fly into Britain on a private jet for a day's butterfly hunting, was eating a picnic in the Philippines which he could not stomach. As politely as he could, he flung the offending portion of shrimps into a nearby banana plant. Within minutes, one of the Emperor's tropical relatives had landed on it. It turned out that the English Emperors too have a taste for the exotic, and enjoy nothing more than dipping their proboscis into shrimpy Far Eastern dishes.

This explained the fetid feast on the tables at Fermyn Woods in the romantic old forest of Rockingham. Oates was hosting the Purple Emperor's Breakfast, a contemporary art event arranged by Fermyn Woods' art gallery (every forest should have a resident artist these days) and he wanted to find out which baits worked best. Carrying a purple notepad and sporting a purple band in his sunhat decorated with a sprig of what he claimed was Sukebind, a fictional flower from *Cold Comfort Farm* which turns people mad in midsummer, Oates was a slightly deranged maître d'. 'Don't go anywhere near the egg gobi fish, that's the plate to avoid,' he cautioned.

I drove to the wood early that morning from the east. This was my first fortnight of butterflying by myself. Dad was on holiday abroad and Lisa was not interested, preferring to spend the weekend at a party with her friends. After the desolate Fens, entering the rolling countryside of Northamptonshire with its grey-green fields of wheat and smooth hillsides topped with large hunks of forest was like diving into cool water. On the map, Rockingham Forest was marked in fragments and appeared oppressed by the urban sprawl of Corby and Kettering. In reality, it was empty and peaceful. There was a wind farm on the horizon which made it feel as if I was travelling through the spacious countryside of central Germany.

William the Conqueror, the Second World War and heavy boulder clay had all helped bring us to Fermyn on the first weekend of July. These woods of Rockingham once stretched from Northampton to Stamford, a medieval hunting forest carved from great estates created by the Conqueror. This was never dense woodland but included villages and their strip fields. Forest was a legal term, referring to land ruled by forest law, which forbade anyone from hunting there or taking timber without permission from the king. Forest law may have been oppressive but it inadvertently helped preserve ancient woodlands rich in flowers and butterflies, even after the law's abolition in 1832.

The hundreds of acres of ancient oaks of Fermyn were a large fragment of the old forest that endured until the Second World War, when it was felled for its timber. Afterwards, under the control of the Forestry Commission, then determined to stamp industrial productivity on English woodlands, it was planted with Norway spruces. For a couple of decades, the spruces soared. Then, suddenly these alien trees stopped thriving in the heavy boulder clay of east Northamptonshire. They began to die off and soon the plantation was useless. Dismayed, the Forestry Commission removed the dead wood, left the few oak trees that had survived the spruces, and let the forest regenerate naturally. On this heavy clay soil, one of the first trees to shoot up is sallow, the food plant of the Purple Emperor caterpillar. Over the last three decades, much of Fermyn had become a sallow jungle. 'The woodland must not only be mixed, it must be dense,' wrote Heslop of the Emperor's requirements.

For centuries, populations of Purple Emperors had been recorded in Rockingham Forest until they were feared lost after the Second World War. It was said that BB, the author of *Brendon Chase*, reintroduced Emperors into Fermyn but he may have only topped up a long-resident population. A few miles to the east are Barnwell Wold and Ashton Wold, two celebrated sites where Victorian collectors waxed lyrical about hunting *iris*. Along with Sussex, this is the stronghold of the Emperor and almost as far north as the butterfly will go. Usually living in large woodlands at very low densities, the long-resident population of *iris* boomed in Fermyn with the recent growth of these lush sallow thickets. At this moment, and for as long as the sallow is tolerated by the Forestry Commission, Oates felt that Fermyn boasted the finest population of Emperors in the country.

The Purple Emperor was 'indolent,' Oates explained, standing by a pile of felled conifers at the entrance to Fermyn Woods. Heslop and his helpers had watched one male, continuously, for ten hours in perfect weather, and observed it was active for a total of 'about ten minutes' during that time. Heslop also, however, noted they could be seen flying at a great height before suddenly closing their wings and diving like a peregrine falcon. As Oates put it, Purple Emperors were 'gloriously unpredictable. They explode into dramatic action. They are capable of doing anything.'

This year, so far, had been an extremely good year for *iris* but it still required an unusual amount of devotion. The technique for spotting an Emperor was unique, claimed Oates: 'You have to forsake all others and yield only to H.I.M.' It was also crucial to pick the right time of day. The Emperor rises at 8 a.m. for a morning perambulation and later descends to woodland rides in mid-morning. By midday, he has usually retired to patrol the treetops.

It was 10 a.m. when we walked down the forest ride towards Oates's table of indelicacies. A final few Norway spruces still stood by the track, as pointless as an ornamental hedge gone to seed. The heat of the previous week had given way to a more typical British summer: a thick shroud of cloud, a hint of rain and a fickle promise of blue sky. After a few minutes strolling down the broad gravelly track, a Purple Emperor swooped high overhead and sailed back into the oak and ash.

I could not believe how easy it had been this time. The butterfly left an unmistakable sense of extreme vigour; it was an energetic, virile, muscular, alpha male. If the White Admiral was pure grace, the Purple Emperor was power and grace. I later read that *iris* tended to stamp this impression on every observer. 'Somehow the build of this fine insect when seen in the hand cannot fail to impress the beholder with a sense of muscular power,' wrote A. M. Stewart in 1912.

A second male flew in, lower this time, and looped around the broad crown of a squat sallow bush. Others soon followed; lightning forays and lordly retreats. They were, explained Oates, searching for a mate. 'They behave like heavily testosterone-laden young men let out for an evening to go clubbing. If they flush a girl out, all hell breaks loose. They are looking for freshly emerged, virgin females. Female virginity doesn't last too long in the Purple Emperor world.' It turns out there is one thing more alluring to an Emperor than the stench of decay and corruption. As E. B. Ford wrote in 1945: 'No attraction among those so far mentioned is as potent as that which the female butterfly exercises for the male; to the Purple Emperor it even surpasses the appeal of a decomposing rat.'

We saw more than a dozen in flight as we made our way towards the banquet of rotting shrimp delights. One roared down low and confronted me, dancing around me, wondering what I was. Its wings made an audible clicking – flick-flick-flick – as it batted around me. I felt under attack, before it sped off with great impatience, as if I was not worth trifling with. It was my first real encounter with an Emperor. And like every object of unrequited love, it treated the lovelorn with something like contempt.

This willingness to confront its foes impressed the Victorians. Michael Salmon retrieved the nineteenth-century recollections of the Revd Walter Wilkinson, who relayed his brother's account of meeting a Purple Emperor after swimming on a hot summer's day: 'He flew *bang* at me. I aimed a blow with my towel, and sent him sprawling on the ground, but before I could hit him again he was up and away. I pursued him in a most excited chase, but of no avail – he gained every step, and left me exhausted in the rear.' A few days later, Wilkinson's brother wrote a second time to say once more he had knocked the Purple Emperor down with his towel and lost it again, before returning with a net, waiting two hours, and catching it easily. Oates, too, had encountered the Emperor's pugnaciousness when one flew –

deliberately – at his face. 'I have been hit in the eye by this butterfly and it necessitated an eye bath,' he said. 'It's a vicious thug.'

In Fermyn Woods, however, male Emperor behaviour seems to have become less aggressive and less territorial than in other forests. 'Perhaps because the population is so much denser they have to be more tolerant,' said Oates, who believes that the Purple Emperor behaves very differently in subtly different woods. Every summer, he hires a cherry picker, a hydraulic platform usually deployed by workmen to repair electricity pylons or clean high windows, to rise into the oaks and study Emperors in the treetops. It has helped him debunk some popular ideas. For centuries, lepidopterists believed all male Emperors gathered at the top of a particularly tall, prominent oak, a 'master tree', picked for its conspicuousness and vigorously fought over. Because the Purple Emperor exists in such low densities, these master trees may help males and females find each other.

According to Oates, this behaviour does exist but only in some forests. A prominent oak may be popular in undulating areas, where trees on higher ground protrude from the canopy, although these are more likely to be groups of trees, rather than just one, which offer the Emperor shelter from the prevailing south-westerly winds. In woodlands on fairly flat ground, such as Fermyn, there are few prominent trees and Emperors do not pick out a master tree. In reality, argues Oates, what the Emperors prefer are 'sacred groves' – sheltered spots between higher trees where they can feed on aphid honeydew, rest and seek mates.

Oates also suggests they may not require oak trees (and, in fact, do not even need woodland: in one spot, they have colonised sallows growing on the embankment of a bypass). 'The myth holds that it is

a species of oak forest and needs oak woods. Wrong. No,' he continued, as we walked through Fermyn: 'What they need is sallows,
particularly the broad-leaved sallow. It is not just quantity of the food
plant with the Purple Emperor, it is quality as well, and we don't yet
know what that quality is.'

When she is laying eggs, the female Purple Emperor appears to
reject certain sallow leaves. Oates fears that in the future, Emperors
could be hit by new tree diseases that damage sallows, or even by the
behaviour of grey squirrels, which can weaken trees and allow them
to become diseased by stripping their bark. The caterpillar hatches in
August, feeds on the tip of a sallow leaf, disdains direct sunlight,
grows very slowly and lives for an unusually long time, right through
until early June the following year. It changes colour with the seasons
to remain camouflaged and eventually grows to the size of a human
adult's little finger.

Like the adult butterfly, the caterpillar assumes an impressive
form. Dru Drury, an apothecary and naturalist, discovered four
Purple Emperor caterpillars in May 1758, 'which in their Shape and
Motion differed from any [species] hitherto discovered; being furnished with two Horns, of the same hard Substance as their Heads,
resembling the Telescopes of a Snail, and in their progressive Motion
seemed rather to glide along like that Animal, than to crawl as most
Caterpillars do'. In its every incarnation, it seems, we have found the
Emperor to be the most regal of all insects. The caterpillar does not
crawl like a grub; he glides, bearing horns for a crown.

We waited by the table and saw more Purple Emperors motoring around the trees above our heads. Higher still, red kites soared on thermals. Briefly, an Emperor alighted on the Thai Boy shrimp paste, and then raced off. Another undertook a cursory inspection of the candle on the table and the cloth. The attractiveness of a white picnic cloth to *iris* has been noted in the past; given that it has also been drawn to bright metallic objects, there should have been a silver service and cutlery as well. To compensate, Oates anarchically smeared some kind of poo on a footpath sign by his table. It was lapped up by a Comma but no Emperors deigned to examine it.

Understandably, given their vulnerability to predation if they descend to the ground, Purple Emperors are easily spooked by the movement of people. The group of butterfly watchers gathered by the table were getting restless and their shifting around was probably enough to scare off *iris*. Two hours passed and the sun refused to shine. In the sky, a Purple Emperor beat up a Purple Hairstreak, a speck in comparison, and similarly dressed in iridescent purple. This elusive small butterfly's fondness for the tops of oaks led one Victorian collector to call it the Emperor's 'attendant knight' and it was the first I had seen this year and for many years. The two purple butterflies seem to squabble in the air – the Purple Hairstreak had been dismissed as 'an inquisitive nuisance to the greater species' by Heslop, which seems a little harsh.

Passing walkers and cyclists gave the table a puzzled glance although most, in a very English way, did not even pause to ask what it was. 'Oh, the butterflies,' said a walker with a shrug. 'There were lots of them on a mud pool further down there.' I wondered whether the English Emperors really did have a taste for shrimp paste. The breakfast had become brunch and as lunch approached it became a moveable feast. Oates and his followers lifted up the tables and parked them by a trailer of timber that smelt of crisp pine sap. Wearily, Oates took a sip of Pimm's. 'Ooh, that's nice,' he said. As someone with a long Methodist ancestry, he endeavoured not to drink on a Sunday. But it was his wife's birthday, after all.

Oates is, in many ways, a disciple of Heslop. He believes the Purple Emperor should become our national butterfly or a national symbol of Englishness (it does not fly in Scotland or Northern Ireland). 'It is as British as the Oak,' wrote Heslop. 'And it has been continuously British probably since the Holocene, perhaps ten thousand years ago.' While Heslop was eccentric and some of his remarkable captures of rare migrant butterflies were so exceptional they have led some to wonder if he was a fantasist, he tirelessly campaigned to conserve the Emperor, helping set up two nature reserves in Somerset and Wiltshire to preserve precious Purple Emperor habitat. He was ahead of his time in understanding the need for the type of conservation management which is taken for granted today. Of one woodland reserve, he wrote, wisely: 'The main purpose is to preserve the Copse in its natural state. But, paradoxically, this cannot be achieved by allowing a manless Nature to take its course.'

Helping Oates at Fermyn was Neil Hulme, a friend and the chairman of Sussex Butterfly Conservation. A fit-looking forty-something, Hulme had the crew cut of an oilman and the tan of someone who cleverly arranged his work as a micro-palaeontologist for oil companies around summers seeking butterflies. Every year, he spotted all the forty-five species found in Sussex. One year, he got to forty-seven, which included two rare migrants: the Queen of Spain Fritillary and the Large Tortoiseshell. Mostly, though, he was in thrall to all things purple and was undertaking some Emperor studies in Fermyn, deploying a Japanese folding bicycle on forest rides so he could speed between Emperor hotspots with maximum efficiency.

In the afternoon, I abandoned the Emperor's breakfast to join Hulme on the corner of a ride deep in the woods, close to an old stand of oaks and a big bushy patch of sallow. Hulme possessed the stillness of an experienced butterfly seeker, smoked a lot of cigarettes and appeared to have a psychic connection with *iris*. He also had a jar of Shito, an evil-smelling fish paste from Ghana. He smeared a circle of the stuff on the gravel ride as we watched several male Emperors swooping around the oaks above our heads. One chased a large dragonfly. Two followed each other and became four, darting through the treetops in a tight formation, pursuing each other in a mad rage. This was a treasured sight – great *iris* hunters have written in the past of seeing three at most together – but I still desperately wanted to see this butterfly land on the ground.

After an hour, an Emperor obliged. It did not pounce on the paste but flew to Hulme's feet, as if he had commanded it. He stood very still, bent low, and took the perfect photograph. Later one dropped onto his boot. It seemed to enjoy the smell. Hulme did not appear to look after his boots. Eventually, one succumbed to Shito's execrable charms. Keeping its wings closed, it strutted purposefully across to the paste, sticking up from the grey gravel track, as jagged and dark as a shark's fin. The underside of its wings looked like a polished slice of tree bark, with a big eyespot emulating the gaze of a hawk.

I knelt down close by, as it began probing the Shito paste with its lemon-yellow tongue. 'Once they've got their proboscis on some-thing, they are not easily spooked,' said Hulme. The sun flickered into life above us, and the Emperor opened his wings. Glorious purple erupted from them. I felt bludgeoned, like a dazed cartoon character seeing stars.

It was banal to ask Hulme why the Emperor seduced him but every Emperor obsessive had a subtly different answer. 'It's like no other but-terfly,' said Hulme. 'It's ballsy, it will even chase birds, it seems to have a personality; the fact it's such a gorgeous looking creature and yet it feasts on fox faeces; all the contradictions.' The Revd Walter Wilkinson, the rector of Hyde whose brother so memorably recounted his first meeting with the Emperor, also relayed his brother's 'pang of sorrow' after killing his first one. Not out of guilt but because he had not bagged a pair. Hulme agreed. 'Today it's done with a camera but it's the same thing with this butterfly – you just want more.'

By the end of the day, I was dizzy with Purple Emperors. I had seen fifty-seven. It felt excessive. I was happy and weary, as if I had been drinking all afternoon in the sunshine. The only way to retain this state would be to keep lapping up more, and that was impossible. Everything had to come to an end. When I went to bed, large purple-and-black butterflies danced over my closed eyelids. I did not know it then, but the curse of the Purple Emperor had already struck again.

45. Purple Emperor, Fermyn Woods, Northamptonshire, 5 July
46. Purple Hairstreak, Fermyn Woods, Northamptonshire, 5 July

15

High summer in the north

Butterflies are symbols of freedom and happiness, sunshine and summer days. They are tokens of romance, not heartache. Could a butterfly stand for love and loss? Some might say a Camberwell Beauty's dark-brown wings are associated with sadness in much of Europe and in America, where it is called the Mourning Cloak, a direct translation of its German name, *Trauermantel*. Any sighting of a Camberwell Beauty in Britain, however, would be far too exciting to be a harbinger of heartbreak. For me, the Purple Emperor had heralded physical pain in the past. Dark, rare and disdainful, it certainly had the power to conjure up emotional pain. What butterfly would you break up to? I thought, obviously, of brown butterflies that flew even when the sun was buried by cloud: a dull Meadow Brown, or a Ringlet, so dark it was almost black. These, though, bounced along every grass verge in the countryside.

They were too common to herald deeper than everyday disappointments.

I had my answer soon enough, sooner than I thought. After getting drunk on Purple Emperors in Northamptonshire, I drove north to the Lake District that evening. From the M6, just past Lancaster, the mountains were served up, high on the horizon, like a fancy birthday cake held aloft by a waiter, flaming orange in the sunset. By the time I got to Kendal, a long slow summer dusk had set in and I found a scruffy pub with a tiny single room for the night. I calculated I might be here some days because the weather forecast was uncertain and the butterfly I was hunting was the most difficult of all the fifty-nine species to see.

To say the Mountain Ringlet is our only Alpine butterfly is correct, but it may give a false impression. When I think of Alpine butterflies, I imagine flowery hay meadows high in the foothills, filled with spectacular white, black and red Apollos or exotic Niobe Fritillaries. The Mountain Ringlet is very dark and very small, much smaller than an ordinary Ringlet. It is a smudge of an insect which inhabits mountainsides and boggy gullies in Scotland and parts of the Lake District. The Mountain Ringlet is our toughest butterfly, stronger even than the long-lived Brimstone, because it endures the harsh climate found on our northern mountains; this butterfly seldom strays below 500 metres. This means, obviously, you have to climb mountains to see it.

Finding the two purple woodland butterflies – the Emperor and his attendant, the Hairstreak – had taken me close to fifty species for the summer. But I would only feel I was on the home straight if I could find a Mountain Ringlet. Butterfly experts rubbed their hands with glee when I mentioned I had yet to see it. Plenty of people, they warned, spend two weeks looking and never find one.

If the sun isn't out – and mostly it isn't on the tops of our mountains – the Mountain Ringlet disappears completely into tussocks of wiry grass. If it gets too windy – and mostly, it is – it retires to invisibility in the vegetation. Even if it gets too hot, above a modest 23°C, say, it goes to ground. Once it is resting up, when the weather is not quite right, there is no way you can kick it up out of the vegetation. A Mountain Ringlet simply won't fly up like ordinary butterflies do if disturbed, so tenaciously do they bury themselves in the grass. Every year, their colonies move around the mountainside, so you don't know exactly where they will be. I had come to the Lake District alone, furnished only with some grid references for where Mountain Ringlets had been seen in previous years, which I had found in a useful report on the website of the Cumbria branch of Butterfly Conservation. None of the sightings were from last year; some were from the 1960s.

I woke up uneasy. I recognised this feeling now. It was pre-sighting tension (PST) and it welled up strongly this summer when I was on my own, in a place where I had never seen a certain species before. PST put me on edge: I felt helpless, I did not know enough about my quarry, I could not be certain of finding it and I was at the mercy of the weather. Experts, such as Oates, were a security blanket; so too were landscapes or nature reserves where I had been before.

There was something else, too. Lisa had seemed a little distant when I departed for this latest two-week stretch away. I was worried I was pushing it a bit. The concept of a butterfly widow amused her at first but perhaps I needed to spend more time with her, doing her things. She had gone away that weekend for a big party with friends. I was not the jealous type but I started to wonder when I arrived in the Lake District the previous night and found one very flat text message in my inbox, in reply to my two enthusiastic ones. She was tired, she said, and was going to bed. She did not even call for a chat.

It was a grey morning and I drove impatiently up Honister Pass. Twiddling the car radio, the only station I could find was a local one. Why did commercial radio speak its own, foreign language? What, for instance, was 'a great crunch-busting deal'? I was in a black mood, and slightly fatigued too, by all the driving, by my emotions and by the artery-clogging cholesterol fest I had enjoyed at the pub that morning.

I pulled over at the top of the pass, by the scar of a slate mine. Groups of visitors were already being herded around on the first tour of the day, wearing white safety helmets that cannot have been entirely necessary. There was an ugly slab of a youth hostel by the mine and a car park where I slammed the car to a halt on the grey gravel. This was possibly the least scenic corner of the Lake District. It was a world away from the magical valley of Borrowdale below, where tiny stone houses in Seatoller village offered B&B and a twee little shop from which walkers spilled onto the narrow road.

But unlike the rest of the crowded, congested Lake District, this landscape emptied of people as soon as you climbed the fell above the slate mine. The isolation suited my mood. I walked onto Fleetwith saddle, where there was said to be a Mountain Ringlet colony. A sheep tearing grass sounded like footsteps behind me. It was grey and properly chilly, although not as bad as forecast. At least it was not raining and there were patches of blue about.

I surveyed the mountainside and meandered across it, intimidated by the task and the outlook. Grass and rocks; bleak and cold. When there are no butterflies in sight, it seems impossible there will ever be any. I scanned the landscape for marshy, sheltered gullies, which is what Jeremy Thomas, tucked in my rucksack, advised me. I could hear his speaking voice – reassuring and authoritative – through the pages of my guidebook since meeting him in Oxford. I did not know how to identify the Mountain Ringlet's food plant, mat grass, but I thought perhaps it resembled purple moor grass, beloved of the Chequered Skipper. It must be spiny and mountainous looking. All the grass up here looked like that.

Two ravens flew over. Come on, croak, I commanded them out loud. One gave an obliging gurgle. It was strangely satisfying. I carried on walking to the top of Grey Knotts. Here, according to my grid references, there had been another colony of Mountain Ringlets in the past. I sat on a rock. I decided I needed some help, and I berated myself for not planning ahead and getting some advice before arriving here. I tiptoed around to the sheltered side of the fell, juggled with my phone until I had one bar of reception, and phoned the numbers of three Cumbria Butterfly Conservation volunteers. None of them were in.

A dull ache in my stomach, I phoned Lisa. Her flat tired text, and her failure to send me any other kind of message during her weekend away with friends, seemed to sum up her half-heartedness about me and her. So I was angry. She was on a train home, she said, exhausted, and did not want to talk. I could tell she had more to say. A lurch, a beat, a pause and she offered no reassurance. She didn't want to have this conversation now, she said. The signal disappeared.

We spoke again, flatly, and agreed to speak the following day. I felt I had been left dangling, high in the fells, not knowing how hard she would trip me up and how much it would hurt when I fell. But I knew I was going to fall. It was a long way down.

I sat on Grey Knotts, and looked out blankly over a sheltered boggy spot between two crags, for another hour. It was a small fell of no particular note. The only reason anyone would climb over it was on the way up to the far more formidable Great Gable, which glowered darkly to the west. There was, however, a restful view into Buttermere, which slips out of the Lake District to the north. Where the Lakes ended, the countryside of chequered fields seemed to dissolve into nothingness and then I realised this was the sea, the Solway Firth, and the hills of Scotland, a blue flick of pen, beyond.

There was a desperate trickle of a small stream, somewhere, and no sign of this Mountain Ringlet. I did not really care any more. This was the curse of the Purple Emperor. The previous day, when I had been counting Emperors, Lisa was still at her party, having a good time. If she thought of me, her butterfly geek of a boyfriend, it was to realise she did not love me enough.

I was alone on a mountain and needed to talk to someone. I phoned my friend Steve to discuss my romantic woes. He encouraged me, gently, as I gazed on the swampy hollow below. The sun poked out from behind a barrage of grey cloud. Was that another bee? I was hallucinating butterflies now. It was tiny and brown. Much smaller than I imagined. It had to be. Was it? I hurtled down the slope, phone in hand. 'Yes, get in!' I started cackling down the phone. 'Yes, yes, yes.' Steve thought I was completely deranged.

Silky brown and busying around very close to the tufty ground, with a curious crablike flight, sidling left and then right, tacking against the breeze, was a Mountain Ringlet. The last of the British butterflies I had never seen before. And there was another. Their wings were faded, more beige than brown, and frayed at the edges. I explained to Steve what the hell was going on. After a minute, the sun went in again and all three disappeared. I saw where one melted away. So I paced the area where they had been flying, carefully kicking tufts of grass. Nothing emerged. They had vanished.

I sat down again. I was wearing a T-shirt, a shirt, a jumper and two waterproofs and I was still shivering and sniffing from a long-running cold. I also felt a tiny warming, a tingle of relief and consolation. I had sat down on the rock overlooking this sheltered boggy shelf between two crags not merely to call Lisa but because it looked to me like the right sort of spot. I had, on my own, on the first day of looking, found the Mountain Ringlet, a species I had never seen before. I may be about to be made a butterfly widower but I could take heart from that modest achievement. Butterflies, said the French naturalist Marcel Roland, give us 'solace for the pain of living'.

After a few minutes waiting, I wondered if I had imagined it all. I really needed to get a photograph, otherwise people might not believe me on this one. When I explained my task to people, the second question they asked – after why? – was can't you just make it up? After two hours of looking up at the sky, watching the clouds slowly move overhead, fickle patches of blue opening and closing before the sun could reach this little hollow, at 3 p.m. the sun finally reappeared. Again, just as if a conductor had raised his baton, the Mountain Ringlets came out to play. This time I saw four. None were smart. All, in fact, were incredibly tatty. One barely had a quarter of its wings left. You could hardly see its orange ringlets. Battered by the wind, the rain and the sharp slithers of grass. Prematurely aged by altitude.

I followed them slowly. When they landed, even in the sun, they would wriggle and worm their way into the tuft of grass. One collapsed in a heap between grass stems as if it had had a fall, its wings crumpled by its side. I had never seen a butterfly behave like this before. It looked like they were enjoying the final hours of their lives. If I had not got up the mountain that day, they may have been dead and gone. Apparently, however, the Mountain Ringlet emerges in pulses: a few hatch out, live and then die off within days, and then another group emerges and so on, over a few weeks in June and July. This is an evolutionary fail-safe: if all the butterflies hatched out at once and were hit by a massive storm, the capriciousness of the weather in our mountains could wipe out a population before it could breed or lay eggs. If the weather killed off one emergence, the butterfly would still get another chance. I wondered if *I* would get one more chance. I doubted it. From now on, for me, the Mountain Ringlet would always be my break-up butterfly.

The afternoon was brightening up even if I was not, so I decided to search for the butterfly originally called the Marsh Ringlet by Victorian entomologist Edward Newman. That name suited it well but the butterfly had since become the Large Heath, which was much more boring and much less descriptive. Newman described

265

how it was 'abundant in the mosses of Witherslack in June and July'.
I had been advised by Matthew Oates to try Meathop Moss, and it
was only when I looked on the map that I saw this marshy bog was
right next to Witherslack and was exactly where Newman meant too.
Even if it was dying off elsewhere, it was a comfort to think the Large
Heath had held on to its family seat here for at least 140 generations.

I had seen this rare butterfly of the north once before, as a
teenager with Dad when we went on a butterfly tour of Cumbria
one July. I can't remember the damp bog where we saw it, I only
remember the dank day and that the year was 1990 because I can
still hear *Test Match Special* on the car radio: England were playing
India and Graham Gooch was racking up a big total. Even though it
was overcast, we saw the Large Heath. It was famed for flying in
overcast weather and even, sometimes, when it was raining. Living in
a damp place, it was not bothered by the wet. Extinct in almost all
of England, except for a couple of sites in the Lakes, Shropshire and
a few waterlogged moors across the north, the Large Heath is found
in several quite different forms, each with its own unique patterning.
It is more common in North Wales and Scotland but I chose to see
it in England because the form here was probably the most striking,
with a number of dark eye spots on the underside of its hindwing.
Like the much more common Small Heath, you never saw it at rest
with its wings open. They always stayed snapped shut.

The evening sunshine was supposed to be a good time to catch a
Large Heath at rest, so I drove south through the Lakes, twisting
along the shores of Lake Windermere until the fells petered out and
the Lake District gave way to Morecambe Bay. On flat land beyond
the busy A590 to Barrow-in-Furness was Meathop Moss.

266

It looked large and inaccessible and I was not sure whether it was a nature reserve or private land. On the map I saw a footpath that took you close to the bog, so I decided to park where the path began, at Kate Farm. In a state of mild torment and irrationality, I was imbuing everything with significance and so it seemed odd that the farm was named after a former girlfriend of mine, who was very dear to me.

Kate Farm was funny and rather forbidding. The public footpath was routed straight through its farmyard, which happened a lot in the Lakes. A battered wooden footpath sign directed you towards a muddy old yard where the cattle slept. To outsiders, walking through the middle of someone's farm feels a bit like tiptoeing through someone's kitchen; but in the old days, when communities were less uptight about what was public and what little was private, everyone would have wandered through the farms.

Someone here, though, did not want people to use the path. Two very muddy and rickety gates blocked the route. The first featured a stiff metal latch you could not pull back easily. The second had to be shouldered and scraped aside, under the baleful gaze of a cow. Another large cow stared at me through a broken windowpane. The only touch of tidiness in this proper working farm was four swallows sitting neatly in line on a telegraph wire.

The public footpath from Kate Farm to Meathop Moss was not well trodden. I passed through a large herd of cattle and I wondered if they would murder me. There had been a spate of dog walkers being trampled to death by cattle in recent months. The path led back towards the main road and as I got closer to the roar of the A590 I veered off the prescribed route and took on the bog. A huge pair of antlers watched me from the hedge, turned and then leapt through gangly marshy rushes. A female red deer followed the antlered beast.

As soon as I entered the bog, I saw it. A Large Heath. Big and brown, it sat in the sun on a reed, its wings snapped shut. It had, however, only one spot on the underside of its forewing and none on its hindwing. It was obviously one of those variations and, annoyingly, I had forgotten to put Jeremy Thomas in my pocket to clarify things.

I stalked it through man-sized hummocks of reeds, with treacherous boggy craters in between. The butterfly went to ground. I peered over the tussock. It had its wings open. Unprecedented! Hang on, no, it was a Meadow Brown. I felt very foolish. Large Heaths never opened their wings at rest. This was an unusually bright female Meadow Brown, quite different from the ones I had seen earlier in the day but definitely not a Large Heath.

The map showed a wood on Meathop Moss and what appeared to be a large clearing in the centre. I decided to head across the bog for the woodland and then the clearing. I stumbled through the bog, scared that Mr Kate Farmer would suddenly appear against the skyline, as angry farmers do in cartoons and films, and discharge his shotgun at me for leaving the footpath. I hated getting in trouble with true countrymen and believed, like Withnail and I, that rural confrontations were best soothed by shouting, 'We're not from London you know.'

I reached what was a lovely old birch woodland. Inside, the bracken was a dark midsummer green and taller than my head. It stained my trousers green as I stumbled over rotting branches and the dead trunks of birch trees. I found the clearing. It was enormous and square, and must have been where a coniferous plantation was removed. One or two pines were still standing and the old stumps of others poked out of the heather, coated in mosses the colour of ochre and mustard. Everything in this rough, cleared space was red, brown and dirty yellow except for the brilliant new baby-green conifers springing up everywhere.

The birch trees had dampened the noise from the main road and the silence, the emptiness and the strange dragonflies gave the clearing the look of an alien moon, another world altogether. Wispy day-flying moths darted up in all directions, followed by the more solid grey-brown outline of a solitary butterfly. It was definitely a Large Heath. I could see the multiple rings on the underside of its wings even as it flew.

I followed four or five for half an hour. It was 6 p.m. and the sun was out properly now, but it was a frustrating butterfly to pursue. I had learned the virtue of stillness when stalking butterflies but the Large Heath would not allow me to get within three metres, no matter how softly and slowly I approached on the springy carpet of heather. I had never seen such a jittery butterfly. It was positively coquettish. I stood still and watched one very deliberately sneak away from me, edging its way round to the other side of a stem of grass, like a child playing hide-and-seek behind a tree trunk.

I had anticipated a long struggle to find the Large Heath and the Mountain Ringlet and so had not planned ahead, except to assume that I would be able to see the Northern Brown Argus while I was in Cumbria. This was the northern cousin of the brilliant and tiny Brown Argus, the little brown job that had got me started on butterflies in the first place. As a hardy, north-country-loving species, it was one of the first butterflies to recolonise Britain after the Ice Age. It had been here for at least 8000 years.

While it was a distinct species, in England the Northern Brown Argus was most easily distinguished from the Brown Argus simply by the fact that their habitats never overlapped: the Northern Brown Argus was found in the Lakes, the Durham coastline and then scattered more commonly across Scotland; the Brown Argus was only found further south. The Northern Brown Argus looked almost exactly the same as the Brown Argus, except that further north one form of the Northern Brown Argus boasted a bright white spot on its forewing instead of a dark brown one.

I had already tried to see it earlier in the summer. On our long drive back to Devon after finding the Chequered Skipper in Scotland, Dad and I had pulled off the M6 for a break at Arnside Knott. This rocky outcrop stood like a huge ship, jutting its limestone prow into Morecambe Bay. It was spectacular, and the spiritual centre of a limestone landscape that was remarkably rich in butterflies. Most people, as I had always done, hammered up and down the M6 for the Lake District, or Scotland, not thinking to turn off into this hidden corner of Cumbria where, ecologically at least, the south met the north. Driving with Dad into the small community of Arnside Knott for the first time, it appeared to be a model society entirely populated by old people. Huge retirement complexes overlooked the mud flats that divided Arnside Knott from Meathop

Moss and Latterbarrow and Whitbarrow beyond. White-haired folk thronged the streets, served by a dinky branch-line railway. Others beetled through the lanes in well-polished cars, heads barely peeping above dashboards. This was the north for southerners, soft and unthreatening.

Following signs to 'The Knott', the road became a track and then a rough car park underneath old yews. Fragments of smaller yews clung to the hillside, extravagantly sculpted by the wind. To the north, the big fells of the Lake District, Helvellyn and Fairfield, were dark blue in the cloud. To the south-west were the uncompromising blocks of Heysham nuclear power station. It was one of those still early summer mornings where all the sounds from the plain below, and the wide limpid sweep of Morecambe Bay, floated upwards: car tyres on tarmac, the call of an oystercatcher, the curse of a fox, a man hammering, a woman's voice, a trundling train.

In Arnside Knott car park, I admired a German shorthaired pointer the colour of milk chocolate, whinnying as it was released from its hatchback prison. We had had two of these handsome and loopy dogs when I was a child and I still fell in love with every one I met. This dog's owners, Richard and Jean Bamber, had come for a walk and Jean kindly took Dad and I to a lower field, where she thought she had already seen Northern Brown Arguses that year.

'Butterflies are magical, I just love them, they are fairies,' she said. 'When I had the children we used to walk down this field and the butterflies would come out. They don't any more. I called it the butterfly field, then I found out it was the Pig Field.'

It was a lovely sheltered meadow but there were no Northern Brown Arguses. Dad and I then circled the steep hill, climbing higher, startling a late-to-bed tawny owl and coming face to face with two watchful roe deer. Their pointed elven ears rotated like satellite transmitters. On the vertiginous south-facing slope that gave us an aerial view of a small castle in the green valley below, we saw Wall Browns and our first Large Skipper of the year. I put my ear to a seething nest of wood ants to hear a rustling noise like the foam of a bubble bath crackling and popping. I vowed to return.

In June, Dad and I had been fractionally too early for the Northern Brown Argus at Arnside Knott. Now, in July, I was in danger of being too late. Two grid references I had jotted down from Cumbria Butterfly Conservation's website for the Northern Brown Argus brought me straight back, the next day, to the other side of the A590 from Meathop Moss. Past a big old black-and-white coaching inn, the old main road traced the bottom of the rocky limestone out-crop of Latterbarrow. After the dual carriageway was built in the 1970s, this became an unused dead end, its cat's eye studs rusting and filling with weeds. It had not taken Latterbarrow many years to strike back against the road. In places its woody tendrils were already halfway across the crumbling tarmac, with adventurous shoots of bramble stretching further. I was in a bleak mood after no further contact with Lisa and found it heartening to imagine that after the Apocalypse it would only be twenty or thirty years before nature recaptured all our roads like this.

At nine in the morning it was already humid but the grass was sodden from last night's rain and the sky was overcast. A Cumbria

Wildlife Trust nature reserve, Latterbarrow was carefully managed. Cattle were grazed here and brambles had been thrashed back by volunteers to maintain its small flowery meadows on the thin soil above the limestone escarpment. Around the edge of the meadow were stunted yews. Despite being ancient indigenous trees, they did not look quite natural to me. I was so used to seeing evergreens as alien invaders in our landscape.

I sat on the bench in the middle of this glorious wild meadow, admiring a solitary dainty white orchid. Only Meadow Browns and one Large Skipper braved the overcast conditions. Even when the sun momentarily emerged, there was nothing else, except a battalion of bees. I waited for more than an hour, filled with foreboding and the usual pre-sighting tension.

It was seven days into July and towards the end of the Northern Brown Argus's flight season. I had not paid this fact much attention, preoccupied with the challenge of finding the Mountain Ringlet. I had also been lulled into a false sense of security by the flight times given in Jeremy Thomas, which, as the man himself pointed out when we met in Oxford, were now rather out of date. His guidebook was published in the 1980s and now some butterflies were emerging a month earlier – and dying off a month earlier too – than the flight periods he gave. This was scary. It suggested that climate change has been so pronounced that it has radically shifted butterfly flight times in less than thirty years.

Had I left it too late? If I had, my best bet now was to drive as fast as I could to northern Scotland, where I hoped the Northern Brown Argus would be showing itself a bit later. In the meantime, I would more modestly walk north from Latterbarrow to another grid reference on the edge of Whitbarrow, some three miles away. I could drive there quickly but I decided to go on foot. I felt guilty about all this driving around, and I was developing a vague and pretentious theory that you saw butterflies best, and truly appreciated them, when you immersed yourself in their landscape and became part of their world too. More pragmatically, the longer you spent outdoors, at walking pace, the more likely you were to see something. It was only geniuses like Oates who spotted White-letter Hairstreaks from the fast lane of a motorway.

At the northern end of Latterbarrow was a gate with a plaque in memoriam to Dr F. H. Day, a geologist and naturalist who died in 1988. He must have been an industrious and practical man who disdained sitting down: no memorial benches for him. I walked up through the slippery yew woods of Witherslack. After about half an hour, on the very edge of Yewbarrow, I entered a small clearing ringed by stands of hazel coppice. The grass was midsummer beige and there were few flowers compared with Latterbarrow. I paused, and saw two Meadow Browns. They were bullying someone much smaller.

I knew instantly what it was. This butterfly was like a German shorthaired pointer for me. A precious memory from childhood. Every time I saw one, I fell in love with it all over again. This was not a Brown Argus, of course, but an identical Northern Brown Argus; the simple fact I was in Cumbria told me this. In flight, it looked silvery and the delicate blue-grey hairs on its underside flashed silvery blue. When it stopped, it was a rich brown and posed very obligingly, opening its wings wide to catch the dull glow of the sun behind the clouds. I followed it and photographed it for fifteen minutes as it struck various poses on grasses and brambles. It was an adorable little thing, all on its own in the clearing.

I was so preoccupied I did not notice something much bigger behind me. When the sun came out more strongly, flashes of gold appeared in all corners of the glade. I had already seen the High Brown Fritillary in Devon with Dad but these limestone habitats around Morecambe Bay were its proper headquarters, its last stand and its best hope of survival. Along with the Duke of Burgundy, the High Brown Fritillary is our most imperilled butterfly. Since butterfly recording began some thirty years ago, its numbers have declined by more than 80 per cent, a 'petrifying' slump in its population according to Matthew Oates.

A big, mobile butterfly dependent on a well-managed combination of violets, bracken and just the right amount of grazing animals, it needs to move around, across large habitats, to survive. Mostly, now, it is stuck in isolated pockets of land, where it is always at risk of extinction. On well-managed nature reserves with a serious conservation effort at its back, some colonies are still inexorably slipping into extinction, although others are holding up and on one site managed by Butterfly Conservation in South Wales the numbers have increased encouragingly.

When I examined another large fritillary on the brambles, I realised it was neither species but a Silver-washed Fritillary, which I was not expecting to see at all. I was convinced I had glimpsed one in Thrift Wood in Essex when I went looking for Heath Fritillaries but I could not be certain, as the big golden butterfly raced beyond the brambles before I could get a proper look. This one, however, was definitely a Silver-washed, the biggest and most elegant flyer of all the fritillaries, a butterfly of our woodlands in midsummer and here right at the northerly limit of its range.

For what seemed like ages, I followed fritillaries – High Brown, Dark Green and Silver-washed – around the glade at Yewbarrow. I found a High Brown laying eggs. It crawled on the ground through blades of grass and appeared to be dropping eggs at random in the warm leaf litter. This looked careless. Surely a mother should be more discriminating? Apparently, however, the butterfly actually carefully probes the dead leaf litter to find appropriate sites. After an hour or so of watching these big fritillaries in the glade I could just about distinguish a High Brown from a Dark Green without needing to see the underside of their wings. The Dark Greens looked more pedestrian somehow, with their slightly more rounded wings. The High Brown Fritillary was not merely elevated by its rarity; its outline was sharper and it possessed a vim and dash that gave it deserved pre-eminence among our northern butterflies.

The day I travelled south, before a final, quiet and painful conversation with Lisa in which she ended our relationship, I sought the sanctuary of Arnside Knott. The old people were still pottering between nursing homes and the Knott, couples who radiated enough love but also enough perseverance – a rarer quality in our impatient society, rich in indulgences and choices – to warm each other through the long decades together. Older still was the great ship of the Knott, and its implacable, defiant yew trees. It felt like an Ark, a refuge for butterflies and a modest place of peace for people too. On the steepest, driest escarpment, where dozens of Graylings now tussled and mated, I found another sign that nature, at least, was solid and reliable. Perhaps the eight-thousandth generation of Northern Brown Argus to fly here, the solitary little butterfly was so grey and ragged it might have single-handedly navigated all those centuries itself.

47. Large Skipper, Arnside Knott, Cumbria, 5 June
48. Mountain Ringlet, Grey Knotts, Cumbria, 6 July
49. Large Heath, Meathop Moss, Cumbria, 6 July
50. Northern Brown Argus, Yewbarrow, Cumbria, 7 July
51. Silver-washed Fritillary, Yewbarrow, Cumbria, 7 July

16

Butterfly burnout

Butterfly burnout was first described to me by Matthew Oates. All spring and summer, lepidopterists count eggs, measure caterpillars, track down pupae, watch butterflies emerge and tick off their favourites, while worrying if their populations are rising or falling. For devotees of the Purple Emperor, such as Oates, July is a particularly frenetic month of early mornings in obscure woods, eyes scrunched against the sun, necks cricked to scour the tops of oak trees. 'By August, you're knackered,' said Oates. 'I'm completely burnt out post Emperor. It is just deckchair, *Test Match Special*, the sound of the distant combine harvester, ash tree and Brown Hairstreak.' According to Oates, the Brown Hairstreak is a perfect late-summer butterfly because it indolently spends hours doing nothing at all in high trees and hedges and can only be monitored with a lot of patience and that aforementioned chair.

Butterfly burnout sounded quite pleasant. A hot day sitting in a wood, or slumped on the Downs, waiting for those final few heat-loving species – the Brown Hairstreak and the Silver-spotted Skipper – that only emerge in late July or August. I never imagined it would hit me as I was hunched in my car in a wood in Surrey, hung-over and miserable, as the rain went ping-ping-ping, mercilessly, on the roof.

I was searching for the Wood White. I had done what seemed like the difficult bit, travelling to Northern Ireland to see Réal's Wood White, where I had learned all about *reali* and *sinapis*, our two, remarkably similar, Wood White species. I realised the English Wood White, *sinapis*, was one of our most endangered species but I knew exactly where it lived, I recognised its unmistakable drunken flight and I understood it needed hot, sunny woodland rides in which to lay its eggs. Seeing it, I thought, would not be a problem. I had not chanced upon it anywhere in June and so was now relying on catching sight of the small second brood that emerged in some of its colonies later in the summer.

When I was a boy, I had seen the Wood White on several occasions while Dad and I were hunting Purple Emperors. It was special, because we did not have it in Norfolk, but not particularly remarkable. I remember seeing it before and after getting excited about spotting my first Silver-washed Fritillary. The Wood White picked its way weakly but indefatigably along a sunny ride in Tugley Wood in July 1988. It looked like one of the easiest butterflies to grab hold of although, as Oates has documented, that great Emperor obsessive Ian Heslop turned the capture of a Wood White into an extreme act of daring, plucking it from a railway line shortly before a train thundered past. 'I jumped down on to the track to the accompaniment of a shout from the railwayman, "Look out, there's a train coming" (and indeed I could feel in my face the draught forced from the tunnel), caught my first Wood White and leapt back on to the plat-form just as the train emerged from the tunnel a few yards away.'

Stephen and Gail Jeffcoate, my dad's friends and Wood White experts, recommended that I return to Tugley to see the Wood White again this year. The wood was part of a rich swath of intimate, forested land close to the villages of Chiddingfold and Dunsfold in Surrey, between the North and the South Downs. Driving along its lanes, you would be blinded by the sudden darkness as you and the road were enveloped by grand old oaks.

Gail gave me precise instructions about which particular ride the Wood Whites favoured this year, and I set off in late July with my friends Matt and Camilla – of White Admiral fame. The weather had turned weird. After the joy of a hot sunny June, it had rained on 15 July, St Swithin's Day (St Swithin's day if thou dost rain/For forty days it will remain) and most of July felt like September. Every day dawned cloudy and blustery with heavy showers between glimpses of sunshine. We parked on a track outside the wood and walked to Lagfold Copse. The wind whispered and bounced its way with us. This was not good. Wood Whites did not like wind. But every woodland butterfly seemed to be flying. We found a sunny, reason-ably sheltered ride, with rank grass and tall thistles and saw Painted Ladies, Commas, Ringlets, Meadow Browns, skippers and a Common Blue. Then we walked past a bramble patch and saw a pair of Silver-washed Fritillaries. Matt was impressed by my binoculars.

We strolled around to the Botany Bay entrance and followed the track down to a stream. We nearly stepped on a blue-black adder, the

first I had ever seen in the wild, and then, to my delight, saw a
White Admiral glide through the trees, so I could show Camilla her
butterfly. In 1803, A. H. Haworth wrote of 'an old Aurelian of
London, so highly delighted at the inimitable flight of *Camilla* that,
long after he was unable to pursue her, he used to go to the woods
and sit down on a stile, for the sole purpose of feasting his eyes with
her fascinating evolutions'. It was a beautiful creature. Finally, on the
ride ahead, I saw the flop of a weak white butterfly. We chased it and
eventually it settled with its wings open by a puddle on the forest
ride. Wood Whites never open their wings when they land. This was
a Green-veined White. We had drawn a blank and turned for home.

When I spoke to the Jeffcoates again, they had been inspecting Wood
White sites in the West Country. The following weekend a friend's
wedding beckoned me westwards, so I called in at the headquarters
of Butterfly Conservation in Dorset, a stroll from the spectacular
stretch of coastline around Lulworth Cove where the Lulworth
Skipper flies.

In his lovely account of his teenage collecting days, the moth
fanatic Philip Allan wrote of his grand tour cycling through Dorset.
'At the top of the hill into Charmouth a man asked me if I had seen
a lion, as one had escaped from a travelling circus the previous night.
As I was armed only with a butterfly-net I took the hill in top gear
and let the road racer race. The initial note of a donkey braying on
the other side of the hedge cause my legs to revolve almost as fast as
the spokes of the bicycle. At Lulworth Cove I lay face downwards on

the grass near the top of the cliff while little brown butterflies flew about me in plenty. But I was chary about harming the colony, so took only six and felt guilty at that.'

The Camberwell Beauty may be long gone from Camberwell, the Scotch Argus can be seen in the Lake District and the Essex Skipper is now a complete misnomer, for it is found across southern England. The Lulworth Skipper, however, is the only British butterfly we can still accurately locate geographically by its name. It is found in its thousands only along a limited stretch of the Dorset and Devon coast. One entomologist estimated that almost one million of the insects fly on rough fields above Lulworth Cove. While most butterflies suffered from the decline of grazing and the myxomatosis-induced decline in rabbit populations, the Lulworth Skipper has benefited, needing longer grass for its egg-laying and its caterpillars.

Butterfly Conservation's homely offices, filled with photographs, paintings and distribution maps of butterflies, are in an old yard belonging to the Lulworth Estate, which owns most of the land around Lulworth. When the charity moved in, it planted different species of buddleia in the gravel yard; a few years ago a rare Monarch called in on the flowers after migrating from North America. As I chatted to Martin Warren, the chief executive of Butterfly Conservation, two Silver-washed Fritillaries hurtled in an expansive circuit around the yard, one circling the other like the death-spin of an X-wing fighter in *Star Wars*. 'They are doing the dancey thing,' said Warren, excitedly. 'That's a scientific term, is it, Martin?' quipped his colleague Nigel Bourn, dryly. Bourn had alerted me to the swarm of Heath Fritillaries in Blean Woods.

Tanned, lean and boyish, Warren is a first-class butterfly scientist who wears his knowledge lightly. He helped save the Heath Fritillary and has studied a number of rare species, including the Wood White. By his reassuring side, there was no anxiety about whether we would find our target. Lulworth Cove was what my dad would call a honeypot. The summer holidays had started and a large car and coach park was heaving with families, mooching between visitor centre and toilet block. It was even busier than usual because Camp Bestival, one of a glut of summer music festivals, was getting under way at Lulworth Castle, right at the charity's doorstep.

Warren and I walked to the cliff top and looked at the Lulworth Crumple, where rock had been pushed into a vertical strata. We then paused to admire the perfect semicircle of Lulworth Cove. The sea was a milky turquoise against the chalk, and small boats were moored in the calm waters of the bay. A line of limestone runs westwards along the coast from here to the Isle of Purbeck. Behind this is clay, and then chalk. At Lulworth Cove the sea breached the limestone, greedily ate out the clay in a wide scoop beyond and was then stopped dead by the chalk, which is more resistant to erosion. Behind the cove is a big chalk grassland hill. Where it is fenced off and grazed, the downland is full of Adonis and Chalkhill Blues. But the Lulworth Skipper only flies on the hazardous side of the fence, right on the cliff edge, where the vegetation is out of reach of sheep and cattle and can grow to its preferred length.

We walked through rough grassland on the edge of the cliffs, admiring the blocky purple head of a pyramidal orchid beneath our feet. The stiff Tor grass rustled like straw in the wind and a gull floated below us in the studiously casual fashion of a rogue. We soon saw a Lulworth Skipper; it was very small and olive-coloured. If Small Tortoiseshells are the Labradors of the butterfly world then skippers are the Jack Russell terriers. I had already seen plenty of examples of Large Skippers and Chequered Skippers aggressively dispatching any rival insect that dared fly past their perches. Like its fellow skippers, the Lulworth Skipper was a fast, robust flyer, scooting low between long grass to avoid the worst of the wind that battered it constantly on the exposed cliffs. Living in such numbers, however, it seemed much less pugnacious than other skippers and was happily taking nectar from yellow ragwort alongside its brethren.

We saw another male and then a female, who was less olive in colour and had the faintest sketch of a circle on her wings, like an aerial photograph of an ancient archaeological site traced out in summer wheat. She was sitting keeping warm. Warren explained that she had probably laid a batch of eggs already and was now maturing her next set of eggs, so she could lay more later in the day. A mother and her teenage daughter and friend, wearing fancy dress in preparation for Camp Bestival, wondered what we were doing, floundering in the rough grass on the cliff edge. 'Are they Brown Admirals or something?' asked the mother. 'We call every butterfly we don't know a Brown Admiral.'

Rather than thousands, we only saw about thirty Lulworth Skippers, probably because they had emerged early and were coming to the end of their flight season. It was a pleasure to roam the clifftops with Warren, who unshowily dispensed amazing facts about butterflies. I learnt many things I felt I should know already. One was that butterflies do not hold their wings open and bask in the sunshine to feel the sun warming their wings. Wings are not like solar panels, and blood does not circulate around them (you can cut the wing off a butterfly and it will not bleed to death). Butterflies keep warm by trapping air around their body, which is why when you look at them closely most butterfly bodies are almost obscenely hairy. When butterflies settle and open their wings on a flat surface, these trap warm air beneath them. This is what warms them up. White butterflies – the Large, Small and Green-veined White, for instance – are a bit different: they always sit with their wings in a stiff 'v' shape. They don't hold their wings flat and outstretched. This is because they are reflective baskers. The sun hits their pale wings at an angle and is directed onto their bodies, which are dark and absorb the heat.

While I was at their headquarters, the lepidopterists at Butterfly Conservation gave me a tip for another Wood White site on the undercliffs at Lyme Regis, so I raced there that afternoon. I only knew the undercliffs from reading *The French Lieutenant's Woman* by John Fowles, where they were an exotic, tangled world of illicit passion. But despite being a butterfly fanatic, Fowles had not woven the Wood White into his story. When I arrived at Lyme, the seaside town and its fossil shops cowered under an enormous storm. After it blew over, I paced impatiently westwards, as instructed, to the undercliff, the collapsed and well-vegetated portion of crumbling coastline of west Dorset and east Devon. Everything was sodden. I ignored notices warning me not to climb the cliffs and scrambled into rough thickets of dripping bramble. It was right on the beach, and it certainly did not feel like a natural Wood White site. The ground underfoot was greasy grey clay, and I could not scale it without sliding and skidding all over the place. Another storm was brewing and, after half an hour, I was defeated for a second time.

My third attempt to see the Wood White came on the journey home, after my friend's wedding. A week earlier, the Jeffcoates had seen plenty of Wood Whites on the undercliffs at Branscombe to the west of Lyme Regis. This village and beach was best known in recent years for scenes of audacious looting as people travelled hundreds of miles in January 2007 to snatch motorbikes and family heirlooms spilled from the stricken ship MSC *Napoli*, which was abandoned just offshore after a winter storm. Another drive and I really had lost patience with the Wood White. I did not want to see it any more; I just wanted to tick it off. I parked in the village and stomped quickly into the woods. Stupidly, I had not taken precise instructions from the Jeffcoates and was relying on books which said Devon's only reliable colony flew on the undercliffs to the west of Branscombe.

The coast path took me through mature trees at the top of the cliff. It was not strictly undercliff – there were some sunny glades. I sweated up and down and round, and saw Speckled Woods and Painted Ladies and Common Blues. I walked down to Branscombe and up the cliffs on the eastern side. Here, the path took me through the undercliff. There were Large Whites and Small Whites and Green-veined Whites but no Wood Whites. I turned back and angrily, and impatiently, tracked down every white butterfly I saw, searched every glade and sunny woodland edge. I knew the Wood White was distinctive but I thought I should check that the Small Whites I was seeing everywhere were not actually Wood Whites. All seemed too vigorous, but then Réal's Wood White in Northern Ireland had been quite lively.

Whenever they landed, they held open their wings to give me a definitive answer: they were not Wood Whites.

Then, finally, on a sunny edge of the woods of Branscombe, there staggered a much smaller white butterfly. At last, I sighed. As simple as that. I moved in to look more closely. It had black veins on exceptionally frayed wings. Oh hell, I cursed. It was a really ancient, tatty Green-veined White.

Apart from the Wood White, I was edging closer to my goal of seeing all fifty-nine species of British butterfly during the course of one summer. Before the Lulworth Skipper became butterfly number fifty-three, I clocked up the Chalkhill Blue, the last of our summer blues to emerge. I had a job in St Albans which I finished early. I had woken that morning after a vivid dream of a Camberwell Beauty. It sat on a buddleia in an everyday location, and I fired off some photographs to prove I had seen it. It was exciting, and very realistic. It seemed a good omen, so even though it was cloudy I skipped off for the rest of the day to pay my first visit to the famed Royston Heath.

The A10 to Royston is a grand old road. It is part of Ermine Street, the great Roman highway that runs arrow-straight, on the map at least, from Bishopsgate in London to Royston, and then on to Lincoln and York. As the A10, it loops up and down the gently rolling hills of east Hertfordshire, sympathetic to the landscape in a way that eludes the modern M11, not far to the east. And yet it was a melancholy drive. I imagined these vast arable fields as they once were: rough pasture and small meadows bordered by hedgerows and trees. This landscape was now a barley desert, bereft of butterflies.

Royston Heath, an isolated fragment of chalk downland just outside Royston, is a grassy slope looking north over the plains of prairie fields, through which winds the River Cam. Known locally as Therfield Heath after a nearby village, it was at the heart of the frenzied final era of butterfly collecting, when small boys and chequebook collectors would flock to the town to hunt the many variations and aberrations of the Chalkhill Blue.

In the early decades of the twentieth century, every room in every hotel and inn around Royston Heath would be booked up in July by hunters seeking to catch Chalkhill Blues as soon as they hatched. As a summer event, it was a bit like a music festival or Wimbledon. Residents would rent their houses to visitors searching for ever more freakish variations, and schoolboys would take specimens to pubs to hawk to chequebook collectors, rich men who drove Bentleys and might fork out £5 or even £50 for a rare aberration. In those days, small children who grew up in the countryside would take to collecting butterflies as naturally as playing conkers.

Thousands of these were caught, killed and laid out on display by one singular individual, a tax accountant called Robert 'Porker' Watson. Porker won wrestling prizes at fairs as a young man before settling down to marry five times, and building himself a house he called Porcorum – 'of pigs'. Defying the disability of being almost blind in one eye, Porker also became an adept and dedicated butterfly hunter.

His spoils can be found in thirteen slightly scruffy mahogany cabinets that give off an unmistakable whiff of mothballs, tucked within the Natural History Museum's collection of 8.7 million dead butter-flies and moths. Sliding smoothly from each cabinet are ten glass-topped drawers, each containing the perfectly preserved dry corpses of 160 small butterflies, pale blue and pinned on cork. If you peer closely, you can see that every one of these 20,800 specimens is subtly different. Some are washed all over in silvery blue; in others, the blue streaks into chocolate brown. Some boast rows of tiny orange studs bordering all four wings; in others, the studs are white and black only. All, however, are exactly the same species: Chalkhill Blues.

By the car park an exceedingly comprehensive noticeboard of the old school variety (the new school eschew geography lessons for pretty pictures of knapweed and butterflies) told the story of the heath before the Chalkhill Blue frenzy began. Chalk deposits of up to 90 metres thick were laid down on what was once a seabed over 100 million years and when the ice retreated 10,000 years ago, but-terflies arrived and so too did man. On the heath is Hertfordshire's oldest monument, a 5000-year-old Neolithic long barrow, as well as Mile Ditches showing an Iron Age presence, and shards of pottery from the Romans. In the seventeenth century King James I was a regular visitor to the heath where he would hunt the soon-to-be-extinct Great Bustard.

In 1892 the biggest influence on the heath in modern times was created: Royston Golf Club. There was an old notice that left every visitor in no doubt that golf took priority over foolish nature lovers who threw themselves in front of flying golf balls. 'The public are warned that a golf ball can cause serious injury and great care should be taken when walking on the course. By order – The Conservators of Therfield Heath.' Golf appeared to dominate this precious fragment, virtually the last sizeable piece of chalk downland in East Anglia. From where I was standing, most of the heath appeared to be golf course. No butterflies can survive on a putting green.

I was still reading the information board when I saw a pale blue butterfly ghosting across the rough grass just below a bunker. It was more beautiful than I remembered. The Large Blue is hailed for its looks but, on a gloomy day, this Chalkhill Blue possessed a luminous power. It was almost as large as the Large Blue but rather than bold wings of blue and black it was as pale as stonewashed jeans from the 1980s. Away from the golf course, flowery grass ran wild between the warts of lumpy old barrows mounds on the downs. Chalk grassland is a lovely and unassuming thing. From a distance, it simply appears to be rank dull yellow grass, with a reddish tinge. Only when you walk into it, and see it close up, do you realise it is a mass of purple knapweed and mauve scabious and, palest of all, harebells as fine as the most precious porcelain.

It was windy and as dark as it could be at 3 p.m. on a summer afternoon. I kicked up a plump pair of red-legged partridges sheltering in the grass. I felt hungry just looking at them. Despite the imminent rain, over the course of the next half an hour I saw at least thirty Chalkhill Blues, nectaring hungrily on almost every prominent flower head. They also blundered up and down grass stems, walking up, tipping them over and almost unbalancing before trotting down again. There was a hint of turquoise close to the body on the chalky underside of the males, and I had forgotten that the striking silvery brown of the females is quite unlike the brown of any other butterfly.

I liked their personalities, in this overcast weather at least. They were obliging, haphazard, clumsy and sociable. They did not seem bothered by each other, or me, preoccupied as they were by the uncomplicated pleasure of nectar. But they also seemed terribly exposed and vulnerable here, on their butterfly island, surrounded by roads, golf and a desolate ocean of barley.

When I mentioned in an email to Matthew Oates that I had not yet seen the Wood White, there was an urgency in his reply. 'Advise: head for 2nd brood WW NOW!' he wrote. The first Saturday in August brought more unsettled weather and a colossal hangover, an unfortunate byproduct of being single again. I had no choice but to head to Tugley Wood. This was becoming an arduous commute and it could not be done on public transport. Instead, I had to drive from north-east London to south-west London, and then to Surrey. It was less than fifty miles but involved either driving across the capital, or taking the car park that was the M25, or risking the notorious Blackwall Tunnel. I tried the tunnel. Three hours later, averaging the sort of speeds a Victorian Aurelian would comfortably attain in his horse and cart, I arrived at a quintessential summer scene in the village of Chiddingfold. Cricketers were playing on the green but the umpire was already looking at the sky and shaking his head. Teenagers had bought ice creams from the village shop but were pulling up their hoodies against the incoming rain.

I was starting to resent all this time spent in Surrey. When I first visited the Surrey countryside on our butterfly trips as a boy, I was amazed that we could pop out of the silent folds of woodland and see a signpost saying 'London 38 miles'. Coming from the rural depths of Norfolk, I had no idea you could live in such apparent peace and yet be so close to the capital. My child's mind pictured London surrounded by a wasteland, like those pictures of the deforested Amazon: all dead tree trunks rising from the ground, surrounded by smouldering piles of rubbish and rubble.

And as a boy, I was impressed by the tidy English beauty of rural Surrey. Now I found it oppressive. The intimacy of the landscape was claustrophobic. Stop on any little lane in Surrey and soon there are dozens of gleaming cars being driven too fast past you. No one waves. On the edge of Tugley Wood, I passed converted farm cottages with a commuter-belt sheen. They had a free-range hen shed, which was guarded by CCTV. Boggis, Bunce and Bean just wanted to shoot Roald Dahl's Fantastic Mr Fox; paranoid residents of Middle England compile CCTV footage of foxy carnage to show at their weekly Neighbourhood Watch meeting. Dotted through the woods, every house had a gate. A horse stood in a paddock wearing what looked like a hijab. 'Warning', said red letters on a white sign. 'Dogs loose in ground.'

By the time I reached the Botany Bay entrance to Tugley Wood, it was pouring down. I had broken my journey at a service station on the M25, wedged with holidaying families wondering whether to buy a cheap surfboard or a cheaper folding chair. At least parked up by the wood, I was on my own. Except for the paranoid denizens of Surrey. And the rain.

Henry Walter Bates rebelled against his mercantile background and became a great Victorian naturalist who travelled to Brazil as a young man with fellow enthusiast Alfred Russel Wallace (he of the Birdwing and headache for the rest of the day) to collect and discover new species of insects and birds. During a decade in South America, he marvelled at the wealth of tropical butterflies and collected 14,000 different mostly insect species, of which 8000 were undiscovered, and sent them home to the British Museum. Bates endured dysentery, yellow fever, malaria and parasites, but most of all he was haunted by loneliness. He wrote and told his brother: 'I was obliged, at last, to come to the conclusion that the contemplation of Nature alone is not sufficient to fill the human heart and mind.'

During my mission to find fifty-nine extremely well-known species of butterfly with the help of experts, maps, a car and satnav, I had endured terrible traffic and love's indulgent grief. Now I had a headache. These trifles were enough to nudge me towards the same conclusion as Bates. Had butterflies caused the breakdown of my relationship with Lisa? Why was life both so interminably long, and yet so frighteningly short? And why would I have to do this awful drive all over again tomorrow and the next day, and probably the day after that, all to see a small white butterfly? What if I had missed the short second brood of the Wood White altogether? My journey to find all fifty-nine species of British butterfly would end at fifty-eight. It was not an heroic failure. It would be an inept failure, especially as the stumbling point was the humble Wood White, and the short-willied form at that.

This was what butterfly burnout felt like.

As the rain ratted and tat-tat-tatted on the roof of my car, the insides of which increasingly resembled a bachelor's bedsit, I consoled myself with a passage from Heslop's book about the Purple Emperor. Frederick Courtenay Selous was a British explorer, hunter, conservationist and man of colonial Africa, who inspired H. Rider

Haggard to create the hero of *King Solomon's Mines*, Allan Quatermain. He was an alpha-male hero and Heslop feted him as 'the greatest big-game hunter who ever lived'. Despite the namby-pamby image of butterfly collecting, Selous was happy to admit to pursuing Purple Emperors. He probably wielded binoculars without shame too. During a trip to Salzburg, Selous endured seven days of frustration, waiting from 12 until 3 p.m. for Purple Emperors. Every day, he was thwarted by the weather: not once did the sun break through the clouds. 'I think that if this sort of thing had continued for another week I should have gone into a chronic state of melancholy and moroseness for the rest of my life, and people would have said, "Ah, he must have had some great disappointment in early life,"' Selous wrote. 'These are the sort of things that rile me more than anything else, for you can't think how I put my whole soul into egg and butterfly collecting when I'm at it, and how I boil up and over with impotent rage at not being able to attain the object of my desires on account of the weather over which I have no control.'

I too had no control over the weather, or the butterflies, or the traffic, or the hearts of those I loved. For some reason, I continued to cling to the idea that I could find what I was looking for if only I was smart enough, and disciplined enough, and organised enough, and knew the right back road through south London. I badly needed to learn not only patience, but acceptance.

It was still raining outside so I turned, as everybody should in such crises, to Enid Blyton. Wisely, I had remembered to lob *Five Go To Billycock Hill*, a Famous Five adventure, into the car boot. I had bought it on eBay because a friend told me it featured a pair of butterfly collectors. By the time I started butterflying, I had grown out of the Famous Five but the argot of Aunt Fanny's lashings of cold ham and boiled eggs was familiar enough, although I had never realised just how much the Five's lives revolved around food. If they lived today, these kids would be raving about Texas BBQ pizzas with cheese-filled crusts and the latest McFlurry flavour and they would be far too obese to hound baddies out of caves.

Of all the portrayals of Aurelians in literature, Blyton's story of Mr Gringle of the butterfly farm and his faithful companion, Mr Brent, is by far the most devastating critique of men in the grip of an obsession with insects. Mr Gringle is 'rather a peculiar figure, untidy, with glasses slipping down his nose, and his hair much too long'. He shambles along with a big butterfly net, and when he meets the Famous Five his 'curiously bright' eyes shine behind his glasses. Here, you imagine, is a man not to be trusted.

He is keen, however, to show the Five around his butterfly farm. While Julian, Dick, George and Anne (and Timmy, if dogs could talk) politely and keenly point out passing butterflies, Mr Gringle answers their questions 'rather coldly', dismisses their innocent belief that moths only fly at night as 'rubbish', confuses George for a boy, and almost knocks her over in his selfish pursuit of a Brown Argus.

At the farm, the butterfly glasshouses are immaculate but the house which Mr Gringle shares with 'my friend Mr Brent' is neglected. Blyton obviously wants us to think Gringle and Brent are gay. 'It was certainly a queer place,' she writes, and the Famous Five later see the pair huddled together, poring over butterfly-breeding charts late at night. So as not to set her young audience wondering too much, she reveals they have a bedroom each.

The crime the Famous Five investigate is the theft of two top-secret military planes from a nearby airfield. Blyton is too cunning to cast the butterfly men as the baddies. These queer lepidopterists are far too weedy to breach national security and steal military secrets. Rather, it turns out, the baddie is the evil son of their housekeeper, and the butterfly men are too myopically wrapped up in their own obsession to notice. Worst of all, these unpatriotic homosexuals accuse the Famous Five of breaking the windows of their glasshouse and threaten to call the police. It is left to Julian to tell these butterfly berks to get a grip, in no uncertain terms: 'We shall be very *glad* to see the police, if you have really sent them after us. Quite a lot has been going on here that you don't know anything about. You've noticed nothing but your butterflies and moths.'

The way butterfly enthusiasts have been cast as eccentrics and even sexual predators over the years is wearily familiar, as is the idea that a love of butterflies is effeminate or even gay. Simon Barnes, the great sports writer and birdwatcher, wrote of his love for butterflies in *The Times* and was puzzled to receive a letter praising his bravery. The following week, he returned to the sissy shame of lepidopterists. 'To say you like butterflies is regarded by some as effeminate. I have made myself a Fotherington-Thomas, the skipping, curly-locked figure of the Molesworth books: "Hello, sky. Hello, clouds!"' he wrote. 'Unmanly? Unwomanly? I think that we all have a profound attachment to the wild world from which we spring, and an important nostalgia for the world we are losing. To like butterflies is an irrefragable aspect of the human condition, and if you can't admit it, it's you, not me who is diminished.'

Three hours passed. Surrounded by a very wet wood, I felt calm;

but I needed a wee. I jumped out of my car and ran across the rough grass by the entrance to the wood. As I scampered, a speck of silver grey rose from the grass. I immediately knew what it was: here was the little brown job, the butterfly that had started everything for me, and which, bizarrely, I had not yet seen that summer. In my hour of desperation, of impatience, frustration and emasculation, here flew the Brown Argus. The brilliant little butterfly that had so entranced me as a child latched onto a stem of grass and sat with its wings closed against the rain. An hour later, I checked again and it was still hanging on the same stem. When the downpour eased for a moment, it opened its tiny wings to reveal its deep rich-brown colour. Cold and wet, I cackled at the ridiculousness of it all.

By 5.15 p.m., it was almost dark, with steady rain that showed no sign of easing. I decided to go for a stroll before returning to do battle with the traffic. I would return for another shift at Tugley Wood tomorrow. Trees spilled great droplets and a slick brown slug with bright-orange trim around the bottom, like the luminous lights boy racers mount under cars, crossed my path. I have appreciated slugs ever since I terrorised my sister by placing them on her swing as a child, so I picked this fellow up and crooned at him and stroked his slimy back. He squirmed in my warm dry hand, and I wondered if I was causing him pain. I put him down and he glided off again, pausing to wriggle from side to side, as if he was a pig scratching an itch by rubbing his back against a gatepost. An old-fashioned plane chugged low overhead and I felt nine years old again and a member of the Famous Five. It had been a long time since I had been scared, on my own, in the middle of nowhere. I crossed the stream and stalked slowly up the hill. I could see a shape on the forest ride ahead of me and I wondered if it was a huge pheasant or a tiny deer. I blinked a droplet of water out of my eye and a white moth shape stumbled into my vision, staggering through the rain ahead of me.

I had seen a ghost. Or had I? There it was again. At last, amazingly, and at a moment when I had absolutely given up hope: a real live Wood White. I was interested in how detached I felt. I had finally reached a state of acceptance: I was not going to see a Wood White that day, I may not see one the following day, I may have missed seeing it altogether and would have to write about my failure. And then it had suddenly appeared. There was probably no link between letting go and getting what you want when you no longer want it, although that paradox seemed to occur often enough in life.

The Wood White settled in the rain, something it would probably not have done in the sunshine, and I watched it taking nectar from a delicate woodland flower. Another, the shape of a droplet of water, hung off a leaf nearby. I was struck by how placid they seemed and how, like any wild thing, they were truly in the moment. This, the ability to just be, and live fully absorbed in the present, was exactly what I got from butterfly watching, and I had forgotten it in my impatient haste to tick off species number fifty-five. These Wood Whites were not raging against the rain, even though it would probably kill them tomorrow. They were patient, biding their time, doing what they could to survive that second, with no thought for the future or the past.

52. Chalkhill Blue, Therfield Heath, Hertfordshire, 21 July
53. Lulworth Skipper, Lulworth Cove, Dorset, 24 July
54. Brown Argus, Tugley Wood, Surrey, 1 August
55. Wood White, Tugley Wood, Surrey, 1 August

17

The final four

After seeing the Wood White, the world felt cleansed and calm. Finding it in such unlikely conditions made me feel that anything was possible. It was the start of August and I only had four butterflies to go: the Scotch Argus, the Adonis Blue, the Silver-spotted Skipper and the Brown Hairstreak. Apart from the Adonis Blue, which I could have seen in May or June during the first of its two summer broods, I was exactly where I should be for the season. The other three butterflies were all late-summer creatures, and seldom flew in great number before August.

The elusive Brown Hairstreak would be the most challenging, but first I had to drive north to seek out the Scotch Argus. I got up at 5 a.m. and beat the traffic to head to Cumbria. Dad and I had visited the old railway line at Smardale Gill nearly twenty years before; I had a dim recollection of walking past a spectacular viaduct and seeing dozens of Scotch Argus butterflies on the wing. I had checked with the Cumbria branch of Butterfly Conservation and the butterfly was still found at Smardale, although when I searched for the Mountain Ringlet and Large Heath in Cumbria in July it had been too early for the butterfly, which does not emerge until the end of that month.

Away from the congestion and caravans of the Lake District, Smardale is proper Cumbria: a secluded valley close to the pretty, unheralded town of Kirkby Stephen. The drive up was eerily smooth. I had been so frustrated and self-pitying the previous day I did not deserve such a favour from the god of traffic. Although the sunny morning in the south gave way to a line of cloud close to Chester, there was no rain when I parked at the entrance to the old railway line at 10 a.m. This track had taken coke from the mines of County Durham across the Pennines to the iron and steel furnaces of Barrow in West Cumbria. When the steelworks closed in 1962, the railway too was scrapped and ash, birch, hazel and willow quickly colonised its steep embankments.

It was a fine day with a hint of late summer. The berries on young rowans were already turning a smudgy orange and the raspberries growing on the railway line tasted good. I did not even reach the viaduct before I saw my first butterfly of the day. Between purple knapweed and UFO-shaped scabious flowers was a delicious dark-chocolate-brown Scotch Argus. I ignored a Dark Green Fritillary to take a photograph of this, perhaps the most handsome of our brown butterflies. A friendly couple from Durham came past; the man was a birder but loved his butterflies and was delighted to see his first ever Scotch Argus.

Further on, I entered the steep grassy meadow overlooking the viaduct. *Five Go To Billycock Hill* must still have been on my mind, because my eyes narrowed when I saw two figures wielding butterfly nets and puffing and sweating up and down the slope. One clumsily waded across the mountain stream to investigate a butterfly on the far bank. I wondered if they were legitimate conservationists or Mr Gringle and Mr Brent, carrying out a nefarious plot that threatened national security and would exterminate the Scotch Argus. However, I was not a member of the Famous Five, so I did not go and ask them what they were doing. I met them later when I was heading home on a narrow lane. Mr Brent had a Butterfly Conservation sticker on the rear window of his car so he can't have been all bad.

Instead of confronting Gringle and Brent, I sat on an old hawthorn with a trunk bleached almost white. It had fallen in the meadow and now looked like it was resting, perfectly alive and happy in this beautiful valley with the brush-brush of stream below and the grunt of a raven above. There were more Dark Green Fritillaries zipping around and, I was amazed to find, dozens of Small Skippers. Even the most up-to-date butterfly book does not record Small Skipper populations in Cumbria. Climate change was quickening their conquest of the north.

I spent two hours in the meadow, in the valley of Smardale, watching the Scotch Argus, the most handsome of the browns. It reminded me of a Mountain Ringlet the way it jittered and bashed its way clumsily through the stiff moor grass, falling and stumbling to rest deep in the turf and well out of the wind. There it would open its wings if it found a hazy glimpse of sun. I had planned to rest overnight in Cumbria but my time with the Scotch Argus had been perfect, so I headed back to London. I took the A66 across the Pennines and headed home down the madness of the A1. The journey seemed as effortless as the flight of fluffy seeds that rose in a blizzard from hundreds of thistles in the central reservation. I was home from my day-trip to see the Scotch Argus, half-demented by the 560-mile drive, at 5.30 p.m.

I had to wait several days for the sun to reappear. As soon as it did, I drove straight to Worthing to meet Neil Hulme, the oilman and Purple Emperor obsessive I had encountered in Fermyn Woods. He looked even more tanned than when I had seen him last. Hulme reckoned we might be able to bag my final three species in one day; but we were thwarted after a morning waiting futilely under blackthorn for the elusive Brown Hairstreak.

He was convinced we would have more luck with the Adonis Blue on Mill Hill, a steep chunk of the South Downs facing west over the Adur valley and the imposing gothic chapel of Lancing College. At the top of the hill, white van men were parked up for lunch when we walked down the precipitous slope, flowery with knapweed and scabious and smelling of warm thyme.

I had saved the best of the blues until last. This dashing electric-blue butterfly had the power to incite great obsession.

Joseph Grimaldi, a renowned entomologist of the early nine-teenth century, was better known as the greatest professional clown of the day. The grandson of 'Iron Legs' Grimaldi, a dancer who gained his nickname by leaping so high he broke the chandeliers in a Paris opera house, Joe Grimaldi first appeared on stage when he was two. His father was a violent pantomimist and ballet master, and his mother danced in the chorus at Sadler's Wells, where Joe began appearing regularly aged three. His father died when he was nine, and later, Grimaldi's wife passed away in childbirth. Joe's surviving son drank himself to death.

Charles Dickens, who edited the clown's memoirs, wrote of Grimaldi's 'unconquerable antipathy to being idle'. Grimaldi buried his heartache in fifty years of clowning, and in the pursuit of butterflies. Here, he was a nonconformist, even among Aurelians: he considered the prized Camberwell Beauty 'ugly' and preferred what he called the Dartford Blue, now known as the Adonis Blue.

Dickens described one June in 1794 when Grimaldi was just fifteen and had to perform every night at Sadler's Wells. When the clown's show ended, he had supper and, shortly after midnight, walked fifteen miles to Dartford. He arrived at 5 a.m. and breakfasted and rested with a friend, and then set out to find the butterfly. After some hours in the field, he 'bottled' just one Dartford Blue. At 1 p.m. he walked back to central London in time for his evening's work at Sadler's Wells. When the panto was over, he was so fired up by capturing one blue earlier in the day that he marched straight back to Dartford again, breakfasted with his mate and resumed his mission. This time, he caught four dozen of the little blue butterflies, before striding back to the theatre on foot to perform again that evening, having not slept properly for at least sixty hours. Like many things in Grimaldi's life, his love of butterflies ended in tragedy: his collection of Dartford Blues was smashed up by burglars who broke into his home when he was rehearsing. Grimaldi was so devastated that he took up pigeon fancying instead.

I may have missed the first generation of Adonis Blue but as a boy

I had always seen the Adonis during its second brood in the summer holidays, when it flew on chalk downs in tandem with its paler cousin, the Chalkhill Blue, as well as the Common Blue and the Brown Argus. It seemed right to see all four species together: the climax of summer on the Downs.

For a few minutes, I wondered if we were too early for the second brood but after seeing plenty of Chalkhills and the more mauve-blue of the Common Blue, we picked up a flash of electric blue that carried a hint of turquoise. Here was Adonis.

Crouched on the hillside as small planes floated into Shoreham airfield below, we watched a male and female Adonis mating. The female's wings were curled at the corners; they had not dried properly. This was a sign she had been grabbed by the male within minutes of her emergence from her pupae that morning. This, in the butterfly world, was not unusual. In some foreign species of *Heliconius* butterflies, the males sit on pupae waiting for the female to emerge. As the butterfly starts to take shape inside, the males become so excited they puncture the pupae and mate with the female inside. Lepidopterists call this 'pupal rape' because it appears that the female has no say in it. This may be an anthropomorphism too far because the female does emit a pheromone to attract males and, from an evolutionary point of view, being able to lay eggs from the very second you emerge from the pupae gives you a competitive advantage against those butterflies who have to wander around for days, searching for a mate.

Like the Adonis Blue, the Silver-spotted Skipper is a chalk downland butterfly that requires short well-grazed natural grassland to thrive. Until this was fully understood by conservationists, both appeared poised to follow the Large Blue into extinction. In the last twenty-five years, grazing with cattle and sheep specifically for conservation has been introduced on the North and South Downs. The heat-loving Silver-spotted Skipper has also benefited from climate change, steadily expanding its range almost every year since its nadir in the 1980s when it was reduced to only a handful of sites. Hulme and I drove east to Newtimber Hill, a precipitous piece of grassy chalk downland that faced west over the spectacular v-shaped valley of Devil's Dyke, the stubby tower of a village church and an expanse of the heavily wooded West Sussex countryside beyond. We parked in a lay-by. 'I bet we will see a Silver-spotted Skipper within five minutes of leaving the car,' said Hulme, as I locked up. We ducked under a barbed-wire fence and sweated up the slope. As soon as we set foot on this steep hill we were swallowed up by flowery grassland and lost sight of the road below. Despite being a few miles from Brighton, and a fine summer afternoon, there was no noise, and no people, only a few cattle over to one side. Hulme pointed out a delicate flower with an indigo head. It was a round-headed rampion, 'the pride of Sussex,' he said, and then I saw a dart of golden brown drop into the grass. It closed its wings, showing off an unmistakable underside: green with sharp silver spots. We had been on the Downs for four minutes.

This skipper was a female with a fat body full of eggs. It must have emerged that morning because it was immaculate. Silver-spotted Skippers usually only fly if the temperature rises above 19°C; much below this and there simply is not the heat to give them the energy to take to the wing. 'This is one of the cutest butterflies,' remarked Hulme, as I lay on my stomach on the springy grass and looked at the skipper through my binoculars. This little skipper had a huge body relative to its wings and the female was so chunky that it looked like she would struggle to fly. Hulme was right about her looks. She had the cutest little cartoon face I had ever seen: the big black eyes of a baby seal and the golden fur of a teddy bear. It was like a poster I had on my bedroom wall as a child, of a Netherland Dwarf, a milky-eyed flop-eared cutie of a rabbit. It was captioned: 'You're no bunny till some bunny loves you.' I was a soft little boy, and unusually fond of trite aphorisms.

There were more Silver-spotted Skippers on the hillside than any other butterfly. We counted seventy-three and watched a male pursue a reluctant female. He followed her and they crash-landed in the grass together. Then he edged alongside her and bent his abdomen around in a semi-circle to latch onto the end of the female's abdomen. It looked as ungainly a manoeuvre as parking on the wrong side of the petrol pump and heaving the nozzle around to the petrol cap on the other side of the car. The female flew off in disgust. You could hear the buzzing sound of her little skipper wings as she fled. Hulme reckoned she was already mated. Indefatigable, the male followed her. He tried the same trick, forcing the female to the ground and then edging apologetically alongside her and curving his abdomen around again. The female wearily rose up and buzzed off. The male did not know when he was beaten, and tried again. This time, the female stayed still. Had she tired of the chase, or finished testing him and found he had enough genetic tenacity to be the father of her babies? The male locked his abdomen to hers, and then shifted into a more comfortable position, so they stood back to back, with what we might call their bottoms firmly attached to each other. I felt a bit uncomfortable watching them through the binoculars (and this time, finally, not because of the binoculars). Unblinking, they sat motionless, making babies, as the sun caught the ripples of the Downs to the west.

We spent what seemed like hours on the hill. Hulme was one of the most energetic butterfly enthusiasts I had ever met, with a boundless enthusiasm for watching, counting and photographing them, fuelled by a constant supply of Silk Cuts and energy drinks. I was sweating and feeling the weariness of a 58-species-in-one-summer veteran with just one butterfly left to find. While we tried to take photographs of skittish skippers, a brilliant yellow butterfly bounced into view. It was a Clouded Yellow, and the golden yellow spots inside the black borders on its wings showed it was a female and less inclined to dash off at high speed like the males. This was a beautiful insect to encounter, and it was a relief to see it properly. My sole sighting on Marsham Heath in Norfolk in July had been exceedingly brief, slightly uncertain and not supported by any witnesses or photographic evidence. On Newtimber Hill, we watched two females as they picked their way around the flowers on the Downs. I had never before noticed the Clouded Yellow's spooky green alien eyes and the veins in its wings that would power it across oceans. They bulged like a wrestler on steroids.

After a slow start, Hulme and I clocked up twenty-six species of butterfly that August day on the Downs – the most butterflies I had ever seen in a day. Hulme, however, was disappointed; a friend had found thirty-one in a day powered only by bicycle. Because so many emerge at different times of the year, and in different parts of the country, it would be hard to get many more than that.

Our success with the cutest butterfly in Britain left just one to see: the Brown Hairstreak. This was pleasingly symmetrical. Finding the eggs of the Brown Hairstreak outside a freezing, snow-bound Bullingdon Prison in Oxfordshire was the first challenge of the year. Catching sight of the adult butterfly, the last British species to emerge in late summer, would be my final task. And the Brown Hairstreak had a deserved reputation as the hardest butterfly in Britain to see.

The first time I tried to see them I went with Hulme to a hedgerow in a hollow by the affluent small town of Steyning in West Sussex. We walked past the tennis courts and the most immaculate allotments I had ever seen, scented with sweet peas and partitioned off with neat lines of orange-flowering runner beans. At the bottom of a meadow where the north slopes of the South Downs petered out was an overgrown hedge of blackthorn in front of some ash trees. The butterfly laid its eggs on blackthorn and hung around the tops of ash trees which, at low points in the landscape, served as its 'master tree' where the males would sunbathe all day, waiting for the more conscientious females to find them.

Voices raised to remonstrate with badly behaved dogs carried on the wind to where we stood and waited under the blackthorn. The last hint of mauve clung to teasel heads. It was humid but the sun was only hazy at best and it was not bright enough to stir the Brown Hairstreaks into action. We patrolled the hedgerow, looking for females who had just unzipped themselves from their pupae and would be sitting, stupefied, on a low branch, drying their wings.

Two miles east along the Downs a tear in the cloud widened into a long blue opening, but the split stubbornly refused to move overhead. 'They are so lazy and dependent on hot summer conditions,' reflected Hulme, smoking another Silk Cut as we waited, conscientiously putting the butt into a little pouch he carried in his pocket. A bad summer can be good for spotting Brown Hairstreaks because if the sun does come out they are more likely to move than in years when they have a glut of sunbathing opportunities and so stay hidden at the top of ash trees.

The Brown Hairstreak might be a common butterfly if we did not flay the blackthorn in our hedges every year, hacking off the eggs laid in the junction of last year's growth. But then its kamakaze caterpillars also throw themselves on the ground to pupate. Shrews love to sniff out Brown Hairstreak pupae. We waited for an hour and a half but the sun wouldn't come out. When it did, two hours later, we raced back to the rough meadow in Steyning to look again. Plenty of Hedge Browns bumbled through the grass below but no Brown Hairstreaks stirred in the trees. I would have to wait for another sunny day to try again.

On the second Sunday of August I rose at 6 a.m. to drive from Norfolk to West Sussex, again to return to the hedgerow near

Steyning where, on the previous day, Neil Hulme reported he had seen Brown Hairstreaks. He was leading a butterfly walk there at 11 a.m. but I arrived early and went down to the hedgerow by myself. There was an autumnal mist on the drive down, the rough meadow was dewy and the sun was struggling to push back the cloud. The crickets in the grass hummed like electricity pylons in damp weather. Within two minutes of standing below the master ash tree I saw what we had failed to find the previous week: a small, dark butterfly-like creature buzzed around the crown of the tree. It had to be a Brown Hairstreak, the fifty-ninth and final species of the summer. And then, a nagging doubt. I could not just walk away now. I was assuming that this was a Brown Hairstreak site and the behaviour of the butterfly I had seen fitted that of the Brown Hairstreak. But it was not a positive identification. And what if what I saw was not a butterfly at all but a moth? What if I had imagined it, I thought after twenty minutes in which I had not seen anything else stir.

Watching so intently, I became attuned to every pinprick in the landscape, the sway of every blade of grass and the blunder of every bee. The only disturbance were shouts of 'heel' and 'leave it' from distant walkers to their dogs. Looking up at the ash again, I finally saw another, similar butterfly, rooting around in the branches in front of the ash, and a third zipped around its crown again. When I had been there for an hour, a small butterfly dashed down from the ash tree and flew haphazardly just over my head and up to the black-thorn hedgerow beside me. I ran after it in the heavy wet grass. It was bright ginger in colour, but it dashed about so randomly I soon lost sight of it against the ash. Another raced along the hedgerow with it. These things were flying like moths.

At 11 a.m., Hulme parked by Steyning's tennis courts, where a group of butterfly enthusiasts assembled. A few years ago, these gentle Sunday rambles would attract about eight hardy obsessives. Today there were forty-six people. I wondered if this reflected the growing popularity of butterflies or the charisma of Hulme. He had clearly injected a lot of energy into the Sussex branch of Butterfly Conservation. Most of the butterfly watchers were retired couples but there were half a dozen people in their thirties and a couple in their twenties. Half the group were experts with zoom lenses and butterfly binoculars but for a sizeable number this was their first trip to watch butterflies. They were lucky to have Hulme as their guide.

We returned to where I had watched what may have been Brown Hairstreaks. Forty-six pairs of eyes would quickly sort it out. They soon spotted a bird of prey, a hobby, flying overhead. But there were no signs of any Brown Hairstreaks in the hedgerow, just the false alarm of a few Hedge Browns. I plucked at the seed heads of thistles. They felt like the soft underbelly of a rabbit. Hulme explained to the group it was easier to find the eggs of the Brown Hairstreak than the butterfly itself. I could vouch for that, having helped count a hundred eggs outside Bullingdon Prison in Oxfordshire that freezing February.

It was past midday when I saw the flash of a butterfly in another high ash, as did an elderly butterfly spotter. We called Hulme over, but he only picked up a bumble bee. It had gone again. No one in the group took credit for spotting it first, but several people began beckoning everyone over to another spot. About seven metres up, on a branch, perched a small, ginger triangle: here, finally, indisputably, and verified by forty-six pairs of eyes, was a female Brown Hair-streak.

She clung on to an ash twig as the breeze got up, displaying her ginger underside with delicate silver tracing and slivers of bright orange. When the wind died down again, she opened her wings wide, showing off the bright orange patches that only occur on the females, against her livery of immaculate chocolate brown. Her name did her a huge disservice: she was far more beautiful than a mere Brown Hairstreak.

She must have only just emerged from her pupae because her wings were yet to be snagged and torn by the blackthorn. She still sported a dapper little set of bright orange tails. Everyone clustered beneath her to take pictures. Every ten minutes she would get up and rearrange herself on another leaf. I watched her for nearly an hour. Then she buzzed erratically over my head and out into the field in a very similar fashion to the moth-like creatures I had watched on my own that morning. Here was confirmation I had not been wrong earlier, but after a summer of practice I had still spotted Brown Hairstreaks without being able to confirm that I had. So I was relieved that the final, fifty-ninth sighting had, even-tually, proved conclusive and not, as I had feared, an uncertain anti-climax.

I drove home feeling strangely drained. I had seen all fifty-nine species of British butterfly in one summer: the first on 15 March and the last on 9 August. It was not a spectacular achievement but it did feel like running a tough marathon. Blessed by the first benign summer for three years, it proved easier to see the butterflies than I imagined but far harder to undertake the journey.

I had driven far too many miles, taken trains, planes, buses, taxis and my own two feet. I had spent more time getting to places than staying in them. I had been soaked, stung, bitten, frozen, sunburned and approached by strangers looking for sex. I had been happy, delirious, lonely, hungover, joyous, irritated, inspired, frustrated, anxious, sad, tense, meditative, calm and worshipful. I was grateful for the time I had borrowed from fascinating people, the information I gleaned from interesting books and the facts I learned from both about our butterflies and their endless capacity to surprise us. Juggling a full-time job and this butterfly mission, I had spent too much money on diesel and too much time in my car. I had not spent enough time with my friends and I had lost my girlfriend.

I had wasted more hours in traffic than savoured in communion with nature. But every time I had got there, and gave myself up to it, the pursuit of butterflies had placed me in the quiet, calm and resolute corners of our countryside, in a state of being where the petty material worries and emotional traumas of the everyday dissolved into the sun and the trees and the dew. Searching for butterflies had given me the gift of becoming, for a moment, here and there at least, a small, harmonious part of the natural world.

Nabokov's words kept coming back to me, the perfect description of the transcendent power of butterflies and what they can do to us: 'And the highest enjoyment of timelessness – in a landscape selected at random – is when I stand among rare butterflies and their food plants. This is ecstasy, and behind the ecstasy is something else, which is hard to explain. It is like a momentary vacuum into which rushes all that I love. A sense of oneness with sun and stone. A thrill of gratitude to whom it may concern – to the contrapuntal genius of human fate or to tender ghosts humoring a lucky mortal.'

56. Scotch Argus, Smardale Gill, Cumbria, 2 August
57. Adonis Blue, Mill Hill, West Sussex, 5 August
58. Silver-spotted Skipper, Newtimber Hill, West Sussex, 5 August
59. Brown Hairstreak, Steyning, West Sussex, 9 August

AUTUMN

18

The Queen of Spain

Freed from the intense cocoon of hunting for fifty-nine butter-flies, August slipped into September before I even noticed and butterflies began passing out of my life. I went for a walk on the North Downs and several dynamic Clouded Yellows crossed my path and three brilliant blues – Common, Chalkhill and Adonis – clustered companionably on a dog turd. My binoculars saw service again from my window in north London when I picked up a flash of brown against the ash tree. Could it be an unprecedented urban sighting of a Brown Hairstreak? No, it was a Speckled Wood. In Brighton, I saw half a dozen Clouded Yellows on the beach on a pre-posterously sunny October day. In Norwich, as 24,000 pairs of eyes followed the bounce of the ball on the football pitch at Carrow Road, a movement against the stadium roof caught my eye: a Small Tortoiseshell tacked into the stand, searching for a warm dry place to spend the winter. Towards the end of November, while writing this, there was a beat of wings at the window. It was grey and cold outside and a Red Admiral was pacing along the street, checking windows and doors like a dogged-but-unsuccessful burglar, looking for a way in, and out of the cold.

I glimpsed a butterfly tattoo on the pale back of a young woman and an advert on the television that deployed butterflies in a rural idyll to sell chips, of all things. But as summer receded and normal life beyond butterfly hunting reasserted itself, each day, and then each week, was punctuated by fewer and fewer butterflies.

At the end of August, I flew to Greenland to write about climate change for work. Painted Ladies had reached Iceland during their great migration earlier that summer and I hoped to record one in the Arctic Circle. For all the talk of melting ice, however, Greenland was chilly and bereft of butterflies. I was away for a week and did not appreciate what I had been missing until I touched down at Heathrow, took the Piccadilly Line to Manor House and emerged into a grimy, billowy afternoon in London. I looked up and, like a flake of sky cut loose, a Large White crossed the road ahead of me. I watched it zigzagging high over a building site and I tasted its freedom and the stale city breeze in its wings. It was, weirdly, one of the most elevated butterfly experiences of the summer. It took me completely out of myself.

It is easy to visualise a world without butterflies. Every year, with the arrival of autumn, butterflies depart as naturally as deep green leaves and grass that is dry enough to sit on. It is less easy to imagine how exactly we are diminished without them.

The disappearances during early autumn can be a warning to us. This warm season is like the cities we now inhabit: a place where every sighting of a butterfly is an event and the wealth of lepidopteral riches our forebears experienced is a swiftly fading collective memory. We are not merely losing butterflies. Many scientists who study the environment fear we are on the brink of triggering a sixth mass-extinction event. The first five – the dinosaurs and all that – were natural. The sixth will be caused by industrialisation, globalisation, the huge growth in human population, the ongoing destruction of the rainforests, the acidification of the oceans and runaway climate change. From blue whales to plankton, millions of species are threatened, many of which we do not yet know exist.

The fifty-nine butterfly species of Britain look pretty insignificant placed next to this. They may be the least of our worries: pretty, and pretty useless compared with bees or even dung beetles. We have served our butterflies well in recent decades. With our natural bias towards caring for beautiful creatures, they have garnered a good portion of our conservation efforts: thanks to them, we have not lost a species of British butterfly since 1979 and the one we let slip, the Large Blue, was successfully reintroduced. Protected from the worst ravages of climate change by our temperate island weather and guarded by sophisticated, relatively well-funded conservation projects, the fifty-nine butterflies of Britain may be among the last insect species we need worry about. Nevertheless, despite this effort, three-quarters of our native butterflies are declining and more than half are classified as threatened species – a higher proportion than birds or plants.

At the start of the year, I was staggered by the Victorian accounts of great swarms of butterflies in our skies: the snow storms of whites that blotted out the sun, the puffs of Clouded Yellows mistaken for poison gas and the delight of the Aurelians who skimmed hundreds of Purple Hairstreaks from the trees. Such scenes are so exotic today that they read as if ripped from the pages of a fantasy novel. Even in recent decades, we have a sense of loss. Ask around, and we all agree there are fewer butterflies now compared with our memories of childhood. However, in this one summer chasing butterflies, I encountered not one but two swarms: 120,000 Painted Ladies in a field on the South Downs and 1300 of one of the most endangered butterflies in Britain, the Heath Fritillary, in a wood in Kent. As a boy, for summer after summer, I tried and failed to find a Purple Emperor and yet in this butterfly year I saw fifty-seven in one day in an ordinary wood in Northamptonshire.

Could this brilliant summer mark the dawn of a new golden age of butterflies? My experiences reflected what was a good year for most of our butterfly species after a disastrous run of dire summers (2008 had been the worst year for butterflies since 1981). While Heath Fritillaries swarmed, another of our most endangered butterflies, the Duke of Burgundy, surprised everyone by turning up as an adult butterfly for a second generation in July and August on Rodborough Common, where I had seen it in May. This was only the third time since 1893 that the Duke emerged anywhere in the UK for a second generation. This success was partly attributed to global warming: because the first generation emerged earlier in the spring, its caterpillars could grow fast enough to produce a second generation later in the year, as it does in warmer parts of

Europe. An unusually large second generation of the Small Pearl-bordered Fritillary also emerged in August, the graceful White Admiral made a surprise reappearance for a second summer generation in the south-east, while a number of species, including the rare Silver-spotted Skipper and the common Small Skipper, were found to have expanded into new locations. Second generations, late in the summer, however, are often bad news for butterflies because their eggs and caterpillars do not have time to develop before the onset of winter. And for many species, this summer of apparent abundance was an upward blip on a relentlessly downward trend. For our rarest butterflies, such as the High Brown Fritillary, the partial recovery brought about by one good summer still left their population far smaller than it had been just ten years before.

The clouds of butterflies I saw were great, historic exceptions. My experiences actually reflected what everyone instinctively suspects: most of us no longer find our summer days routinely animated by dozens, let alone swarms, of butterflies. When I was not specifically looking for butterflies, I hardly saw any. When I was seeking them out, far more often than the times I saw swarms or scores were the occasions when I found only single butterflies. Visiting reserves well known for good populations of particular species, I only ever saw one Black Hairstreak, one Swallowtail, one Silver-studded Blue, and less than half a dozen Northern Brown Arguses, White-letter Hairstreaks, Purple Hairstreaks, Large Heaths, Mountain Ringlets, Small Blues, Wood Whites, Pearl-bordered Fritillaries and Small Pearl-bordered Fritillaries. What the Victorian lepidopterist Edward Newman said of rare migrants now rings true for most of our butterflies: angels' visits are few and far between.

September sped away, as it always did. Time goes quicker when the nights are closing in; every day brings fewer minutes of light than the previous one. I was beginning to close the drawer on my reignited passion for butterflies, and put them out of my mind for winter, when I heard of a late invasion of Clouded Yellows along the south coast. The weather had been still, calm and fine, and hundreds of a new generation had hatched, joining those still crossing the Channel. When I called Neil Hulme, the energetic chairman of Sussex Butterfly Conservation who had helped me see the late-summer butterflies like the Silver-spotted Skipper and the Brown Hairstreak, he mentioned an even more tantalising prospect than hundreds of Clouded Yellows: there were rumours of a Queen of Spain Fritillary on the wing in West Sussex.

To consider looking for a sixtieth British species of the summer was greedy. For that potential sixtieth sighting to be a Queen of Spain Fritillary was the stuff of fantasy. To see one of these rare migrants really was to witness an angel's visit. This butterfly was rarer than the most elusive of my fantasies, the Camberwell Beauty. Over the past three centuries, there have been barely 500 sightings of the Queen of Spain Fritillary in Britain, according to historical records. It is a European fritillary first found in 1710 and years passed without a single sighting of it. A run of warm summers in the 1940s saw a flurry of seventy-five recorded, but over the next four decades barely a handful were found in our countryside. Weirdly, in the mid-1990s, it bred for a couple of summers at Minsmere nature reserve on the Suffolk coast and then vanished again, just as inexplicably.

I had my fifty-nine and I thought nothing more of it. One Friday afternoon in October, however, Hulme emailed with surprising information: he had organised a last-minute trip to a wood on the edge of Chichester where an immigrant female Queen of Spain Fritillary had apparently bred. One had been spotted here in July and, more than two months later, a dog-walker had chanced upon half a dozen of the butterflies over a few fine days, by a field of maize.

I was stuck in Cheltenham for work. I could have cancelled my plans, risen at the crack of dawn, spent a fortune on a new train ticket and made my way to Chichester, but I did not. I had seen my fifty-nine and the weather forecast was not good. Then Saturday dawned dazzling and I sat in a park in Cheltenham, bitterly regretting not going the extra mile to see the Queen of Spain Fritillary. I regretted it even more when I texted Hulme. 'Only two left now!' he texted back. 'Out celebrating!' Would there still be two of the butterflies flying on Sunday?

I was surprised by the urgent tug of desire inside me to go to Chichester. I cancelled my Sunday plans and set out in the car on my own. It was another interminable stop-start-stop affair for an hour and a half. Roadworks, dozy Sunday drivers, buses pulling out, cyclists pulling in, aggressive vans, taxis, lane closures, speed cameras and a twenty-minute poke-shunt-shove-inch-jerk at the back end of a bus. Finally I was slungshot onto the A3 and away, shaking off the last tendrils of the capital like autumn cobwebs.

As the traffic melted away, so too did the sunshine. By Guildford, a heavy mizzle had set in. The traffic, the weather and the route into Surrey took me straight back to that grotty day in August when I had sought out the Wood White. All the conditions were the same and yet everything had changed. I was not burned out or frustrated or anxious and I did not mind the traffic. I wondered if I had truly learned the state of acceptance inside or whether it was because everything had really changed outside. It was a new season, I had seen all fifty-nine species and, completely unexpectedly, I was back with Lisa again. I did not know whether this was a happy ending but I appreciated such gifts: another chance, the sunshine of late autumn and one last expedition of the year to hunt for the Queen of Spain Fritillary.

Just where the suburbs of Chichester began, I turned right into a small lane and flicked off my headlights as I came to a halt in the muddy gloom under the trees by Brandy Hole Copse, fourteen acres of sweet chestnut coppice over the haphazard hillocks of some Iron Age earthworks. Hulme had not told me precisely where he had seen the two butterflies the day before. He seemed to want to keep that information to himself, and was too busy to join me. I had the grid reference he gave out for his guided walk I had missed the previous day and I was perfectly content on my own. Would the Queen of Spains have died overnight? They could not have found much sun or nectar to keep them going.

Under heavy grey skies, I walked slowly into the woodland and sniffed the sour smell of damp, dead chestnut leaves. It had been two months since my last butterfly trip. The landscape had moved from summer to autumn. Everything had changed and yet, rather like a person you had not seen for decades, nothing was wholly different. There were still traces of summer in the hardness of the ground and the stubborn green of old oak leaves. The stillness of a wood in autumn is, however, quite unlike the stillness of summer. The deathly quiet of midsummer was over; birds had begun to sing again and seemed busy preparing for winter. The rain, when it came, was soft. Most obviously of all, leaves were turning yellow, orange and red, and there were no butterflies.

I stopped in a clearing. Underfoot were matt brown acorns and spiny balls of sweet chestnuts, as prickly as hedgehogs. I started at the beat of a butterfly wing in my peripheral vision. It was a leaf, slowly twirling to the ground. In spring I had mistaken floating blossom for butterflies. Now it was falling leaves.

I ran my fingers over a yellow puffball pushing up through the green-and-red tartan of autumnal bramble leaves. I picked at one last blackberry but the Devil is said to spit on them when September ends. The berry tasted of rainwater. A square of wood had been nailed to a tree stump, under a small beech, to make a seat. I sat there and waited. A beech leaf curled in supplication at my feet. This looked, to me, like the best spot for a Queen of Spain Fritillary. Not that I knew anything about their behaviour. It just seemed the most promising place for any butterfly.

It was fifteen minutes before I saw an insect of any description: a fly, busying its way around the canopy of an oak. In the next hour, I spotted a bee, a crow, a pigeon and a great tit, but the woods were empty of butterflies. There was no nectar anywhere. By the edge of Brandy Hole Copse was a triangular field of thistles. This must have been popular with the Painted Ladies a month ago. Where the thistle heads had been as soft as rabbits' ears in August, they now hung stiff and tatty after a good autumnal soaking. A blackbird went pink-pink-pink in the hedge as if night might be falling, even though it was only 2 p.m.

The naturalist Frohawk studied the Queen of Spain in captivity, rearing a hundred eggs to the pupal stage. Of these, eighty died before the butterflies emerged in late September. 'There is no doubt that the late autumn English climate is quite unsuited for the existence of this species,' he concluded. In Sussex, the Queen of Spains had disappeared, and no wonder. It was mid-October and it was starting to rain. I sat some more and then gave up. It was a long slow drive home. I could not expect the butterfly year to end with a flourish; the natural order of things, autumn itself, was a melancholy anti-climax.

On Monday I did something I had never done before: I pulled a sickie. Waking with a jolt at 7.30 a.m., the brightness in the room told of a cloudless pale-blue sky beyond my drawn curtains. I checked the weather forecast on my laptop in bed. A round yellow sun hung over Sussex all day. I picked up the phone and told a white lie. An unprecedented sixtieth butterfly of the summer was more important than work, I reasoned with myself. I would make it up to my bosses.

Neil Hulme had been very generous to me but he was keeping a tight rein over this butterfly. His apparent possessiveness was actually his concern that rogue butterfly collectors – 'netsmen', he called them – might hear about the sighting and swoop on it, especially if it was breeding. So while he agreed to meet me that afternoon, he revealed that the butterfly had not actually been seen at the grid reference he had previously given out for Brandy Hole Copse, near Chichester. Where I had searched the previous day, in the grey, had not been the right spot. I had wasted my time trying to see it alone. I had to accept I was in Hulme's hands. He obviously felt responsible for this rare and precious thing, and I must do what he said.

He was busy and said we should meet at 3 p.m. With the autumn days cooling early, I was worried this would be too late. I was driving along the lanes of Sussex at 2 p.m. when he called. I broke the law and answered my phone. He was at Brandy Hole Copse and was watching a Queen of Spain at that very moment.

'Your sixtieth species is guaranteed,' he hollered with characteristic enthusiasm. I was not so sure. It was a migratory butterfly. It could fly off.

'Don't let it get away,' I said.

'I'll keep the dragonflies at bay,' laughed Hulme.

Oh, no. Another hazard I had not thought of. A dragonfly likes nothing better than feasting on a butterfly. I had convinced myself I was pretty relaxed about a bonus sixtieth species. Now I was getting sucked into caring again. I desperately wanted to see this butterfly. I put my foot down on the accelerator.

When I got to Brandy Hole Copse, it was still a wonderfully lucid autumn day. I phoned Hulme. He did not answer. I grabbed my bag and camera from the boot and then, thankfully, he called me back. He was watching a Queen of Spain, he said, and he was in the triangular field just beyond the sweet chestnut coppice. So I had walked through the right spot on the previous day after all. I knew exactly where to go. I ran.

In the scruffy field, Hulme and three other members of Butterfly

Conservation were warily circling a phantom, invisible from a distance. I nearly tripped on low brambles, shook Hulme's hand, and there glided an elegant medium-sized fritillary. It flew like a Heath Fritillary, but was larger and stronger, with a more definite shape. This slightly faded, male Queen of Spain Fritillary had very distinctive blunt, squared off hindwings and was very obliging, settling on the low brambles and basking in the autumn sunshine with its wings stretched wide. When I lay on the ground and peered up at the underside of its wings, I could see they were decorated with large, irregular silver panels, which distinguished it from other, more ordinary British fritillaries. A kestrel arrowed overhead, a female pheasant flapped up with a great fuss and the sun was like a warm hand on the back of my jeans.

'This is THE season,' sighed Hulme.

Uncharitably, I felt a twinge of suspicion. My arrival at this remarkable scene felt a bit like those gullible collectors of old, who would receive a tip-off from a scurrilous butterfly dealer about a rare sighting and race to a wood, where the dealer had just released a butterfly he had bred in his greenhouse. Finding this Queen of Spain Fritillary so easily, in such an incongruous spot, without any flowers nearby, was almost too neat. Unlike the collectors of old, I was not paying anyone. But was a modern-day breeder playing God and trying to establish this butterfly in Britain? There are a small number of obsessives who release captive bred butterflies in strange spots. Imagine the ego rush of going to a wood and seeing 'your' butterfly, which you put there, breeding happily the next summer. I had seen this already once this year, on Warham Camp, an Iron Age fort near my home in Norfolk. Miraculously, on this tiny patch of chalk grassland, Chalkhill Blues had been found for the second successive summer. It was sixty miles from their nearest site, an island in seas of barley, so the butterfly must have been introduced by a breeder. Butterfly Conservation disapproved of such meddling, unless it was undertaken in a planned and monitored way, like the reintroduction of the Large Blue. Unauthorised reintroductions play havoc with organised conservation efforts and most end in failure.

'Have you just put the Queen of Spain here for me?' I laughingly asked Hulme.

'I'm more prepared to believe they are from Mars than they are captive bred,' replied Hulme. He suddenly sounded fierce. 'Anybody who doubts it is simply jealous because they didn't see it.'

He explained why he believed this Queen of Spain was the natural-born offspring of an immigrant female sighted in Brandy Hole Copse in July. Hulme said that after arriving on our shores, these immigrant butterflies would tend to follow rivers inland. In this case, a mated female – departing from a colony in Normandy to expand the range of her species – would have followed the fingers of Chichester harbour inland. We were at the top of one of those fingers.

If these Queen of Spains were captive releases, they would have all looked the same age. But rather than seeing a few butterflies all at once, people had seen butterflies of different ages over a period of several weeks. The staggered emergence of these butterflies suggested they were hatching out, one by one, in a natural way, depending on how quickly the caterpillars had developed. The timing perfectly fitted the life cycle of eggs laid by the Queen of Spain spotted in July.

Butterflies bred in captivity tended to be dumped in an inappropriate environment near no suitable food plant. What really clinched this case was when Hulme and his colleagues at Butterfly Conservation found wild pansies on the edge of the adjacent maize field. Wild pansy and field pansy are what Queen of Spain caterpillars like to eat most of all. 'That's the missing piece of the puzzle,' Hulme concluded with a flourish. It was a convincing case. Queen of Spain Fritillaries had bred in Britain. This was sensational. I stood in the sunshine and tried to take it all in.

It has long puzzled lepidopterists why this graceful, powerful migrant has failed to establish itself in this country when there were large colonies on sand dunes just the other side of the Channel, in Holland and further north into Scandinavia, as well as across most of Europe. Now, as our summers warm up, this was one contender to become our sixtieth resident species. 'It is a butterfly which is definitely coming this way,' said Hulme. 'Within the next two decades they will become residents in the UK if certain climatic trends continue. This is one species, quite possibly the first one, which will set up home here.'

What does the future hold for butterflies in Britain? Climate change, in theory, should help sunshine-loving insects. The vast majority of our butterflies are found in southern England. From the Adonis Blue to the Lulworth Skipper, many of our fifty-nine species are living at the northernmost limit of their natural range. As the world warms, they should colonise new habitat further north. Milder winters will enable more butterflies to live in Britain all year round. The Red Admiral is one beneficiary already: it survives winters in the south where it once perished.

For many of our native butterflies, however, climate change will be their biggest challenge yet. When I met Jeremy Thomas, the saviour of the Large Blue, in Oxford, he chose his words with characteristic scientific care. 'Climate change is one of the biggest disasters facing everyone. Life for the Large Blue has got a little bit easier because it's got a little bit warmer. Because about 80 per cent of British butterflies are at the northern edge of their range, and butterflies are confined to the extreme south, for the next decade or two or three we should be seeing climate change helping butterfly populations in Britain and to some extent mitigating the harmful effects of habitat losses,' he said. But, Thomas concluded abruptly, if the world warms beyond 2–3°C and 'the fundamental ecosystems' crack up then 'it all goes pear-shaped' for butterflies – and everything else.

As every lepidopterist points out, the impact of climate change will be complex. Our northern species, such as the Mountain Ringlet and the Scotch Argus, will be imperilled by a warming world. Many other butterflies will be affected in ways we have not yet predicted. Erratic weather and sudden storms may destroy newly hatched butterflies like the fragment of a Heath Fritillary I found battered by the rain on Exmoor. Wetter summers, or droughts, may kill caterpillars or stop adults breeding and laying eggs.

Most dangerously of all, climate change may herald milder conditions that allow new pests, predators and diseases to infiltrate the countryside and attack our butterflies, like *Sturmia bella*, the parasitic fly first recorded in Britain in 1998 that is now munching its way through the chrysalises of our Small Tortoiseshells. Tom Brereton, one of a number of young scientists working for Butterfly Conservation, is in charge of monitoring population numbers and crunching all the data received from volunteer butterfly recorders like my dad.

'Whichever way you look at it, it's linked back to the climate,' he explained. Climate change makes their conservation far more complicated. Invasive weeds in particular have multiplied through milder winters and crowd out butterfly food plants. Grass, brambles and bracken – with which many rare fritillaries have a delicate relationship – are sprouting back more vigorously than in the past. Even where coppiced, woods are growing more dense and tangled. Grassland, moorland and woodland will need different types of grazing or clearing more regularly. Brereton believes that much of our current conservation management will not work in the future. 'With climate change, species are changing their habitats and their requirements are changing as well. It can be fatal to manage for what a butterfly needed twenty years ago. We need to keep on the ball with understanding what species need because their requirements are changing as the earth warms up.'

Our rare butterflies may have been successfully preserved on tiny nature reserves but add a couple of degrees and these reserves are no longer suitable. In a warmer world, on our fragmented isles, the nearest good habitat may be fifty miles away. Many of our smallest butterflies are surprisingly robust flyers but even when energised by fine weather most will struggle to colonise new areas when they live on pockets of land surrounded by conifers or motorways or deserts of barley. The Black Hairstreak's stubborn refusal to move beyond its small slice of central England is just one example of how butterflies can fail to find suitable new habitat even when it is just around the corner. 'If you had an intact countryside, butterflies should be going through the roof, but the species can't move through the countryside like they once would have done,' explained Brereton.

As it gets warmer, the Scotch Arguses of Arnside Knott in Cumbria will struggle to find a cooler habitat; they already live in splendid isolation forty miles from the nearest colony and hundreds of miles from decent expanses of suitable countryside in Scotland. Then there is the Swallowtail, our biggest butterfly, stuck on the Norfolk Broads. It is widely expected that the freshwater lakes of the Broads will become saltmarsh and even open sea within a hundred years, as sea levels rise. The Swallowtail and its food plant will die out unless we move it to similar marshy habitats many miles inland. These places are not only miles from its current confinement; they do not yet exist. If we want our grandchildren to see Swallowtails in the wild, we will have to meticulously create artificial reserves on a large enough scale to allow for the survival of the milk parsley upon which this notoriously picky species depends.

Conservation can be a depressing business, and Matthew Oates likes to encourage people with his motto: never underestimate a butterfly. Some appear to be able to adapt quickly: the Duke of Burgundy moved from being a woodland butterfly to a pre-dominantly grassland one in less than fifty generations during the twentieth century. 'Butterflies are continuously changing their habits and trying to adapt to new situations imposed upon them because of changes in landscape and climate. The problem is the pace of change plus the fragmentation of habitat,' he said. Other lepidopterists are less positive about the capacity of butterflies to adapt; some apparent adaptations, suggests Martin Warren, are simply a drastic decline in a butterfly in a certain habitat alongside that species being belatedly discovered clinging on in a previously overlooked landscape.

Oates is intrigued by the challenge of saving the Swallowtail, which has evolved into a unique subspecies, *britannicus*, during its confinement in Britain. Oates could see it being moved from the Norfolk Broads to an expanded, recreated wetland reserve in the Cambridgeshire Fens, where it was driven to extinction less than a century ago. But even this solution could be complicated by climate change. 'There is also the possibility of *gorganus*, the European subspecies of the Swallowtail, colonising from the Continent. You could be faffing around trying to save *britannicus*, which breeds on a single rather neurotic wetland plant, and this other subspecies comes in and breeds on all kinds of plants in Kent and then the two subspecies might breed and hybridise themselves out.' Oates grinned, savouring the irony of it. 'That really would be superb.'

The difference between *britannicus* and *gorganus* may be reduced, in physical terms, to the size of its thorax and wings. For us, however, the distinctiveness of *britannicus* is more emotional and more profound. If we allowed climate change to erase the Swallowtail from the Norfolk Broads, we would lose far more than a skinny-bodied subspecies: we would lose a living link to our biological history, a butterfly that was part of Darwin's life, and an insect that offers us something unique and special. As Oates pointed out, it is hard to beat the experience of watching a Swallowtail on milk parsley lording it over the insects, birds and butterfly watchers of Hickling Broad or Catfield Fen. 'All that will go. All the aesthetics of the Broadland experience in June would be lost,' said Oates, 'and you would instead see a big European Swallowtail batting about diffusely on brownfield wastelands in the south of England.'

In our disenchanted world, we may no longer believe butterflies are our souls but even the least romantic person would see them as harbingers of sunshine and summer days. As John Masefield wrote: 'Like floating flowers, Came butterflies, the souls of summer hours.'

As our summers change, so too will our butterflies.

The trees glowed gold around Brandy Hole Copse and we stood and watched the last Queen of Spain Fritillary of the year. I felt sorry for this one, left on its own, born into an unsuitably chilly foreign land just as the nights grew colder.

And then we saw another golden butterfly, flying high and then swooping in lower. We gave chase, stumbling across the field. It settled and Hulme quickly identified it as a female Queen of Spain. This insect was larger than the male we had been watching. It had the immaculate look of a freshly emerged specimen, as shiny as a conker, with pristine white borders and a tinge of green spreading out from its furry body. While territorial males stay in one spot, females roam. This one took off into the oak trees and gave us the slip. Twenty minutes later, it reappeared. The faded male we had been watching all afternoon flew up to chase away this rival. Oh, it then seemed to say, discovering it was not a rival but a female. How did they know? Did they smell each other? Some butterfly species are exceedingly well studied but many are not. There are so many butterfly mysteries still to discover.

Time was short. They dived down together and shuffled about in the dead grass. A short struggle ended when the male reversed his abdomen into the female, who crouched still and then shifted around a bit. We were now watching something that no one had ever seen in the wild in Britain before: two Queen of Spains mating. 'We mustn't get too close,' said Hulme, his eyes widening boyishly. 'We literally could stop the future population in its tracks if we break the pairing. This is British butterfly history unfolding before our very eyes.'

It seemed a miracle that these two insects had met in a random, foreign field, in the middle of October. The male, I murmured out loud, was probably in despair: cold, and alone, he must have given up hope of ever finding a female. 'That's the thing I love about butterflies,' remarked Hulme. 'They never give up.'

A plane turned high overhead, moaning in the autumn silence. After twenty-five minutes, the butterflies broke apart and the male staggered off. The female sat there, resting, allowing us to lean in and admire her. As she lay flat out, we could see tiny traces of spilt male sperm on her body, glistening in the afternoon light. If she survived the night, she would lay her eggs the next day. This was not merely a perfect symbol of how the changing climate will irrevocably alter the butterfly life in our countryside, for better as well as for worse: it was not beyond the bounds of possibility that this single butterfly, my sixtieth species of the summer, could be the first generation of a new resident species, the first in a vanguard of

Continental butterflies tempted by warmer summers and milder winters to try their luck across the Channel.

As an evening chill sank onto the meadow, the female Queen of Spain flew up and settled at the very top of a sweet chestnut to catch the final fingers of the setting sun. With binoculars, I could just, just, just pick out the triangle of the roosting butterfly against the golden leaves and the sky. As the sun sank beyond our horizon, its silver pearls sparkled for a final moment in what seemed like the last sunlight of the year.

THE SIXTY BUTTERFLIES OF 2009
(IN CHRONOLOGICAL ORDER)

1. Small Tortoiseshell, Sheringham, Norfolk, 15 March
2. Brimstone, Sheringham, Norfolk, 15 March
3. Comma, Ashburton, Devon, 22 March
4. Peacock, South Pool, Devon, 22 March
5. Large White, Stoke Newington, London, 5 April
6. Holly Blue, Fulham, London, 18 April
7. Small White, Ham Lands, London, 18 April
8. Orange Tip, Ham Lands, London, 18 April
9. Speckled Wood, Ham Lands, London, 18 April
10. Green-veined White, Ham Lands, London, 18 April
11. Grizzled Skipper, Waterford Heath, Hertfordshire, 20 April
12. Red Admiral, Waterford Heath, Hertfordshire, 20 April
13. Green Hairstreak, Rodborough Common, Gloucestershire, 23 April
14. Small Heath, Rodborough Common, Gloucestershire, 23 April
15. The Duke of Burgundy, Rodborough Common, Gloucestershire, 23 April
16. The Dingy Skipper, Rodborough Common, Gloucestershire, 23 April

17. Pearl-bordered Fritillary, Aish Tor, Dartmoor, Devon, 8 May
18. Small Copper, Aish Tor, Dartmoor, Devon, 8 May
19. Wall Brown, Start Point, Devon, 9 May
20. Small Pearl-bordered Fritillary, Start Point, Devon, 9 May
21. Common Blue, Start Point, Devon, 9 May
22. Painted Lady, Start Point, Devon, 9 May
23. The Glanville Fritillary, Brook Bay, Isle of Wight, 31 May
24. Réal's Wood White, Craigavon Lakes, Northern Ireland, 1 June
25. The Marsh Fritillary, Murlough Dunes, Northern Ireland, 2 June
26. Chequered Skipper, Glasdrum Wood, Scotland, 3 June
27. Large Skipper, Arnside Knott, 5 June
28. Marbled White, Rodborough Common, Gloucestershire, 5 June
29. Small Blue, Rodborough Common, Gloucestershire, 5 June
30. Dark Green Fritillary, Aish Tor, Devon, 6 June
31. High Brown Fritillary, Aish Tor, Devon, 6 June
32. Heath Fritillary, Halse Combe, Exmoor, Somerset, 8 June
33. Meadow Brown, Wells-next-the-Sea, Norfolk, 10 June
34. Swallowtail, Hickling Broad, Norfolk, 13 June
35. Large Blue, Green Down, Somerset, 16 June
36. Black Hairstreak, Whitecross Green Wood, Oxfordshire, 20 June
37. Ringlet, Whitecross Green Wood, Oxfordshire, 20 June
38. White-letter Hairstreak, Ponders End, London, 22 June
39. Clouded Yellow, Marsham Heath, Norfolk, 4 July
40. Small Skipper, Kelling Heath, Norfolk, 4 July
41. Essex Skipper, Kelling Heath, Norfolk, 4 July
42. Hedge Brown, Kelling Heath, Norfolk, 4 July
43. Grayling, Kelling Heath, Norfolk, 4 July
44. White Admiral, Kelling Heath, Norfolk, 4 July
45. Silver-studded Blue, Kelling Heath, Norfolk, 4 July
46. Purple Emperor, Fermyn Woods, Northamptonshire, 5 July
47. Purple Hairstreak, Fermyn Woods, Northamptonshire, 5 July
48. Mountain Ringlet, Grey Knotts, Cumbria, 6 July
49. Large Heath, Meathop Moss, Cumbria, 6 July

50. Northern Brown Argus, Yewbarrow, Cumbria, 7 July
51. Silver-washed Fritillary, Yewbarrow, Cumbria, 7 July
52. Chalkhill Blue, Therfield Heath, Hertfordshire, 21 July
53. Lulworth Skipper, Lulworth Cove, Dorset, 24 July
54. Brown Argus, Tugley Wood, Surrey, 1 August
55. Wood White, Tugley Wood, Surrey, 1 August
56. Scotch Argus, Smardale Gill, Cumbria, 2 August
57. Adonis Blue, Mill Hill, West Sussex, 5 August
58. Silver-spotted Skipper, Newtimber Hill, West Sussex, 5 August
59. Brown Hairstreak, Steyning, West Sussex, 9 August
60. The Queen of Spain Fritillary, Brandy Hole Copse, Chichester, West Sussex, 12 October

BUTTERFLY FAMILIES

There are often changes in how taxonomists classify butterflies but British species are usually placed in the following groups:

Hesperiidae
With their chunky bodies and small wings, the Skippers tend to resemble and are closely related to moths: Chequered Skipper (*Carterocephalus palaemon*), Small Skipper (*Thymelicus sylvestris*), Essex Skipper (*Thymelicus lineola*), Lulworth Skipper (*Thymelicus acteon*), Silver-spotted Skipper (*Hesperia comma*), Large Skipper (*Ochlodes faunus*), Dingy Skipper (*Erynnis tages*) and Grizzled Skipper (*Pyrgus malvae*).

Papilionidae
Often spectacular butterflies with distinctive tails, Britain's sole representative is the Swallowtail (*Papilio machaon*).

Pieridae
The Whites actually include yellow butterflies such as the Brimstone and the Clouded Yellow: Wood White (*Leptidea sinapis*), Réal's Wood White (*Leptidea*

reali), Clouded Yellow (*Colias croceus*), Brimstone (*Gonepteryx rhamni*), Large White (*Pieris brassicae*), Small White (*Pieris rapae*), Green-veined White (*Pieris napi*) and Orange-tip (*Anthocharis cardamines*).

Lycaenidae
A large family of butterflies found all over the world, these blues, hairstreaks and coppers tend to be small and lively: Green Hairstreak (*Callophrys rubi*), Brown Hairstreak (*Thecla betulae*), Purple Hairstreak (*Neozephyrus quercus*), White-letter Hairstreak (*Satyrium w-album*), Black Hairstreak (*Satyrium pruni*), Small Copper (*Lycaena phlaeas*), Small Blue (*Cupido minimus*), Silver-studded Blue (*Plebeius argus*), Brown Argus (*Aricia agestis*), Northern Brown Argus (*Aricia artaxerxes*), Common Blue (*Polyommatus icarus*), Chalkhill Blue (*Lysandra coridon*), Adonis Blue (*Lysandra bellargus*), Holly Blue (*Celastrina argiolus*) and Large Blue (*Maculinea arion*).

Nymphalidae
There are more than 6,000 members of this butterfly family around the world. These striking butterflies include our colourful garden-loving Peacocks, Red Admirals and Small Tortoiseshells. The Fritillaries are also part of this family, which is distinguished by its members having just two pairs of active legs. The third pair are small arm-like things that are used for tasting food. The Nymphalidae in Britain include the Satyrinae (see p. 343) and the following butterflies: White Admiral (*Limenitis camilla*), Purple Emperor (*Apatura iris*), Red Admiral (*Vanessa atalanta*), Painted Lady (*Cynthia cardui*), Small Tortoiseshell (*Aglais urticae*), Peacock (*Inachis io*), Comma (*Polygonia c-album*), Small Pearl-bordered Fritillary (*Boloria selene*), Pearl-bordered Fritillary (*Boloria euphrosyne*), Queen of Spain Fritillary (*Issoria lathonia*), High Brown Fritillary (*Argynnis adippe*), Dark Green Fritillary (*Argynnis aglaja*), Silver-washed Fritillary (*Argynnis paphia*), Marsh Fritillary (*Euphydryas aurinia*), Glanville Fritillary (*Melitaea cinxia*) and Heath Fritillary (*Melitaea athalia*).

Satyrinae

A subfamily of Nymphalidae, these are the Browns, except for the Marbled White – a Brown which is white! The Satyrinae in Britain are: Speckled Wood (*Pararge aegeria*), Wall Brown (*Lasiommata megera*), Mountain Ringlet (*Erebia epiphron*), Scotch Argus (*Erebia aethiops*), Marbled White (*Melanargia galathea*), Grayling (*Hipparchia semele*), Gatekeeper (*Pyronia tithonus*), Meadow Brown (*Maniola jurtina*), Small Heath (*Coenonympha pamphilus*), Large Heath (*Coenonympha tullia*) and Ringlet (*Aphantopus hyperantus*).

Riodinidae

These mostly tropical butterflies are also known as the metalmarks. Taxonomists debate this endlessly but Britain is sometimes said to have just one member – the Duke of Burgundy (*Hamearis lucina*), which is also regularly placed in other butterfly families as well.

WATCHING BUTTERFLIES: HOW AND
WHERE TO FIND THEM

If you want to watch butterflies, I heartily recommend you join Butterfly Conservation (www.butterfly-conservation.org), a fantastic and friendly charity. There are local branches all around the country which organise days out and butterfly recording. These have their own websites on which members share information about sightings; this is the best starting point for discovering butterflies near you.

It can be hard to track down rare butterflies without knowing exactly where to look in a particular nature reserve so it is handy to get advice from Butterfly Conservation members. Butterfly Conservation has bought its own nature reserves and also does a lot of conservation work and management of sensitive nature reserves. You could also join the National Trust, the RSPB or your local wildlife trust; between them, these charities manage many great butterfly sites.

You may like the sound of some of the places I visited but there are thousands of other beautiful places blessed with butterflies. Residents of Wales, Yorkshire, north-east England and the Midlands will find the following list of sites I visited in 2009 extremely limited, because I omitted to visit their fine regions! I hope they will not take offence – they too have many excellent butterflying hotspots.

Like much of our countryside, the sites I enjoyed are precious. If they were swamped with insensitive visitors, they would be ruined. Forgive me for stating the obvious but please, if and when you visit these, or any other nature reserve, tread carefully. Leave your dog at home and perhaps the mobile phone too. I have not always set the perfect example here, but it is best to stick to the footpath and not trample down grassland or flowers. And you may enjoy the countryside more if you get out for an early morning or a late evening or even on an overcast day when you have a woodland or a meadow to yourself.

Some nature reserves where rare butterflies are found are closed to the public during sensitive times of the year, most notably most Large Blue sites in Somerset. The main Large Blue sites open to the public are Collard Hill (National Trust) and Daneway Banks (Gloucestershire Wildlife Trust). While Fermyn Woods is still good for Purple Emperors, this butterfly has expanded its range into Lincolnshire, Cambridgeshire and the rest of East Anglia. According to Matthew Oates, the best place in 2017 for Emperors was Knepp Wildland, a rewilded farm in West Sussex – there are plenty of public footpaths through this special place.

Greater London

Ham Lands, Twickenham

Nature reserve managed by Richmond council.

For: Orange Tip, Small White, Green-veined White, Speckled Wood, Comma, Holly Blue and other common spring butterflies.

Getting there: a pleasant walk from Teddington railway station; passenger ferry across the Thames. OS map grid reference: TQ166718.

Durant's Park, Ponders End, Enfield

Public park.

For: White-letter Hairstreak.

Getting there: a short walk from Southbury railway station. OS reference: TQ356967.

More information: There are dozens of parks across north and south London, including green spaces in Battersea, Hackney and Islington, where White-letter

Hairstreaks can be seen if you have binoculars and patience. Join the Middlesex and Hertfordshire or Surrey branch of Butterfly Conservation to find out the best locations.

The Home Counties and the south
Aldbury Nowers, Hertfordshire
National Trust site with management by Hertfordshire and Middlesex Wildlife Trust.
For: Grizzled and Dingy Skipper, Green Hairstreak, Marbled White.
Getting there: Tring railway station is less than a mile away. OS grid reference: SP950130.

Blean Woods, Kent
Rough Common is part of this National Nature Reserve.
For: Heath Fritillary.
Getting there: two miles from Canterbury West railway station. OS grid reference: TR120594.
More information: while parts of the huge Blean complex of woods are privately owned, others are open to the public and owned and managed by Natural England, the Woodland Trust and the RSPB.

Brook Bay / Compton Bay, Isle of Wight
Coastline owned by the National Trust, open to the public.
For: Glanville Fritillary.
Getting there: parking in the National Trust car parks at Shippards Chine, Compton Chine and Brook Bay. OS grid reference: SZ375850.

Denbies Hillside, Surrey
North Downs grassland.
For: Adonis Blue, Chalkhill Blue, Clouded Yellow, Grizzled Skipper, Dingy Skipper, Silver-spotted Skipper.
Getting there: a lovely three-mile stroll from Westhumble railway station. OS grid reference: TQ141503.

Mill Hill / Shoreham Bank, West Sussex
Steep chalk grassland on the South Downs.
For: Adonis Blue, Chalkhill Blue, Clouded Yellow, Dingy Skipper, Grizzled Skipper.
Getting there: two miles from Shoreham-by-Sea railway station. OS grid reference: TQ212067.

Newtimber Hill, West Sussex
Chalk grassland on the South Downs, owned by the National Trust.
For: Silver-spotted Skipper.
Getting there: five miles from Hassocks railway station. OS grid reference: TQ265125.

Steyning, West Sussex
Public footpath and open access land around old rifle range.
For: Brown Hairstreak.
Getting there: six miles from Shoreham-by-Sea railway station; parking on road by the tennis courts and allotments in Steyning. OS grid reference: TQ172112.

Therfield Heath / Royston Common, Hertfordshire
Public heathland with footpaths around golf course.
For: Chalkhill blue.
Getting there: one-mile walk from the railway station at Royston. OS grid reference: TL345405.

Tugley Wood, Surrey
Woodland with public footpaths.
For: Purple Emperor, Wood White.
Getting there: five miles from Witley railway station; limited parking on roads around the wood. OS grid reference: SU986331.

Waterford Heath, Hertfordshire
Hertfordshire and Middlesex Wildlife Trust reserve in old quarry.
For: Grizzled Skipper.
Getting there: a mile and a half from Hertford railway station. OS grid reference: TL318150.

Central and eastern England
Bernwood Forest, Oxfordshire
Large woodland open to the public.
For: Black Hairstreak, Brown Hairstreak, Purple Emperor, White Admiral.
Getting there: twelve miles from Oxford railway station. OS grid reference: SP611118.

Fermyn Woods, Northamptonshire
Country park and woodland, open to the public.
For: Purple Emperor, White Admiral, Purple Hairstreak.
Getting there: six miles from Corby railway station; park on lane at the north entrance to the wood. OS grid reference: SP965855.

Hickling Broad, Norfolk
Lake and wetlands which form a Norfolk Wildlife Trust nature reserve. For: Swallowtail.
Getting there: nearest railway station at Worstead is about ten miles away. Parking at reserve OS grid reference: TG428222.

Kelling Heath, Norfolk
Heathland close to the coast.
For: Silver-studded Blue, White Admiral.
Getting there: nearest railway station is Sheringham, four miles away, although steam trains on the North Norfolk Railway stop at Weybourne, close to the heath. OS grid reference: TG099418.

Marsham Heath, Norfolk
Heath and woodland.
For: Silver-studded Blue.
Getting there: nearest railway station is Worstead, ten miles away. OS grid reference: TG171239.

Whitecross Green Wood, Oxfordshire
Ancient woodland nature reserve.
For: Black Hairstreak, Brown Hairstreak.
Getting there: twelve miles from Oxford railway station. OS grid reference: SP605145.

The south-west
Aish Tor, Devon
Open moorland bordered by National Trust land. Public access via footpaths. For: Pearl-bordered, Small Pearl-bordered and Dark Green fritillaries. Green Hairstreak, Silver-washed Fritillary. The rare High Brown Fritillary is also clinging on here.
Getting there: thirty minutes' drive from Newton Abbot and Totnes railway stations. Parking in the Dart Valley between Poundsgate and Holne. OS grid reference: SX705705.

Bin Combe Exmoor, Somerset
Rough moorland close to Dunkery Beacon, owned by the National Trust. For: Heath Fritillary.
Getting there: thirty miles from Tiverton Parkway railway station. OS grid reference: SS909408.

Collard Hill, Somerset
Grassland; rare Large Blue nature reserve open to the public.
For: Large Blue.
Getting there: close to Street, twelve miles from Castle Cary railway station. OS grid reference: ST488340.

Lulworth Cove, Dorset
Coast path and clifftops.
For: Lulworth Skipper.
Getting there: five miles from Wool railway station, parking at Lulworth Cove.
OS grid reference: SY825805.

Rodborough Common, Gloucestershire
National Trust-owned Cotswold grassland.
For: The Duke of Burgundy Fritillary, Small Blue, Adonis Blue, Marbled White, Green Hairstreak, Dingy Skipper.
Getting there: a couple of miles' walk from Stroud railway station. OS grid reference: SO851036

Start Point, Devon
Spectacular coastal public footpath.
For: Small Pearl-bordered Fritillary, Wall Brown and migratory butterflies including Painted Ladies.
Getting there: Totnes is the nearest railway station, then half an hour in a car. OS grid reference: SX832370.

Scotland and the north
Allt Mhuic, Loch Arkaig
Butterfly Conservation nature reserve.
For: Chequered Skipper, Pearl-bordered Fritillary, Scotch Argus. Getting there: twenty miles north of Fort William. OS grid reference: NN121912.

Arnside Knott, Cumbria
National Trust nature reserve.
For: Scotch Argus, Northern Brown Argus, Grayling, High Brown Fritillary, Dark Green Fritillary.
Getting there: a scenic one-mile walk from Arnside railway station. OS grid reference: SD450774

Glasdrum Wood, Argyll
National nature reserve.
For: Chequered Skipper, Pearl-bordered Fritillary, Small Pearl-bordered Fritillary.
Getting there: close to the A828 Oban to Fort William road, with buses from both towns. OS grid reference: NN003458.

Grey Knotts, Cumbria
Steep mountainside with rough public paths.
For: Mountain Ringlet.
Getting there: twenty-five miles from Penrith railway station. Park at youth hostel on Honister Pass. Steep mountain walk. OS grid reference: NY220124.

Latterbarrow and Yewbarrow, Cumbria
Grassland and woodland managed by Cumbria Wildlife Trust.
For: Northern Brown Argus, High Brown Fritillary, Dark Green Fritillary.
Getting there: park on the old road by the Derby Arms, just off the A590. Nearest railway station is Grange-over-Sands. OS grid reference: SD445831 and SD435851.
More information: There is more than one Latterbarrow and more than one Yewbarrow in Cumbria!

Meathop Moss
A bog and Cumbria Wildlife Trust nature reserve.
For: Large Heath.
Getting there: reserve entrance on the eastern side of Meathop Moss. Nearest railway station is Grange-over-Sands. OS grid reference: SD447820.

Smardale Gill, Cumbria
National nature reserve along disused railway with stunning viaduct. For: Scotch Argus.
Getting there: three-mile walk from Kirkby Stephen railway station. OS grid reference: NY735065.

Northern Ireland
Craigavon Lakes, Armagh
City park with rough grassland.
For: Réal's Wood White (today known as the Cryptic Wood White).
Getting there: nearest railway station is Lurgan. OS grid reference: J050580.

Montiaghs Moss, Antrim
National nature reserve, pronounced 'munchies'.
For: Réal's Wood White (or the Cryptic Wood White), Large Heath.
Getting there: five miles from Lurgan railway station. OS grid reference: J090650.

Murlough, County Down
National Trust nature reserve with dunes and grassland by sandy beach.
For: Marsh Fritillary, Réal's Wood White (or the Cryptic Wood White).
Getting there: regular daily bus service, Ulsterbus 20, Belfast to Newcastle, alight at Lazy BJ Caravan Park. Belfast Central railway station 25 miles away. OS grid reference: J394338.

Useful websites
Butterfly Conservation
www.butterfly-conservation.org

UK Butterflies
www.ukbutterflies.co.uk
Online database run by Pete Eeles with excellent species information, photographs of all life stages and database of good butterfly sites.

RECOMMENDED READING, REFERENCES AND BIBLIOGRAPHY

Recommended Reading

Butterfly guidebooks

There are phone apps for butterfly ID but I like a robust physical field-guide. There are plenty of pocket guidebooks available. For a heftier but definitive guide, the best is Jeremy Thomas and Richard Lewington's *Butterflies of Britain and Ireland* (revised edition 2010). One of the best new guides to British butterflies is *The Butterflies of Sussex* by Michael Blencowe and Neil Hulme (2017). It is focused on Sussex sites and butterflies but is useful for anyone butterflying in southern England. It combines brilliant photography with fascinating history, field craft and up-to-date science.

Butterfly history and memoir

There's been a wonderful little resurgence in narrative non-fiction about butterflies since *The Butterfly Isles*. Matthew Oates's *In Pursuit of Butterflies: A Fifty-Year Affair* (2015) is evocative, inspiring and eccentric in equal measure. Peter

Marren's *Rainbow Dust: Three Centuries of Delight in British Butterflies* (2015) is an elegantly written history of butterfly obsession and butterflies in culture. Marren co-authored an earlier work, Michael Salmon's *The Aurelian Legacy: British Butterflies and Their Collectors*, to which I'm indebted for its excellent history of butterfly collecting. It's out of print but can be found online. Miriam Rothschild's *Butterfly Cooing Like a Dove* (1991) is a sideways look at butterflies in literature and art. Robert Michael Pyle has written the epic American version of *The Butterfly Isles* – *Mariposa Road: The First Butterfly Big Year* (2010), a rather more impressive pursuit of hundreds of species.

Butterflies in literature

Vladimir Nabokov must be the most talented writer to also have been a serious lepidopterist: he wrote scientific papers specialising in the blues of North America, named several species and is now honoured in the names of dozens of butterflies. Butterflies flit through much of his writing. In *Lolita*, for instance, Humbert and Lolita spend time between 'Snow' and 'Elphinstone' in Colorado. Both are names of mountain-loving butterflies: Snow's Copper and *Elphinstonia charlonia* or the Greenish Black-tip. There's a short story, 'The Aurelian', in *Nabokov's Dozen*. The best summary of Nabokov's feelings for butterflies come in chapter six of his memoir, *Speak, Memory*. This is also reprinted in the fascinating scholarly work, *Nabokov's Butterflies*, edited by Brian Boyd and Robert Michael Pyle.

The idea that catching beautiful insects is a metaphor for male desire to possess and subdue female beauty is an obvious one and has been well used over the years. The scariest account of an obsession with butterflies is John Fowles's well-written thriller, *The Collector*. Despite being a lepidopterist himself, Fowles gave a particularly unflattering portrait of a butterfly lover turned stalker and kidnapper. More recently Fiona Mountain gave Eleanor Glanville well-deserved fame with a bodice-ripping historical novel about her troubled life.

Unsurprisingly, butterflies make frequent appearances in children's books. My favourite is B.B's *Brendon Chase*, a gripping, nostalgic tale of three boys who run away from home and live rough in the woods in the idyllic 1920s. I enjoyed it as a boy but was surprised by the beauty of B.B's nature writing when I returned to it as an adult. Enid Blyton's *Five Go to Billycock Hill* is a bit of fun if you want to see how butterfly collectors were viewed by mainstream society in the 1950s and 1960s.

Bibliography

H. G. Adams, 1871, *Beautiful Butterflies* (Groombridge and Sons)

P. B. M. Allan, 1943, *Talking of Moths* (The Montgomery Press)

P. B. M. Allan, 1980, *Leaves from a Moth-Hunter's Notebook* (E. W. Classey)

Jim Asher, Martin Warren, Richard Fox, Paul Harding, Gail Jeffcoate and Stephen Jeffcoate, 2001, *The Millennium Atlas of Butterflies in Britain and Ireland* (Oxford University Press)

B. B., 1944, *Brendon Chase* (Jane Nissen Books)

J. H. Bell, c.1934, *Days With A Butterfly Net* (Watkins and Doncaster)

Enid Blyton, 1957, *Five Go to Billycock Hill* (Hodder and Stoughton)

Brian Boyd and Robert Michael Pyle (eds), 2000, *Nabokov's Butterflies* (Allen Lane)

C. R. Bristow, S. H. Mitchell and D. E. Bolton, 1993, *Devon Butterflies* (Devon Books)

Eric Carle, 1969, *The Very Hungry Caterpillar* (World Publishing Company)

John Clare, 2003, *Selected Poems* (Faber and Faber)

W. S. Coleman, 1860, *British Butterflies* (Routledge)

R. L. H. Dennis, 1977, *The British Butterflies: Their Origin and Establishment* (Classey)

Charles Dickens, 2007, *Memoirs of Joseph Grimaldi* (Pushkin Press)

C. Donovan, 1936, *A Catalogue of the Macrolepidoptera of Ireland* (Cheltenham and London)

A. Maitland Emmet and John Heath, 1990, *The Butterflies of Great Britain and Ireland* (Harley Books)

E. B. Ford, 1945, *Butterflies* (Collins)

Margaret Fountaine, 1980, *Love Among the Butterflies* (Penguin)

John Fowles, 1963, *The Collector* (Vintage Classics)

Richard Fox, Jim Asher, Tom Brereton, David Roy and Martin Warren, 2006, *The State of Butterflies in Britain and Ireland* (Pisces Publications)

Michael Frayn, 2003, *Spies* (Faber and Faber)

W. Furneaux, 1916, *Butterflies and Moths* (Longmans)

Charles A. Hall, 1938, *A Pocket-Book of British Butterflies, Moths and Other Winged Insects* (Adam and Charles Black)

Moses Harris, 1766, *The Aurelian or Natural History of English Insects, Namely Moths and Butterflies* (Salem House Publishers, 1986)

I. R. P. Heslop, G. E. Hyde and R. E. Stockley, 1964, *Notes and Views of the Purple Emperor* (The Southern Publishing Co.)

A. E. Hodge, 1919, *The Young Collector's Guide to Butterfly and Moth Collecting* (Arthur Pearson)

Tove Jansson, 1961, *Finn Family Moomintroll* (Puffin)

Henry Guard Knaggs, 1869, *The Lepidopterist's Guide* (Bibliobazaar)

Torben B. Larsen, 2003, *Hazards of Butterfly Collecting* (Cravitz)

Peter Laufer, 2009, *The Dangerous World of Butterflies* (The Lyons Press)

Laurie Lee, 1959, *Cider with Rosie* (Penguin)

S. A. Manning, 1965, *A Ladybird Book of Butterflies, Moths and Other Insects* (Wills and Hepworth)

E. Mansell and L. Hugh Newman, 1968, *The Complete British Butterflies in Colour* (Ebury Press)

Fiona Mountain, 2009, *Lady of the Butterflies* (Preface Publishing)

Vladimir Nabokov, 1967, *Speak, Memory* (Penguin)

Vladimir Nabokov, 1990, *Nabokov's Dozen* (Penguin)

David Newland, 2006, *Discover Butterflies in Britain* (WILDGuides)

Edward Newman, 1871, *An Illustrated Natural History of British Butterflies* (William Tweedie)

L. Hugh Newman, 1954, *Butterfly Farmer* (The Country Book Club)

Matthew Oates, 2000, 'The Duke of Burgundy – Conserving the Intractable, *British Wildlife*, vol. II, pp. 250–7

Matthew Oates, 2004, 'The Ecology of the Pearl-bordered Fritillary in Woodland', *British Wildlife*, vol. 15, pp. 229–36

RECOMMENDED READING, REFERENCES & BIBLIOGRAPHY

Matthew Oates, 2005, 'Extreme Butterfly Collecting: a biography of I. R. P. Heslop', *British Wildlife*, vol. 16, pp. 164–71

Robin Page, 2003, *The Great British Butterfly Safari* (Bird's Farm Books)

Miriam Rothschild, 1983, *Dear Lord Rothschild* (Hutchinson)

Miriam Rothschild, 1991, *Butterfly cooing like a Dove* (Doubleday)

Sharman Apt Russell, 2003, *An Obsession With Butterflies* (Arrow)

Michael A. Salmon, 2000, *The Aurelian Legacy – British Butterflies and their Collectors* (Harley Books)

Michael A. Salmon and Peter J. Edwards, 2005, *The Aurelian's Fireside Companion – An Entomological Anthology* (Paphia Publishing)

Linda Sonntag, 1980, *Butterflies* (Hutchinson)

C. Stefanescu, 1997, 'Migration patterns and feeding resources of the Painted Lady butterfly, in the northeast of the Iberian peninsula', *The Zoological Miscellany* 20.2 pp 31–48

Jeremy Thomas, 1980, 'Why Did the Large Blue Become Extinct in Britain?' *Oryx*, 15, pp. 243–7

Jeremy Thomas, 1986, *Butterflies of the British Isles* (Newnes Country Life Books)

Jeremy Thomas and Richard Lewington, 1991, *The Butterflies of Britain and Ireland* (Dorling Kindersley)

J. A. Thomas, D. J. Simcox and R. T. Clarke, 2009, 'Successful Conservation of a Threatened Maculinea Butterfly', *Science*, 325, pp. 80–3

Hana Volavkova (ed.), 1993, *I Never Saw Another Butterfly – Children's Drawings and Poems from Terezin Concentration Camp, 1942–1944* (Schocken Books)

Specific references in the chapters

Probably to the frustration of some readers I have not always quoted the source of information in the chapters because I did not want to disrupt the flow of the story. More information (and credit!) is given here.

Chapter 1

Some of the examples of how butterflies symbolise our souls around the world come from Sharman Apt Russell's *An Obsession with Butterflies*. Linda Sonntag's *Butterflies* is also good for the global symbolism of butterflies.

Chapter 2

Frederick William Frohawk's dream is taken from Michael Salmon's *The Aurelian Legacy*. The meaning of the first butterflies of the year as explained by the Snork Maiden is from Tove Jansson's *Finn Family Moomintroll*. Miriam Rothschild wrote about yellow butterflies in *Butterfly cooing like a Dove*. Dr Owen Lewis of Oxford University was speaking about the impact of the fly *Sturmia bella* on the Small Tortoiseshell at Butterfly Conservation's annual symposium in 2009; his work is available at: http://users.ox.ac.uk/~zool0376/small-tortoiseshell.htm

The entomological hoax with the Brimstone is recounted in Salmon's *The Aurelian Legacy*.

Chapter 3

Nabokov wrote of his desire for a 'flying seat' in *Speak, Memory*. Peacocks hissing is well explored by correspondence reprinted in *The Aurelian's Fireside Companion* by Michael Salmon and Peter Edwards. William Swainson's recommendation for a 'little boy' to carry a butterfly collector's clobber comes from Salmon's *The Aurelian Legacy*.

Chapter 4

More information about Charles and Walter Rothschild can be found in *Dear Lord Rothschild* by Miriam Rothschild. W. S. Coleman's account of chasing butterflies comes from his entertaining and very Victorian 1860 guidebook, *British Butterflies*.

Chapter 5

Matthew Oates' paper for *British Wildlife*, 'The Duke of Burgundy – Conserving the Intractable', is the source of information about the Duke of Burgundy's scarcity. The latest information on its scarcity was provided by Martin Warren at Butterfly Conservation.

RECOMMENDED READING, REFERENCES & BIBLIOGRAPHY

Chapter 6
The white butterflies seen at Calais is from Salmon; the nineteenth century invasion of Small Whites was noted by L. Hugh Newman in *Butterfly Farmer*. The observations of a Painted Lady migration from a nineteenth-century explorer travelling along the Sudanese Red Sea coast comes from Torben Larsen via Sharman Apt Russell's *An Obsession with Butterflies*.

Chapter 7
P. B. M. Allan writes about the detective work in uncovering the story of Eleanor Glanville in *Leaves from a Moth-Hunter's Notebook*. Sharman Apt Russell also summarises Glanville's life in *An Obsession with Butterflies*. Elizabeth Harper's plight of an entomologist's wife is reprinted by Salmon and Edwards.

Chapter 9
P. B. M. Allan discusses fraud and butterfly collecting in a chapter on The Kentish Buccaneers in *Talking of Moths*. Salmon's *The Aurelian Legacy* is the source for Abel Ingpen's creepy killing instructions.

Chapter 10
The quotes from Henry Seymer and Stainton are drawn from Salmon's *The Aurelian Legacy*. The best up-to-date account of how the Large Blue was saved is found in the 2009 article in *Science* by J. A. Thomas, D. J. Simcox and R. T. Clarke.

Chapter 11
The S. G. Castle Russell quote was dug out by Matthew Oates. Once again, Salmon is the source of other accounts of butterfly swarms.

Chapter 12
Fergus Ogilvie's observations about cuckoos' love for Swallowtail caterpillars is related via Frederick William Frohawk in P. B. M. Allan's *Talking of Moths*.

Chapter 13

The story of Albin's Hampstead Eye and collecting on Hampstead Heath is nicely related by Salmon in *The Aurelian Legacy*, as is the anecdote about Dandridge and the Purple Emperor and Siegfried Sassoon's encounter with a Camberwell Beauty.

Chapter 14

The definitive, dated and hugely entertaining book about the Purple Emperor is Heslop, Hyde and Stockley's *Notes and Views of the Purple Emperor*. Matthew Oates' paper, 'Extreme Butterfly Collecting: a biography of I. R. P. Heslop', captures the eccentricity and appeal of Heslop's Emperor obsession. Oates and Heslop are a rich source of expertise about the Emperor and where it appears in literature and poetry as well.

Chapter 16

The life story of Robert 'Porker' Watson is told by Salmon in *The Aurelian Legacy*. I read about the explorer Henry Walter Bates on the internet and found more in Sharman Apt Russell's *An Obsession with Butterflies*.

Chapter 17

Joseph Grimaldi's biography was written by Charles Dickens and is still in print. It is also available online.

Chapter 18

The facts on the Queen of Spain sightings in Britain came from A. Maitland Emmet and John Heath's *The Butterflies of Great Britain and Ireland* and also from a draft of an unpublished paper by Neil Hulme and Dr Mike Perry, 'Evidence of Immigration and Subsequent Breeding by the Queen of Spain Fritillary Butterfly (*Issoria lathonia*) at Chichester, West Sussex, in 2009'.

ACKNOWLEDGEMENTS

I am particularly grateful to Matthew Oates and Martin Warren, outstanding communicators of butterfly science who generously helped me find rare butterflies and kindly read my manuscript. Any errors that remain are my own doing. Jeremy Thomas talked me through the story of the Large Blue with typical generosity and modesty. Energetic and entertaining, Neil Hulme helped blow away butterfly burnout. Maurice Hughes was a superb host in Northern Ireland. Stephen and Gail Jeffcoate were a great help with Wood Whites; Andrew Middleton with the White-letter Hairstreak. Thank you to Michael Walter at the RSPB, Geoff Martin at the Natural History Museum and Nigel Bourn and David Redhead of Butterfly Conservation. It was also a pleasure to meet so many lovely butterfly enthusiasts and BC members during the year.

A special thanks to my agent, Karolina Sutton at Curtis Brown, who started me off and has offered constant support and encouragement, and to my brilliant editor, Sara Holloway. Sara and the team at Granta – including Philip Gwyn Jones, Sarah Wasley, Christine Lo, Kelly Pike, Iain Chapple, Pru Rowlandson and Brigid Macleod – have been fantastic.

Thanks to my bosses at the *Guardian*, Emily Wilson and Clare Margetson, for their patience and interest. I would also like to thank Suzanne Barkham, Lisa Walpole, Beth Rigby and Hannah Pool for their encouragement, and John Barkham, the best butterfly companion of all.

ILLUSTRATIONS

INDEX